Origins and Development of Congress

CONGRESSIONAL QUARTERLY INC.

Congressional Quarterly Inc.

Congressional Quarterly Inc. is an editorial research service and publishing company serving clients in the fields of news, education, business and government. Congressional Quarterly, in its basic publication, the CQ *Weekly Report*, covers Congress, government and politics. Congressional Quarterly also publishes hardbound reference books and paperback books on public affairs. The service was founded in 1945 by Henrietta and Nelson Poynter.

An affiliated service, Editorial Research Reports, publishes reports each week on a wide range of subjects. Editorial Research Reports also publishes hardbound and paperback books.

Editor: Robert A. Diamond
Contributors: Michael A. Carson, Mary Cohn, Ed Johnson, William Korns, Mary Neumann. **Art Director:** Howard Chapman. **Production Manager:** I. D. Fuller. **Assistant Production Manager:** Kathleen E. Walsh.

Library of Congress Cataloging in Publication Data

Congressional Quarterly Inc.
  Origins and development of Congress.

  Bibliography: p. 309

  Includes index.

  1. United States.   Congress.   I. Title.

JK1021.C56   1976   328.73´09   76-18295

ISBN 0-87187-094-0

Table of Contents

PART I

Constitutional Beginnings

PART II

History of the House of Representatives

PART III

History of the Senate

Preface

Although the United States Congress is 187 years old, there have been surprisingly few comprehensive histories about this branch of government. Since 1936, only two books have been published covering the entire span of congressional history for both chambers of Congress—*The Story of Congress, 1789-1935,* by Ernest Sutherland Bates, published in 1936 and *The American Heritage History of the Congress of the United States,* published in 1975.

Apart from these two works, the history of Congress is widely scattered in countless memoirs and specialized studies confined to brief periods of congressional history or to either the House or the Senate or to particular institutions of Congress (for example, the committee system) or to issues before Congress (for example, foreign policy). There is a need, therefore, for a compact one-volume history of Congress covering the institution from its origins in colonial America through the major reforms that have swept Congress in the 1970s. *Origins and Development of Congress* endeavors to meet that need.

The Introduction provides an overall survey of congressional history from the Constitutional Convention of 1787 through the Watergate crisis of 1972-74. Part I covers the colonial background of Congress, the debates on the powers of Congress at the Constitutional Convention, the struggle for ratification and the first elections under the Constitution. Parts II and III present comprehensive histories of the House of Representatives and the Senate since 1789. Parts II and III are divided into major historical periods; for each period, there is a detailed discussion of congressional leadership, procedural changes, political party developments, major political issues and relations with the President. Reference notes and a selected bibliography appear at the end of the book.

Robert A. Diamond
May 1976

Introduction

The 55 delegates who gathered in Philadelphia in the summer of 1787 faced a challenge of no mean proportions: how were they to devise a system of government that would bind 13 sovereign and rival states into one firm union without threatening the traditional freedoms for which the American colonists so recently had fought?

Americans, with their predominantly English heritage, were wedded to the principles of representative government and personal freedom that had developed in England from the time of Magna Carta. They had gone to war against the mother country to preserve their freedoms from the encroachments of centralized power.

But independence had brought new problems. Men's allegiance still was directed toward the states, and most were reluctant to yield state sovereignty to any superior governmental power. The Articles of Confederation, the first basic law of the new nation, reflected this widespread distrust of centralized power. Under the Articles the United States was little more than a league of sovereign states, bickering and feuding among themselves. The states retained control over most essential governmental functions, and Congress—in which each state had one vote—was the sole organ of central government. So limited were its powers that it could not levy taxes or regulate trade, and it had no sanction to enforce any of its decisions.

Introduction

The inadequacies of the Articles of Confederation, brought into sharp focus by Shays' Rebellion in 1786, gave impetus to a growing movement for governmental reform that culminated in the Philadelphia convention the following year. There the delegates voted to create a new national government consisting of supreme legislative, judicial and executive branches of government.[1] *(Footnotes, p. 297)*

In the Constitution that emerged from these deliberations, the concept of government by consent of the governed formed the basic principle; accountability was the watchword. The rights of the people were to be protected by diffusing power among rival interests.

The Constitution strengthened central authority, but national powers were carefully enumerated and other powers were reserved to the states and the people. The Constitution provided for a President, to be chosen by electors in each state, a national judiciary and a legislature of two chambers. The House of Representatives was to be popularly elected, while the Senate which shared certain executive powers with the President, was to be chosen by the state legislatures. Under the terms of the Great Compromise between the large and small states, representation in the House was to be proportional to a state's population and each state was to have two votes in the Senate. The national plan chosen by the delegates along with the separation of powers between the three branches of government created a system of checks and balances.

Writing in *The Federalist Papers,* James Madison explained the delicate relationship between the federal and state governments and the division of power within the system. He stated: "In the compound republic of America, the power surrendered by the people is first divided between two distinct governments, and then the portion allotted to each subdivided among distinct and separate departments. Hence a double security arises to the rights of people. The different governments will control each other, at the same time that each will be controlled by itself."[2]

The final draft of the Constitution provided a broad framework for the new government. Thus for nearly 200 years the document has proved flexible enough to meet the nation's changing needs without extensive formal revision. Although many modern governmental practices would seem alien to the authors of the Constitution, the basic structure continues to operate in much the way they planned it. Madison realized the importance of "maintaining in practice the necessary partition of power among the several departments." He wrote that this could best be done "by so contriving the interior structure of the government as that its several constituent parts may by their mutual relations, be the means of keeping each other in their proper places."[3]

Separate Roles of House and Senate

The House because of its popularity with the people was expected by Alexander Hamilton to be "a full match if not an overmatch for every other member of the government."[4] The Senate was originally designed to serve as a restraining influence on the House. But each chamber was given special power not shared by the other. The Senate's special authority over appointments and treaties was counterbalanced by the right of the House to originate all revenue bills.

At first the House, under the leadership of Madison and later under Henry Clay, was the preeminent chamber of Congress, but the Senate quickly emerged as a powerful legislative force. In the years preceding the Civil War it was the chief forum for the discussion of national issues, and in the post-Reconstruction era it became the dominant arm of the government. The House, as its membership increased, was compelled to adopt a variety of procedures that diminished the power of individual representatives but assured its ability to act when action was desired. The Senate remained a comparatively small body which found elaborate institutional structures unnecessary for the deliberation that it saw as its paramount function.

In his book, *Congressional Government,* written in 1885, Woodrow Wilson stated: "It is indispensable that besides the House of Representatives which runs on all fours with popular sentiment, we should have a body like the Senate which may refuse to run with it at all when it seems to be wrong—a body which has time and security enough to keep its head, if only now and then and but for a little while, till other people have had time to think. The Senate is fitted to do deliberately and well the revising which is its properest function, because its position as a representative of state

3

sovereignty is one of eminent dignity, securing for it ready and sincere respect, and because popular demands, ere they reach it with definite and authoritative suggestion, are diluted by passage through the feelings and conclusions of the state legislatures, which are the Senate's only immediate constituents. The Senate commonly feels with the House, but it does not, so to say, feel so fast. It at least has a chance to be the express image of those judgments of the nation which are slower and more temperate than its feelings."[5]

Wilson's concept of the Senate might have been satisfactory to the framers of the Constitution, but in the twentieth century it would no longer serve. As the Progressive era advanced, an increasingly restive public demanded more genuinely popular government, and in 1912 the Senate reluctantly agreed to a constitutional amendment providing for the direct election of senators. The House, too, felt the pressures of the times: the power of the Speaker which "Czar" Thomas B. Reed had established in the name of party responsibility in 1890 was dismantled under the banner of popular rule in 1910.

The Seventeenth Amendment, by taking senatorial elections out of the hands of the state governments, blurred the constitutional distinction between the Senate and House, and from the time of its adoption in 1913 the Senate came more and more to resemble the lower chamber. At times it, rather than the House, would appear to be the more representative legislative body. Both chambers, however, were subject to continuing charges that they failed to represent the will of the electorate. Although members of Congress ran for office as Republicans or Democrats, the absence of unity within the national parties precluded party responsibility in legislative action. Moreover, the institutional characteristics of Congress itself often prevented a legislative majority from working its will. Campaigns against the seniority system, under which senators and representatives rose to power within their respective chambers, the Senate filibuster and secrecy in congressional activities all represented attempts to make Congress more accountable to the people. The same goal prompted demands for reapportionment of the House of Representatives to make congressional districts more nearly equal in population.

Congress and Presidential Power

The growth of presidential power in the twentieth century, spurred by a major economic depression, two world wars, the Korean and Indochina conflicts, posed a threat to the viability of Congress as a coequal branch of government. As the volume and complexity of government business increased, legislative initiative shifted from the Capitol to the White House, and Congress with its antiquated procedures often found that it was no match for the tremendous resources of the executive branch. By passing reorganization acts in 1946 and 1970 Congress sought to restore its equality in the three-branch federal partnership. But repeated clashes over spending, war and treaty powers marked congressional resistance to executive encroachment upon the powers delegated to Congress by the Constitution. One peak was Congress' overriding of President Nixon's veto of the War Powers Act of 1973, the first legislation ever to define and limit the commander-in-chief's constitutional role in making war.

Then, all that went before was eclipsed by the most momentous constitutional confrontation since the Civil War—Watergate. Before expiring abruptly after some two years of mounting national agony, the great scandal had ultimately tested the powers of executive, legislative and judicial. As a mesmerized nation and world watched the events in Washington from the Watergate burglary on June 17, 1972, until the Nixon resignation on Aug. 9, 1974, the paramount question became: Can the Constitution withstand the strains tearing at its 185-year-old structure?

The Supreme Court played a crucial role when it ruled unanimously that the President had no power to withhold evidence in a criminal trial. Nixon obeyed the court and surrendered the evidence, certain White House tape recordings. In quick order, the House Judiciary Committee approved three articles of impeachment against Nixon, the new evidence further gravely incriminated him, and 16 days after the court decision, he became the first President in history to resign the office.

In his brief inaugural address, President Ford proclaimed, "Our Constitution works." In accord was historian Henry Steele Commager who wrote that the process of inquiry by the courts and Congress had resulted in a vindication of the constitutional system and of the principle of separation of powers.

But others were not so convinced, fearing the Nixon resignation before completion of the impeachment process amounted to back-door subversion of the Constitution. One was a Judiciary Committee member, Rep. John Conyers Jr. (D Mich.), who foresaw a future Congress recoiling from the agony of exercise of the impeachment power by concluding "that impeachment can never again succeed unless another president demonstrated the same, almost uncanny ability to impeach himself."[6]

PART I

Constitutional Beginnings

Chapter 1

Colonial Background

When the Federal Convention met in Philadelphia in 1787 to consider revising the Articles of Confederation, the reasons for seeking a more effective form of national government for the newly independent United States of America seemed manifest and pressing. The exact form that government should take was by no means clear, however, and substantial compromise was required before agreement could be reached.

What finally emerged as the Constitution of the United States nevertheless reflected in good measure the shared experience of men who had grown up in a colonial America that was predominantly English in origin, and who had finally rebelled against English sovereignty when that seemed the only way to preserve the freedom they had come to expect as a part of their English heritage.

Almost a century passed between Columbus' voyage of discovery in 1492 and Sir Walter Raleigh's attempt in 1587 to plant the first English settlement in the New World—the ill-fated "Lost Colony" on Roanoke Island in what is now North Carolina.[1] By then, Spain had seized the Caribbean and much of South and Central America (with its gold and silver) and had placed outposts in Florida. But at the beginning of the 17th century, most of North America was still unexplored, Spain's power was on the wane, and England was primed for colonial venture. *(Footnotes, p. 297)*

English Dominance

Private initiative was the prime mover behind settlement of America by the English during the 17th century, when all of the 13 colonies except one were founded. Several were started by promoters with an eye to profits or the creation of new feudal domains. Religious strife underlay the "Great Migration" of Puritans to New England (and the West Indies) during the repressive reign of Charles I (1625-49).[2] Poverty drove many others to take a chance on America. Whatever the motive for settlement, though, it was entirely a private undertaking, receiving little more help from the state than a charter to the land to be settled.

The English achieved their dominant position along the Atlantic seaboard in two waves of colonization. Virginia, Maryland and the New England colonies were founded before 1642, when the outbreak of civil war in England absorbed English energies. After restoration of the monarchy in 1660, the English added New York, New Jersey, Pennsylvania, Delaware and the Carolinas. Georgia, the 13th colony, was founded in 1733. By 1700, the colonies had a population of 200,000—largely of English origin—stretched along a thousand miles of coast from Maine to the Carolinas.

Roots of Self-Government

By the time Jamestown was founded in 1607, Englishmen had already attained significant rights and privileges. English justice was grounded on a solid body of common law that included the right to trial by jury, and no Englishman could be deprived of life, liberty or property without due process in the courts. The first colonists brought with them the models of English courts and other organs of local government.

The long English struggle for the right of self-government was also well-advanced by the beginning of the 17th century. The Crown was still supreme, and it would take the beheading of Charles I in 1649 and the dethroning of James II in 1688 to assure Parliament ascendancy over the King. Already, though, the two houses of Parliament—the Lords and the Commons—symbolized the principle of government by law and representative assembly, and this principle too was soon transplanted to America. In 1619, the Virginians (then about 1,000 in number) elected 22 "burgesses" to a General Assembly.³ After Virginia became a royal colony in 1624, the governor and council were appointed by the King, but popular representation in the assembly was retained.

The organizers of the Massachusetts Bay Company carried matters considerably further when they voted to transfer the entire enterprise and its charter as "one body politique and corporate" to New England.⁴ On their arrival in 1630, the officers promptly established themselves as the government of the Bay Colony, subject only to annual election thereafter by the stockholder-colonists. The founders of Massachusetts thereby asserted a right to full self-government that neither the King nor Parliament had contemplated or would be prepared to challenge for another 50 years.

The great distance that separated England from America was itself a major factor in promoting a spirit of independence and self-reliance among the early colonists. Many of those drawn to America were predisposed to resist authority in any event, and this attitude was reinforced by the free availability of land and the harshness of frontier living. In New England, where entire congregations of Puritans had often emigrated and settled together in a town of their own, the town meeting became a unique instrument of self-government that was exceptionally democratic for the times.

Origins of Conflict with England

England left the colonies pretty much to themselves initially, but it was not for lack of a concept of the role they would be expected to play. Under the prevailing economic doctrine of the times—mercantilism—the central goal of any nation-state was self-sufficiency, and it was taken for granted that all profits of empire should accrue to the benefit of the mother country. Thus the English were quick to try to monopolize the trade in Virginia tobacco, the first American product to find a wide market. And in 1660 they began systematic efforts to exploit colonial trade, with the first of a series of Acts of Trade and Navigation.

These laws were designed to maximize English profits on the transport of colonial imports and exports and the

11

marketing of major colonial products. They required all trade between England and the colonies to be carried by English or colonial-built ships manned by English subjects; stipulated that colonial imports from other countries in Europe first be landed and reloaded at English ports; and prohibited exports of specified colonial products to countries other than England. Tobacco was the first of these enumerated items, and eventually every important American export except salt fish was added to the list.

The trade acts were not without some benefit to the colonies. But in exchanging their raw products for English manufactures, the colonists rarely found the terms of trade to their advantage. When tobacco prices collapsed in the 1660s, for example, Virginians had no recourse against the English merchants who raised the prices of goods sent in exchange. This situation was aggravated by England's continuing refusal to permit its coins to circulate in the colonies. To get specie (gold or silver), the colonists had to sell their products in the West Indies or other markets.

The trade acts were met with widespread evasion in the colonies; smuggling, bribery and the use of false documents were commonplace. New Englanders, who ran a chronic deficit in their balance of trade with England, were especially resourceful in evading the trade acts. Massachusetts went so far as to refuse to obey them, asserting that the laws of England "do not reach America" because the colonies were unrepresented in Parliament. For this and similar acts of defiance against English authority, the Bay Colony's charter was annulled in 1684.[5]

When James II came to the throne in 1685, England moved to strengthen colonial administration by consolidating the New England colonies, New York and the Jerseys into one Dominion of New England; for three years these colonies were ruled by Sir Edmund Andros as Governor-general with the aid of an appointed council but no representative assembly. The colonists bridled at being taxed without their consent and were quick to overthrow Andros and other dominion officials as soon as they received word of the Glorious Revolution of 1688 and the expulsion of James from England. The concept of the Dominion was promptly abandoned.

The accession of William and Mary in 1689 marked the beginning of a transfer of power from the Crown to Parliament and of a series of colonial wars that ended in 1763 with the English in control of all of America east of the Mississippi. Mercantilist aims continued to dominate English colonial policy throughout this period, and new restrictions were placed on colonial trade. But the American colonists went on growing in numbers, economic strength and political assertiveness.

Growth of the Colonies

Between 1700 and 1760, large families and new immigrants boosted the colonial population from 200,000 to about 1,700,000. Persons of English stock were in the majority over-all and among colonial leaders; the first Adams came in 1636, the first Washington in 1656, the first Franklin in 1685. Other major ethnic groups in 1760 were the Scotch-Irish (estimated to number 280,000) and the Germans (170,000), whose forebears had started coming to America toward the end of the 17th century. Finding the best land along the seaboard already taken, most had moved on to settle the back country between tidewater and the Appalachians.

Even more numerous in the American population of 1760 were an estimated 310,000 Negro slaves. The Spaniards brought the first African slaves to the New World in the 16th century; a Dutch ship brought the first 20 to Virginia in 1619. The English saw nothing wrong in slavery, and the Puritans regularly took Indians as slaves and sold them in the West Indies.

Slaves helped to meet a chronic shortage of labor in colonial America at a time when most colonists wanted and could easily get their own land. Slavery eventually declined in the North, where it became unprofitable, but it flourished in the plantation economy of the South; the number of slaves in Virginia, the Carolinas and Georgia grew rapidly during the 18th century. Americans vied with the English slave traders in meeting the demand. Yankee slavers were especially successful in trading New England rum for Africans, who were then sold in the West Indies for sugar and molasses with which to make more rum.

Profits from slave labor and the slave trade thus added to a prosperity that was sustained by a rise in prices for colonial produce in England and the rest of Europe. In 1731 exports leaving Charleston included 42,000 barrels of rice,

13

14,000 barrels of pitch, tar and turpentine, and 250,000 deerskins. Virginia and Maryland shipped more tobacco, while Pennsylvania found a growing market for its wheat and flour. The fur trade was centered in New York. The New England colonies exported large quantities of ship timber and lumber of all types along with salt fish and meat.

Most of the colonial products were not competitive with those of England, but when competition did appear, restrictions followed. The Woolens Act of 1699 barred sale of colonial cloth outside the place where it was woven. Parliament in 1732 banned the export of hats from one colony to another. To protect English exports of iron and steel products, the colonies in 1750 were ordered to stop building various kinds of mills. After the British West Indies complained that the Americans were buying cheaper sugar and molasses from the French, Parliament passed the Molasses Act of 1733, placing a stiff duty on imports from the French islands. For the most part, however, these restrictions were poorly enforced and easily evaded by the Americans.

Governors vs. Assemblies

As the American population and economy grew, so did the problems of English colonial administration. All of the colonies were permitted to elect their own assemblies after the Dominion of New England collapsed in 1689, but only Connecticut and Rhode Island kept the right to elect their governors as well. The governors of the eight royal colonies were appointed by the King and those of the five proprietary colonies with the King's approval. And it was these royal and proprietary governors who had primary responsibility for enforcing English laws and regulations in America.

The governors were armed with great legal authority. They had the right of absolute veto over colonial legislation, the authority to terminate and dissolve assemblies, and the power to dismiss judges and create courts, long after the Crown had been stripped of these prerogatives in England. But the real power of the governors was effectively limited by their dependence on the colonial assemblies (in almost all cases) for their salaries and operating revenues. "In this situation, many governors chose simply not to 'consider anything further than how to sit easy,' and to be careful 'to do nothing, which upon a fair hearing...can be blamed.'

Because the surest way to 'sit easy' was to reach a political accommodation with local interests, they very frequently aligned themselves with dominant political factions in the colonies. Such governors sought to avoid disputes with the lower houses by taking especial care not to challenge their customary privileges and, if necessary, even quietly giving way before their demands."⁶

The powers of the assemblies, though nowhere carefully defined by charter or statute, grew steadily. In time they claimed and exercised the right to lay taxes, raise troops, incur debts, issue currency, and otherwise initiate all legislation. They commonly passed only short-term revenue bills, stipulated in detail how appropriations were to be spent, tacked riders on essential money bills, and vied with the governors for control of patronage.

Claiming prerogatives similar to those of the British House of Commons, the assemblies made the most of their power of the purse to extract concessions from the governors. When one governor asked for a fixed revenue for five years, the assembly demanded the right to appoint every official to be paid from the grant.

Some governors came to feel "impotent to carry out either imperial directions or their own projects against the exorbitant power" of the assemblies. "The too great and unwarrantable encroachments of the assemblies," declared Governor Lewis Morris of New Jersey, "make it necessary that a stop some way or other should be put to them, and they reduced to such proper and legal bounds as is consistent with his majesty's prerogative and their dependence."⁷

If the governors found it impolitic to veto some colonial legislation, it could still be killed by the royal disallowance. Acts so vetoed included ones that discriminated against religious minorities, assessed duties on the products of neighboring colonies, authorized unbacked issues of paper currency, and restricted the slave trade. But preventing the assemblies from taking unwanted action was not the same as winning their support for imperial projects, as the English found out during their wars with the French.

During these wars English requisitions on the colonies for men, money and supplies were honored by the assemblies slowly, in part or not at all, especially in those colonies that were not under fire. New York and Pennsylvania were notorious for continuing to trade with the

French in time of war. But all of the colonies resisted imperial direction in some degree and cherished their independence one from another. Not one of the assemblies ratified the Albany Plan of Union of 1754, although it had been drafted primarily by Benjamin Franklin with the approval of representatives from seven of the 13 colonies. The Plan was designed to create "one general government" in America.

Growth of Colonial Indignation

The French and Indian War (1754-63) doubled the national debt of England (to 130 million pounds), quadrupled the prospective costs of administering the greatly enlarged empire in America (to 300,000 pounds a year), and helped thereby to put the government of George III, crowned in 1760, on a collision course with the colonists. To the mercantilists in Parliament, it now seemed logical to plug the loopholes in trade controls and to make the colonies pay a share of the costs of imperial overhead. The shift in English colonial policy began in 1763 when George Grenville became prime minister.

Grenville's first step was to set aside the claims of Virginia and other colonies to portions of the vast lands taken from the French. By the Proclamation of 1763, the entire region between the Appalachians and the Mississippi, south of Quebec and north of Florida, was reserved for the Indians. And the English adhered to this policy despite strong pressures from highly placed speculators (including Benjamin Franklin) who promoted the settlement of such proposed inland colonies as Vandalia, Charlotiana and Transylvania.

At the same time, Parliament began to strengthen enforcement of trade controls. Admiralty courts, which tried smuggling cases without juries, could now move such trials to Halifax in Nova Scotia at considerable cost to those whose goods and ships were detained. Colonial issues of paper money, which had been permitted during the war, were banned by the Currency Act of 1764. And to lighten the British tax load, Grenville pushed three other laws through Parliament.

● The Revenue Act of 1764, to defray the expenses of defending, protecting and securing the colonies, cut in half the widely evaded duty laid on foreign molasses in 1733 but placed new duties on such colonial imports as wine, silk and linen. It also enumerated more colonial products, including hides and skins, that could be exported only to England.

● The Quartering Act of 1765 required the colonies to contribute to the upkeep of the 10,000 troops England planned to station in America. The colonies were to supply them with barracks or other quarters and with some of their provisions and were to pay a part of the money costs.

● The Stamp Act of 1765 required that revenue stamps costing up to 20 shillings be affixed to all licenses, legal documents, leases, notes and bonds, newspapers, pamphlets, almanacs, advertisements and other documents issued in the colonies. Passed on March 22, the law was to take effect Nov. 1 and was expected to yield 60,000 pounds a year.

None of these measures sat well with the Americans, but opposition focused on the Stamp Act as the first direct tax ever laid on the colonies by Parliament. Americans believed they could be taxed only by their own assemblies and that the Stamp Act, which was taxation without representation, was unconstitutional. The Virginia House of Burgesses so resolved at the urging of Patrick Henry, while the Massachusetts House of Representatives called for an intercolonial meeting to be held in New York in October.

The Stamp Act Congress was attended by 28 delegates from nine colonies. They affirmed their allegiance to the Crown, asserted their right as Englishmen not to be taxed without their consent, noted that the colonists were not represented in the House of Commons, and concluded that "no taxes ever have been or can be constitutionally imposed on them, but by their respective legislatures." The delegates urged Parliament to repeal the Stamp Act and other recent laws that had "a manifest tendency to subvert the rights and liberties of the colonists."

The English insisted that Parliament represented and acted in behalf of all Englishmen. But they could not ignore the sharp drop in exports that followed a colonial boycott of English goods or the attacks on royal officials by colonial mobs calling themselves "Sons of Liberty." When it became clear in 1766 that the Stamp Act could not be enforced, it was repealed. But Parliament, through a Declaratory Act, asserted its authority to legislate for the colonies "in all cases whatsoever" and declared colonial resolves to the contrary to be "utterly null and void."[8]

The Intolerable Acts

Following repeal of the Stamp Act, Chancellor of the Exchequer Charles Townshend proposed an increase of customs receipts to get the needed revenue. Parliament passed laws in 1767 laying new duties on imports by the colonies of paper, lead, glass, paint and tea; reorganizing the customs service in America; and authorizing broad use of general search warrants known as Writs of Assistance to ferret out violations. The Townshend Acts were greeted by a new outbreak of protests, colonial merchants revived their nonimportation agreements, and the adverse effects on English business again persuaded Parliament to retreat. When Lord North came to power in 1770, all of the Townshend duties except the one on tea were repealed. Most of the colonists were appeased, trade revived, and for three quiet years England and the colonies lived in relative harmony.

To American radicals like Samuel Adams of Massachusetts, this period of calm foreshadowed a further attack on colonial liberties, for the English had begun to pay the salaries of the royal governors and other officials from their increased customs receipts, thus freeing them from the hold of the assemblies. Adams, Patrick Henry, Thomas Jefferson and others, who now questioned the right of Parliament to legislate for the colonies in any respect, formed committees of correspondence that became the underground of the resistance movement.

The quiet years ended abruptly in 1773 when the faltering East India Company was authorized to dump a surplus of tea on the American colonies by undercutting the price of tea smuggled in from Holland. Colonial merchants, foreseeing ruinous competition, joined the radicals in protesting the Tea Act, and everywhere the colonists prepared to boycott the first shipments. In Boston, however, Adams and John Hancock urged direct action, and on Dec. 16, 1773, a mob disguised as Indians boarded three tea ships and dumped their cargoes into the harbor.

The Boston Tea Party alarmed many Americans who opposed British policy, but it also provoked the English government into a series of coercive acts that drove the colonists together. On March 25, 1774, the House of Commons ordered the Port of Boston closed until the city paid for the tea thrown into the harbor. That order was followed by laws revising the Massachusetts charter to strengthen royal control and transferring to England the trials of colonists charged with murder.

To these Intolerable Acts Parliament added one that alienated most of Protestant America by giving to the French-Canadian—and Catholic—royal province of Quebec all of the land west of the Appalachians lying north of the Ohio River and east of the Mississippi. The Quebec Act of June 22 was regarded as another punitive measure by most colonists and helped to muster broad support for a "general congress of all the colonies" proposed by the Virginia and Massachusetts assemblies.[9]

First Continental Congress

Every colony except Georgia (whose governor blocked the selection of delegates) was represented at the First Continental Congress, which met in Philadelphia on Sept. 5, 1774. Describing the Congress in a letter to his wife, John Adams wrote: "The business of the Congress is tedious beyond expression. This assembly is like no other that ever existed.... Every man upon every question must show his oratory, his criticism and his political abilities."[10] Conservative Joseph Galloway of Pennsylvania hoped to conciliate the English, while radical Samuel Adams wanted to defy all British controls. As the session continued, more and more delegates joined in the movement to protest and repudiate British policies toward the colonies.

The turning point came when Paul Revere arrived with the Suffolk Resolves, adopted by a convention of towns around Boston, which called on Massachusetts to arm itself against efforts to "enslave America" and urged Congress to adopt economic sanctions against England. To Galloway, these "inflammatory resolves...contained a complete declaration of war against Great Britain," and many others agreed. But most delegates felt compelled to register their support of Massachusetts. By a vote of six colonies to five they set aside Galloway's plan (based on the Albany Plan of Union of 1754) to give Parliament and a colonial legislature joint control over American affairs, and endorsed the Suffolk Resolves.[11]

The Congress then adopted a Declaration of Rights and Grievances against all British acts to which "Americans cannot submit" and approved a wide-ranging nonimportation, nonconsumption and nonexportation agreement or "Association" as "the most speedy, effectual and peaceable" means of swaying England. Locally elected committees were directed to enforce this commercial boycott by publicizing violations so that "all such foes to the rights of British-America may be publicly known and universally condemned as the enemies of American liberty." On Oct. 22, 1774, the Continental Congress adjourned, after agreeing to meet again the following May if necessary.

King George III declared that the colonies were "now in a state of rebellion; blows must decide whether they are to be subject to this country or independent." While the Earl of Chatham and Edmund Burke hoped conciliation was possible, they held firmly to "the view that the British Parliament was supreme over the colonies, that the authority of the empire could not be surrendered."[12] In the colonies patriot forces began to gather arms and supplies to train militia, and in Massachusetts they soon controlled all of the colony outside of Boston where the Governor, Gen. Thomas Gage, was installed with 5,000 troops.

On April 19, 1775, Gage sent 1,000 of these men to destroy patriot stores in Lexington and Concord. They were met by minutemen, firing broke out, and the British lost 247 in dead and wounded before getting back to Boston. These turned out to be the opening shots of the Revolutionary War, although more than a year was to pass before the Americans were sufficiently united to declare their independence.

Chapter 2

Revolution and Confederation

When the Second Continental Congress met on May 10, 1775, in Philadelphia, most of the delegates still hoped to avoid both war and independence. Faced with pleas for help from Massachusetts, the delegates agreed in mid-June to raise a Continental Army of 20,000 men, to ask the colonies for $2-million (in proportion to their population) for the army's support, and to make George Washington (a delegate from Virginia) the army's commander-in-chief.

Soon afterward, however, the Congress approved a petition to George III (drafted by John Dickinson) asking for "a happy and permanent reconciliation" between the colonies and England. The delegates also adopted a Declaration of the Causes of Necessity of Taking up Arms (drafted by Dickinson and Jefferson) in which they disavowed any desire for independence but resolved "to die free men rather than live slaves."[13]

The King's response, on Aug. 23, was to proclaim a state of rebellion in America. The British began to hire mercenaries in Germany and to incite the Iroquois against the colonials, while Congress authorized an expedition against Canada and efforts to contact other nations for aid. Yet the legislatures of five colonies took positions against independence that autumn. Pennsylvania's delegation to the Congress was told to "utterly reject any proposition...that may cause or lead to a separation from our mother country or a change in the form of this government."[14]

The British gave no signs of retreating, however, and the appearance in January 1776 of Thomas Paine's pamphlet "Common Sense" marked the beginning of what was to be a rising demand for independence. Paine argued that it was time for Americans to stand on their own feet, for there was "something absurd in supposing a continent to be perpetually governed by an island" and "it is evident that they belong to different systems: England to Europe, America to itself." Paine also put the onus for the colonies' troubles on the King rather than Parliament.[15]

Declaration of Independence

Pressure on the Congress to act reached a climax when, on June 7, 1776, Richard Henry Lee of Virginia introduced a resolution stating that "these United Colonies are, and of right ought to be, free and independent States."[16] Jefferson, John Adams, Franklin, Roger Sherman and Robert Livingston were named to draw up a declaration, but it was largely Jefferson's draft that was presented on June 28. Lee's resolution was adopted July 2; Jefferson's Declaration was then debated and slightly amended (to strike out an indictment of the British slave trade, for example) before it was approved July 4 by all of the delegations except New York's, which later voted for it after receiving new instructions.

The greater part of the Declaration—and the most important to Americans at that time—consisted of a recitation of every grievance against English colonial policy that had emerged since 1763. The grievances were presented as facts to prove that George III was seeking "the establishment of an absolute Tyranny over these States" and to justify their decision to dissolve "all political connection" with Britain. But it was the preamble that was to exert the greatest influence on others as a statement of political philosophy with universal appeal. Rooted in the concept of natural rights as developed by such philosophers as Thomas Hooker and John Locke, the preamble made these assertions:

"We hold these truths to be self-evident, that all men are created equal, that they are endowed by their Creator with certain unalienable Rights, that among these are Life, Liberty and the pursuit of Happiness. That to secure these rights, Governments are instituted among Men, deriving their just powers from the consent of the governed. That whenever any Form of Government becomes destructive of these ends it is the Right of the People to alter or to abolish it, and to institute new Government, laying its foundation on such principles and organizing its powers in such form, as to them shall seem most likely to effect their Safety and Happiness."

In conclusion, the signers, who styled themselves "the Representatives of the united States of America, in General Congress, Assembled," declared that "these United Colonies are, and of Right ought to be Free and Independent States," that as such "they have full Power to levy War, conclude Peace, contract Alliances, establish Commerce, and to do all other Acts and Things which Independent States may of right do," and that in support of this stand "we mutually pledge to each other our Lives, our Fortunes and our Sacred Honor."

Formation of State Governments

The Declaration of Independence committed the colonies to wage a war that was already under way and that would drag on for more than five years before England gave up the struggle. The Declaration also put an end to tolerance of the many Americans who remained loyal to the King; Tories who refused to sign an oath of allegiance to the United States suffered imprisonment and confiscation of property; as many as 80,000 fled to Canada and England. At home, the Declaration put to immediate test the capacity of the patriots to govern.

As early as the fall of 1774, Massachusetts had set up a provisional government in response to the Coercive Acts. As revolutionary sentiment grew, patriots took control of provincial assemblies and conventions, and the royal governors and judges began to leave. New Hampshire adopted a constitution in January 1776, South Carolina followed suit in March, and on May 10 the Continental Congress advised all of the colonies to form new governments. All except Massachusetts and the self-governing charter colonies of Connecticut and Rhode Island had done so by July 4, 1777, first anniversary of the signing of the Declaration of Independence. Four days later, Vermont, not previously a separate colony, declared its independence and adopted a constitution. Connecticut and Rhode Island did not get around to replacing their colonial charters by state constitutions until 1818 and 1842, respectively.

The new state constitutions of the Revolutionary period emerged in various ways. Those of South Carolina, Virginia and New Jersey were drafted by legislative bodies without explicit authorization and put into effect without popular consent. Those of New Hampshire, Georgia, Delaware, New York and Vermont were authorized but were not submitted to the voters for approval. In Maryland, Pennsylvania and North Carolina the constitutions were authorized and ratified by the voters. Only Massachusetts and New Hampshire (which wrote a new constitution in 1784 to replace the one adopted in 1776) employed what was to become the standard method of electing a constitutional convention and putting the product to a vote of the people.

Although they varied in detail, the new constitutions reflected a number of concepts held in common by Americans of the period. All were written, because the unwritten British constitution had been a source of such contention between the colonists and England. All included or were accompanied by some kind of "Bill of Rights" to secure those English liberties that George III had violated, such as freedom of speech, press and petition and the rights of habeas corpus and trial by jury. All paid tribute to the doctrine of separation of powers between the legislative, executive and judiciary, as it had been developed in England after the revolution of 1688 and expounded by Montesquieu's *Spirit of Laws*, published in 1748.

Separation did not mean balance, however, and most of the constitutions betrayed the colonists' great fear of executive authority, born of their many conflicts with the Crown and the royal governors. Executive power was weakened in every state except New York, Massachusetts and New Hampshire, and the governors of only two states were given the power of veto. In most cases the state legislature appointed the judiciary, although efforts were made to protect the independence of judges by preventing their arbitrary removal.

Power under most state constitutions was lodged in their legislatures. Ten of these were bicameral (Pennsylvania, Georgia and Vermont had one house), with the lower house predominant. Virginia's constitution provided, for example, that: "All laws shall originate in the House of Delegates, to be approved of or rejected by the Senate, or to be amended, with consent of the House of Delegates; except money bills, which in no instance shall be altered by the Senate, but wholly approved or rejected."[17]

All of the constitutions recognized the people as sovereign, but few entrusted them with much power. The Pennsylvania constitution (copied by Vermont), written by radicals who came to power early in 1776 after a major reapportionment of the colonial assembly, was the most democratic. It replaced governor and upper chamber with an executive council from whose ranks a president was chosen. Its members could serve no more than three years in seven while assemblymen were limited to four years in seven, to guard against establishing an aristocracy. There were no property qualifications for voting or for holding office.

Most other states adhered to prerevolutionary limits on suffrage. Ownership of some amount of property was generally required as a qualification to vote, and more was required to hold office. The property qualification for state senator in New Jersey and Maryland was 1,000 pounds, in South Carolina 2,000 pounds. Most states also imposed religious qualifications for public office.

Articles of Confederation

When Richard Henry Lee called for a declaration of independence on June 7, 1776, he proposed also that "a plan of confederation be prepared and transmitted to the respective Colonies for their consideration and approbation."[18] On June 11 Congress agreed and named a committee of 13 (one from each colony) to undertake the task. The plan recommended, based on a draft by John Dickinson, was presented July 12, but it was not until Nov. 15, 1777, that Congress, after much debate and some revision, adopted the Articles of Confederation and Perpetual Union.

The Articles reflected the dominant motive of Americans who were rebelling against British rule—to preserve their freedoms from the encroachments of centralized power. Even as Congress was struggling with tenuous authority to prosecute the war (and it gave Washington dictatorial powers over the army in December 1776), few of the delegates or other American leaders were prepared to entrust a national government with any power that would diminish the sovereignty and independence of the states. Thus the scope of federal authority was not a central issue in the design of the confederation.

Constitutional Beginnings

What was at issue was the relative standing of 13 rival and jealous states. Would they be represented equally in the national legislature (as they were in the Continental Congress and as the smaller states desired) or in proportion to their population (as the larger states wished)? Cost of a national government would have to be shared, but on what basis—wealth, population or (as the southerners insisted) the white population only? States without claims to lands west of the Appalachians thought Congress should control the area; those with claims were reluctant to give them up.

As finally adopted, the Articles conferred less authority on the national government than had been proposed in the Albany Plan of Union of 1754. They did little more than legalize what Congress was already doing by sufferance of the states. Congress remained the sole organ of government; the states retained their equality in Congress, having one vote each; and of the specific powers delegated to Congress the most important could not be exercised without the assent of nine of the 13 states.

The delegated authority included the power to declare war, enter treaties and alliances, raise an army and a navy, regulate coinage and borrow money. Congress was empowered also to regulate Indian affairs, establish a postal service, and adjudicate disputes between the states. But it had no power to tax (other than to charge postage); the costs of government would be allocated to the states in proportion to the value of their land and improvements as determined by Congress. The states were also to be assigned quotas for troops in proportion to the number of white inhabitants. But in no case did Congress have any power to compel the states to comply.

The Articles provided that Congress be composed of from two to seven delegates from each state (and from Canada if it chose to join). The delegates were to be selected annually and paid by the states, and they could serve no more than three years in any six. Members of Congress were barred from holding any federal post for pay and were immune from arrest while in attendance and from action for anything said in debate—provisions that were later incorporated in the Constitution. A Committee of the States (with one delegate from each) was authorized to act for Congress during a recess on such matters as did not require the assent of nine states.

Congress was authorized to appoint committees and civil officers necessary for managing the affairs of the United States. Following ratification, Robert Livingston was named as Secretary of Foreign Affairs, Robert Morris as Superintendent of Finance, and Gen. Benjamin Lincoln as Secretary of War. But the Articles made no provision for a federal executive or judiciary, gave Congress no sanction by which to enforce any of its decisions, left control of taxation and tariffs with the states, and required the unanimous consent of the states to adopt any amendment.

Final ratification was delayed by the reluctance of Maryland, New Jersey and Delaware to act until the states with western claims agreed to cede them to the national government. Cession of state claims did not actually begin until 1784, but it was clear by the start of 1781 that the states would cede, and Maryland, the last holdout, ratified the Articles March 1, 1781. Congress proclaimed them to be in effect the same day.

Trials of the Confederation

Adoption of the Articles of Confederation did nothing to relieve the chaotic state of federal finances. Of $10-million requisitioned by Congress in the first two years, the states paid in less than $1.5-million. From 1781 to 1786, federal collections averaged half a million a year, which was barely enough to meet current expenses. After two years as Superintendent of Finance, Robert Morris resigned in 1783, saying "our public credit is gone."[19] The foreign debt of the United States increased from less than $8-million in 1783 to more than $10-million in 1789, plus almost $1.8-million in unpaid interest.

Congress recognized the need for some independent financial authority even before the Articles took effect. A month earlier, it had asked the states for authority to levy a duty of 5 per cent on all imports. But it took unanimous agreement to amend the Articles, and the proposal died in 1782 when Rhode Island rejected it. In 1783 Congress again asked for the power to levy import duties, and this time New York refused approval.

Peace put an end to the destruction and drain of war, but it also underscored the weakness and disunity of the now sovereign and independent American states. As agreed in the peace treaty with England, Congress in 1783 recommended that the states restore property confiscated from the Loyalists, but few of them took any steps to do so. And instead of helping British merchants to recover their prewar debts (as the treaty obligated them to do), many of the states enacted laws to make recovery more difficult. The British, in turn, refused to evacuate several posts on the American side of the border with Canada.

The inability of Congress to force the states to comply with terms of the peace treaty contributed to the refusal of England, France and Spain to enter commercial treaties with the Confederation. Lacking any authority over trade, Congress was unable to retaliate when the British in 1783 closed Canada and the British West Indies to American shipping, and the attempts of the states to retaliate individually failed completely. The weakness of the Confederation also encouraged Spain to close the Mississippi to American ships in 1784 and to intrigue for the secession of frontier areas north of the Floridas.

Congress was equally powerless to help resolve a postwar conflict between debtors and creditors that was aggravated by a depression and a shortage of currency. Most of the states stopped issuing paper money and set out to pay off their war debts by raising taxes. At the same time, merchants and other creditors began to press for the collection of private debts. Squeezed on all sides, debtors (who were mostly farmers) clamored for relief through state laws to put off the collection of debts and to provide cheap money.

In response to this pressure, seven of the states resorted to paper money issues in 1786 during the worst of the depression. Debtors put over their entire program in Rhode Island where creditors, compelled by law to accept repayment in highly depreciated paper money, fled the state to avoid doing so. But in Massachusetts, where the commercial class was in power, the state government refused to issue paper money and pressed forward with a deflationary program of high taxes; cattle and land were seized for debts, debtors crowded the jails, and all petitions for relief were ignored.

Out of this turmoil came Shays' Rebellion of 1786, an uprising of distressed farmers in central Massachusetts led by Daniel Shays. Although the rebellion was put down by state militia in fairly short order, there was a good deal of sympathy for the rebels. Their leaders were treated leniently, and a newly elected legislature acted to meet some of their demands. But the rebellion aroused the fears of many Americans for the future, pointed up another weakness of the Confederation (for Congress had been unable to give Massachusetts any help), and gave a strong push to the gathering movement for governmental reform.

Chapter 3

The Constitution

The state of the union under the Articles of Confederation had become a source of growing concern to leading Americans well before Shays' Rebellion shook the confidence of a wider public. In voluminous correspondence beginning as early as 1780, George Washington, John Jay, Thomas Jefferson, James Madison, James Monroe and many others expressed their fear that the union forged in blood could not survive the strains of internal dissension and external weakness without some strengthening of central authority.

To Washington, writing in 1783, it was clear "that the honor, power and true interest of this country must be measured by a Continental scale, and that every departure therefrom weakens the Union, and may ultimately break the band which holds us together. To avert these evils, to form a Constitution that will give consistency, stability, and dignity to the Union and sufficient powers to the great Council of the Nation for general purposes" was a challenge to every patriot.[20]

How to form such a constitution was not yet clear. Opinions varied widely as to what would be "sufficient powers...for general purposes." Alexander Hamilton, in 1780 (when he was only 23), thought Congress should be given "complete sovereignty" over all but a few matters.[21] But Congress had ignored proposals of its own committees in 1781 that it seek authority to use troops "to compel any delinquent State to fulfill its Federal engagement" and to seize "the property of a State delinquent in its assigned proportion of men and money."[22] And when there was wide agreement on giving Congress authority to levy a federal import duty, the effort to amend the Articles foundered on the rule of unanimity.

At Hamilton's urging, the New York assembly asked Congress in 1782 to call a general convention of the states to revise the Articles. The Massachusetts Legislature seconded the request in 1785. Congress studied the proposal but was unable to reach agreement. Then, in 1785, Virginia and Maryland worked out a plan to resolve conflicts of those two states over navigation and commercial regulations. This gave Madison the idea of calling a general meeting on commercial problems. In January 1786 the Virginia Assembly issued the call for a meeting in Annapolis in September.

Nine states named delegates to the Annapolis Convention, but the dozen who assembled represented only five states—New York, New Jersey, Pennsylvania, Delaware and Virginia. Rather than seek a commercial agreement from so small a group, Madison and Hamilton persuaded the delegates to adopt a report, Sept. 14, that described the state of the Union as "delicate and critical." The report recommended that the states appoint commissioners to meet the next May in Philadelphia "to devise such further provisions as shall appear to them necessary to render the constitution of the Federal Government adequate to the exigencies of the Union."[23]

The proposal was deliberately vague. Madison and Hamilton knew that many others would oppose giving the central government much more power. And some, they knew, preferred the alternative of dividing the union into two or more confederations of states with closer economic and political ties. Southerners were convinced that this was the ultimate objective of John Jay's offer to Spain to give up free navigation of the Mississippi in return for trading concessions of interest to New England. Monroe (a Virginia delegate to Congress) saw it as part of a scheme "for dismembering the Confederacy and throwing the states eastward of the Hudson into one government."[24]

The Virginia Assembly, prodded by Madison and Washington, agreed on Oct. 16, 1786, to send delegates to

Philadelphia, and six other states took similar action before Congress, on Feb. 21, 1787, moved to retain control of the situation. Its resolution endorsed the proposed convention for the purpose of reporting to Congress and the several legislatures its recommendations. Officially, therefore, the convention was to be no more than advisory to Congress.

Soon after the Philadelphia Convention opened on May 25, 1787, the delegates were asked to decide whether to try to patch up the Articles of Confederation or to ignore them and draw up a new plan of government. Congress, the state legislatures and many of the delegates expected no more than a revision of the Articles that would somehow strengthen the Confederation without altering the system of state sovereignty. But Madison and others who had worked to bring about a convention were convinced of the need for fundamental reform.

The Virginia Plan

These nationalists had come prepared, and on May 29 they seized the initiative. Edmund Randolph, acting for the Virginians, introduced 15 resolutions that added up to a plan for a new "National Government" of broad powers. The Virginia Plan called for a "National Legislature" of two houses, one to be elected by the people and the other by members of the first; a "National Executive" to be chosen by the Legislature; and a "National Judiciary." The legislature would have power to legislate in all cases where the states were "incompetent" or would interrupt "the harmony of the United States," and to "negative" state laws contrary to the articles of union. And the states would be represented in both chambers in proportion to their wealth or white population.[25]

The Convention moved at once into Committee of the Whole to consider the Randolph resolutions. They clearly envisaged a central government that, unlike that of the Confederation, would operate directly upon the people and independently of the states. It was to be a "national government" in contrast to the "merely federal" system that had been tried and found wanting. What the Virginians had in mind, though, was a system in which national and state governments would exercise dual sovereignty over the people within separate and prescribed fields. Randolph said that his plan "only means to give the national government power to defend and protect itself—to take, therefore, from the respective legislatures of states no more sovereignty than is competent to this end."[26]

Such a dual system was unknown in 1787. To many delegates the term "national government" implied a unitary or consolidated regime of potentially unlimited powers that would extinguish the independence of the states. However, on May 30, with only Connecticut opposed and New York divided, they adopted Randolph's proposition "that a National Government ought to be established consisting of a supreme Legislative, Executive and Judiciary." This opening commitment by most of the delegates then present reflected the air of crisis in which they met.[27]

The next step of the Committee of the Whole was to take up and approve several of the specific proposals of the Virginia Plan. As the debate proceeded, some members from smaller states became alarmed by the insistence of the larger states on proportional representation in both houses of the proposed Legislature. Under one formula, this would have given Virginia, Pennsylvania and Massachusetts—the three most populous states—13 of 28 seats in the Senate as well as a similar share of seats in the House. This spelled domination to those accustomed to the equality of states which prevailed in the Congress of the Confederation, and in the Convention as well.

To Luther Martin of Maryland, such a plan meant "a system of slavery which bound hand and foot ten states of the Union and placed them at the mercy of the other three." John Dickinson of Delaware declared that "we would rather submit to a foreign power than submit to be deprived of an equality of suffrage in both branches of the Legislature, and thereby be thrown under the domination of the large states." New Jersey would "never confederate" on such a basis, said William Paterson, for "she would be swallowed up" and he would "rather submit to a monarch, to a despot, than to such a fate."[28]

The New Jersey Plan

On June 11 the Committee voted, six states to five, to constitute the Senate on the same proportional basis as the House. That decision led Paterson and others to draft a purely federal alternative to the Virginia Plan. The New Jersey Plan, presented June 15, proposed amending the Articles of Confederation to give Congress authority to levy import duties and to regulate trade. It would have provided also for a plural executive to be chosen by Congress and for a federal judiciary. It proposed that treaties and acts of Congress "shall be the supreme law," and that the executive be authorized to "call forth the power of the Confederated States" to enforce the laws if necessary. But the plan would have left each state with an equal voice in Congress and most of the attributes of sovereignty.

Paterson argued that his plan "accorded first with the powers of the Convention, and second with the sentiments of the people.... Our object is not such a Government as may be best in itself, but such a one as our constituents have authorized us to prepare and as they will approve." The nationalists rejected this concept of their responsibility; as Hamilton put it, the Union was in peril, and "to rely on and propose any plan not adequate to these exigencies, merely because it was not clearly within our powers, would be to sacrifice the means to the end."[29]

Madison was the last to speak against the New Jersey Plan, pointing up serious problems of the Confederation for which it offered no solution. On June 19 the delegates were asked to decide whether the Randolph resolutions "should be adhered to as preferable to those of Mr. Paterson."[30] Seven states voted yes and only three states no. That settled the issue of partial versus total reform; a clear majority of the delegates were now committed to abandoning the Articles and to drafting a new constitution.

The Great Compromise

The task was to take three months. There were few points of unanimity among the 55 men participating. Delegates from the same state were frequently divided and, as a result, occasionally unable to vote. The records of the Convention also reveal that, although the nationalists won over a majority to their cause at an early stage, the original Virginia Plan was unacceptable in many of its details. The Constitution could not have been written without some degree of willingness on all sides to compromise in the interests of designing a workable and acceptable plan.

This became evident soon after defeat of the New Jersey Plan when the small states continued to demand and the large states to oppose equal representation in the

Senate. On July 2 the Convention split five to five on this issue, with Georgia divided. Faced with a deadlock, the Convention named a committee to seek a compromise. It proposed on July 5 that, in return for equality of state representation in the Senate, the House be given sole power to originate money bills, which the Senate could accept or reject but not modify. This formula was finally approved July 16, five states to four, with Massachusetts divided and New York not voting because two of its three delegates had departed never to return. On July 24 a Committee of Detail was appointed to draft the Constitution according to the resolutions adopted by the Convention.

Without the Great Compromise the Convention would have collapsed. As Madison pointed out, however, "the great division of interests" in America was not between the large and small but between the northern and southern states, partly because of climate but "principally from the effects of having or not having slaves."[31] Although the southerners were for the most part supporters of a strong central government, they were determined to limit its power to discriminate against the South's special interests in slavery, agricultural exports and western expansion. This stand necessitated other compromises that accounted for some of the key provisions of the new plan of government.

What finally emerged Sept. 17 as the Constitution of the United States was a unique blend of national and federal systems based on republican principles of representative and limited government. It met the basic objective of the nationalists by providing for a central government of ample powers that could function independently of the states. It also met the concerns of states' rights supporters by surrounding that government with checks and balances to prevent the tyranny of any one branch.

The text of the Constitution does not follow the order in which the separate provisions were developed. The Convention moved generally from decisions on broad principles to questions of detail and precision. But the interdependent nature of the various parts of the plan made for frequent reconsideration of decisions in one area to take account of subsequent decisions in another but related area. As a result, many of the provisions were altered or added in the final weeks of the Convention. How the major provisions were developed is described in chapters four through six.

Chapter 4

The Structure of Congress

The Convention's early decision that a national government, if formed, should consist of three branches—legislative, executive and judicial—was undisputed. This division of governmental functions had been recognized from early colonial times and was reflected in most of the state constitutions. The failure of the Articles of Confederation to separate the functions was generally recognized as a serious mistake. The decision as to three branches also implied broad acceptance of the principle of separation of powers, although most of the provisions of the Constitution that gave effect to the principle were adopted on practical rather than theoretical grounds.

The Virginia Plan called for a legislature of two houses, according to a practice initiated by Parliament, followed by most of the colonial governments and retained by 10 of the 13 states. The Continental Congress and the Congress of the Confederation were unicameral, but once the Convention had decided to abandon the Articles there was little question that the new Congress should be bicameral. As George Mason saw it, the minds of Americans were settled on two points—"an attachment to republican government (and) an attachment to more than one branch in the Legislature."[32] Only Pennsylvania dissented when the Committee of the Whole voted for two houses, and the Convention confirmed the committee's decision, June 21, by a vote of seven states to three.

Election of the House

The nationalists insisted that the new government rest on the consent of the people rather than the state legislatures. So they held it essential that at least "the first branch" or House be elected "by the people immediately," as Madison put it. The government "ought to possess...the mind or sense of the people at large," said James Wilson, and for that reason "the Legislature ought to be the most exact transcript of the whole society." The House "was to be the grand depository of the democratic principles of the government," said Mason.[33]

Those who were suspicious of a national government preferred election of the House by the state legislatures. "The people immediately should have as little to do" with electing the government as possible, said Roger Sherman, because "they want information and are constantly liable to be misled." Elbridge Gerry was convinced that "the evils we experience flow from the excess of democracy," while Charles Pinckney thought "the people were less fit judges"[34] than the legislatures to choose members of the House. Election by the legislatures was twice defeated, however, and popular election of the House was confirmed June 21 by a vote of nine states to one.

Election of the Senate

The Virginia Plan proposed that the House elect the "second branch" or Senate from persons nominated by the state legislatures. There was little support for this plan because it would have made the Senate subservient to the House. Most delegates agreed with Gouverneur Morris that it was to be the Senate's role "to check the precipitation, changeableness and excesses of the first branch."[35] (The role of representing the states emerged later, after the decision for equal representation.) Neither was there any support for the view of Madison and Wilson that the people should elect the Senate as well as the House. Election of the Senate by the state legislatures was carried unanimously in Committee of the Whole, June 7, and confirmed June 25 by a Convention vote of nine states to two.

Basis of Representation

The Virginia Plan called for representation of the states in both House and Senate in proportion to their wealth or

37

free population. This proposal led to the revolt of the small states, which was ended by the vote of July 16 for equal representation of the states in the Senate. But while the principle of proportional representation in the House was never seriously challenged, the idea of basing it on wealth or the free population raised questions that led to adoption of important qualifications.

To retain southern support for proportional representation in the Senate, Wilson had proposed on June 11 that the House be apportioned according to a count of the whole number of free citizens and three-fifths of all others (meaning slaves) except Indians not paying taxes. This formula (first proposed in Congress in 1783) was adopted with only New Jersey and Delaware opposed. Then on July 9 the Convention decided that the new Congress should have power "to regulate the number of representatives upon the principles of wealth and number of inhabitants."[36] Since southerners regarded slaves as property, this led northerners who wanted representation to be based on population alone to ask why slaves should be counted at all.

As a result, on July 11 the Convention voted, six states to four, to exclude blacks from the formula of June 11. At this point Gouverneur Morris proposed that the power of Congress to apportion the House according to wealth and numbers be subject to a proviso "that direct taxation shall be in proportion to representation,"[37] and the proviso was adopted without debate. The slave issue now appeared in a different light, for it seemed that the South must pay for any increases in representation it would gain by counting slaves. So the northerners dropped the opposition to the three-fifths count demanded by the southerners, and on July 13 the Convention restored that provision.

Because it was now agreed that representation was to be based solely on population (counting all whites and three-fifths of blacks), the word "wealth" was deleted from the provision adopted July 9. This resolution of the question gave five free voters in a slave state a voice in the House equivalent to that of seven free voters in a non-slave state, according to Rufus King, but it was "a necessary sacrifice to the establishment of the Constitution."[38]

Size of Congress

The committee that recommended equal representation in the Senate on July 5 also proposed that each state have one vote in the House for every 40,000 inhabitants This proposal precipitated the debate on representation discussed above, during which it was decided to let Congress regulate the future size of the House to allow for population changes and the admission of new states. Upon reflection, however, it was seen that under this arrangement a majority in Congress would be able to block a reapportionment and even to change the basis of representation for slaves. Northerners and southerners now agreed that the periods and rules of revising the representation ought to be fixed by the Constitution.

Randolph was the first to propose a regular census, and on July 13 the Convention adopted the plan, finally incorporated in Article I, Section 2, linking the apportionment of representatives to an "enumeration" every 10 years of the "whole number of free persons...and three fifths of all others." On Aug. 8 it was decided that the number of representatives "shall not exceed one for every 40,000," a figure that was lowered to 30,000 on the last day of the Convention. Until the first census should be taken, the size of the House was fixed at 65 representatives allotted as set forth in Article I.[39]

The size of the Senate was fixed on July 23 when the Convention considered and adopted (with Maryland alone voting against it) a proposal that the body should "consist of two members from each state, who shall vote per capita." A proposal to allow each state three senators had been turned down on the ground that it would penalize poorer and more distant states, and that "a small number was most convenient for deciding on peace and war," as Nathaniel Gorham put it. The idea that senators should vote individually rather than as a delegation came from Gerry, who wanted to "prevent the delays and inconveniences" that had occurred in Congress under the unit rule for voting.[40] Although this provision was at odds with the decision that the states should be equally represented in the Senate, it was accepted with little objection and included in Article I, Section 3.

Terms of Office

There was strong attachment in the Convention to the tradition of annual elections—"the only defense of the people against tyranny," according to Gerry. But Madison argued that representatives would need more than one year to become informed about the interests of other states, and his proposal of a three-year term for the House was adopted June 12. Many delegates still wanted more frequent elections. "The Representatives ought to return home and mix with the people," said Sherman, for "by remaining at the seat of Government they would acquire the habits of the place which might differ from those of their constituents." On reconsideration June 21, the Convention compromised on biennial elections and a two-year term for representatives.[41]

The delegates also changed their minds about the Senate, agreeing first to a term of seven years although the terms of state senators varied from two to a maximum of five. When this decision was reviewed, alternatives of four, six and nine years were considered. Charles Pinckney opposed six years because senators would be "too long separated from their constituents, and will imbibe attachments different from that of the state." But having decided in biennial elections for the House, the Convention voted June 26 to make it a six-year term in the Senate with one-third of the members to be elected every two years.[42]

Qualifications of Voters

The report of the Committee of Detail, Aug. 6, provided that the qualifications of electors for the House should be the same as those required by the states for "the most numerous branch" of their own legislatures. Because property and other voting qualifications varied widely from state to state, no uniform standard seemed feasible. When Gouverneur Morris proposed giving Congress power to alter the qualifications, Oliver Ellsworth replied: "The clause is safe as it is—the states have staked their liberties on the qualifications which we have proposed to confirm."[43] A proposal by Morris and others to limit the franchise to those who owned land was rejected, and on Aug. 8 the Convention adopted the committee proposal without dissent.

Regulation of Elections

The Committee of Detail also proposed that the states regulate the times and places of electing senators and representatives, but that Congress retain the power to change the regulations. The states should not have the last word in this regard, said Madison, since "it was impossible to foresee all the abuses that might be made of the discretionary power." The Convention adopted this provision Aug. 9 but amended it Sept. 14 by adding "except as to the places of choosing Senators," who were to be elected by the state legislatures. The purpose of the change was to "exempt the seats of government in the states from the power of Congress."[44]

Qualifications of Members

The Convention decided in June on a minimum age of 30 for senators and 25 for representatives. The Committee of Detail added two more qualifications: United States citizenship (three years for the House, four for the Senate) and residence within the state to be represented. Fearful of making it too easy for foreigners to be elected, the Convention lengthened the citizenship requirement to seven years for representatives and nine years for senators, after voting down 14 years as likely (in Ellsworth's view) to discourage "meritorious aliens from emigrating to this country."[45]

Some delegates wanted to require residence in a state for a minimum time, from one to seven years. Mason feared that "rich men of neighboring states may employ with success the means of corruption in some particular district and thereby get into the public councils after having failed in their own state."[46] But these proposals were voted down, and it was left that "no person shall be a representative (or senator) who shall not, when elected, be an inhabitant of that state in which he shall be chosen."[47]

The Convention debated the desirability of a property qualification. Most of the state constitutions required members of their legislatures to own certain amounts of property. Dickinson doubted "the policy of interweaving into a Republican Constitution a veneration of wealth."[48] But on July 26, by a vote of eight states to three, the Convention instructed the Committee of Detail to draft a property qualification. As reported, this would have given Congress authority to establish "uniform qualifications...with regard to property." But when the provision was debated on Aug. 10, it was rejected and there was no further effort to include a property qualification.[49]

There was even less disposition to include a religious qualification, although all of the states except New York and Virginia imposed such a qualification on state representatives. The Convention's outlook on this point was made clear when, in debating an oath of office on Aug. 30, the delegates adopted without dissent Charles Pinckney's proviso (which became a part of Article VI) that "no religious test shall ever be required as a qualification to any office or public trust under the United States."[50] The only qualifications established by the Constitution for election to Congress, therefore, related to age, citizenship and residence.

Pay of Members

The Virginia Plan wanted members of the National Legislature to be paid "liberal stipends" without saying who should pay them. To the nationalists, however, one of the weaknesses of the Confederation was that members of Congress were paid by their states. So on June 12, after submitting "fixt" for "liberal," the Committee of the Whole agreed that in the case of representatives "the wages should be paid out of the National Treasury." But on June 22 Ellsworth moved that the states pay. Randolph opposed the change, saying it would create a dependence that "would vitiate the whole system." Hamilton agreed, saying "those who pay are the masters of those who are paid." The motion was rejected, four states to five.

When the pay of senators was discussed on June 26, Ellsworth again moved that the states pay. Madison argued that this would make senators "the mere agents and advocates of state interests and views, instead of being the impartial umpires and guardians of justice and general good." Ellsworth's motion was again defeated, five states to six. Despite this, the Aug. 6 report of the Committee of Detail provided that the pay of senators and representatives should be "ascertained and paid" by the states. But Ellsworth and others had now changed their minds, and on Aug. 14 the Convention voted, nine to two, to pay members out of the national treasury.

Whether the amount of pay should be fixed in the Constitution was another matter. To let Congress set its own wages, said Madison, "was an indecent thing and might, in time, prove a dangerous one." Ellsworth proposed five dollars a day. Others thought the decision should be left to Congress, although Sherman was afraid the members would pay themselves too little rather than too much, "so that men ever so fit could not serve unless they were at the same time rich." On Aug. 14, however, the Convention voted to give Congress full authority to fix its own pay by law.[51]

Eligibility to Office

Because of the attachment of several states to the theory of rotation in office, the Articles of Confederation had provided that "no person shall be capable of being a delegate for more than three years in any term of six years."[52] This rule had forced out of Congress some of its better members and was widely criticized. The Virginia Plan proposed, nevertheless, that members ought to be incapable of re-election for an unspecified period after the expiration of their term of service, and to be subject to recall. But this provision was eliminated in Committee of the Whole, without debate or dissent, and no further effort was made to qualify the eligibility of representatives or senators for re-election.

Whether members of Congress should be eligible to hold other office was debated at much greater length. Under the Articles, a delegate was not "capable of holding any office under the United States for which he, or another for his benefit, receives any salary, fees or emolument of any kind."[53] But the Congress had appointed many delegates to diplomatic and other jobs, and the practice had created much resentment. There was also a general concern over the office-seeking propensities of state legislators. So the Virginia Plan proposed making any member of Congress ineligible to any office established by a particular state, or under the authority of the United States during the term of service and for an unspecified period after its expiration.

Although this provision—with the time of one year inserted in the blank—was adopted in Committee of the Whole, June 12, the Convention reconsidered and modified it several times before the final form was approved on Sept. 3. Delegates who wanted to shut the door on appointments saw them as a source of corruption. "What led to the appointment of this Convention?" asked John Mercer, and answered: "The corruption and mutability of the legislative councils of the states."[54] Those opposed to too many strictures feared they would discourage good men from running for Congress. "The legislature would cease to be a magnet to the first talents and abilities," said Charles Pinckney.[55]

The compromise that emerged was a twofold disqualification. Members could not be appointed during their terms to federal offices created during those terms or for which the pay was increased, and no one holding federal office could be a member at the same time. The provision, incorporated in Section 6 of Article I, made no reference to state office or to ineligibility following expiration of a member's term.

Regulation of Congress

Section 5 of Article I included four provisions for the regulation of House and Senate that originated with the Committee of Detail and were only slightly modified in Convention.

● The provision that "Each House shall be the Judge of the Elections, Returns and Qualifications of its own Members..." was found in the constitutions of eight states and was agreed to without debate.

● The provision that "Each House may determine the Rules of its Proceedings, punish its Members for disorderly Behaviour, and, with the Concurrence of two-thirds, expel a Member" was amended to require a two-thirds vote for expulsion. The change, proposed by Madison because "the right of expulsion was too important to be exercised by a bare majority of a quorum," was approved by a unanimous vote.

● The provision that "Each House shall keep a Journal, and from time to time publish the same..." stemmed from a similar provision in the Articles. When Madison proposed giving the Senate some discretion in the matter, Wilson objected that "the people have a right to know what their agents are doing or have done, and it should not be in the option of the legislature to conceal their proceedings."[56] The Convention voted to require publication of the Journals of each House, but with the proviso "excepting such parts as may in their judgment require secrecy." The clause also provided for recording the "yea" and "nay" votes of members, although some delegates objected that "the reasons governing the votes never appear along with them."

● The provision that "Neither House, during the Session of Congress, shall, without the Consent of the other, adjourn for more than three days, nor to any other Place than that in which the two Houses shall be sitting," was agreed to after brief debate. Most of the state constitutions had similar provisions, reflecting a common commitment to legislative independence born of colonial experience with the right of royal governors to suspend and dissolve the assemblies.

Chapter 5

Powers of Congress

The Virginia resolutions proposed that the National Legislature be empowered—

"to enjoy the Legislative Rights vested in Congress by the Confederation and moreover to legislate in all cases to which the separate States are incompetent, or in which the harmony of the United States may be interrupted by the exercise of individual Legislation;

"to negative all laws passed by the several States, contravening in the opinion of the National Legislature the articles of Union; and

"to call forth the force of the Union against any member of the Union failing in its duty under the articles thereof." *(See p. 32)*

These proposals reflected the great concern of the nationalists with the powerlessness of Congress under the Confederation to protect the interests of the United States at large against the "prejudices, passions and improper views of the state legislatures,"[57] in the words of Dickinson. Madison deplored "a constant tendency in the states to encroach on the federal authority, to violate national treaties, to infringe the rights and interests of each other, to oppress the weaker party within their respective jurisdiction."[58] So it seemed essential that, in addition to adequate authority to legislate for the general interests of the Union, the new national government should possess the power to restrain the states and to compel their obedience.

When these proposals were first discussed May 31, some delegates wanted an exact enumeration of powers before voting, but the first of the Virginia resolutions was approved after brief debate without dissent. The second, granting a power to negate state laws akin to the royal disallowance of colonial laws, was also approved without debate or dissent. When the third resolution was called up, however, Madison moved to set it aside because he feared that "the use of force against a state would look more like a declaration of war than an infliction of punishment."[59] Although the New Jersey Plan contained a similar provision, there was no further consideration of this power by the Convention.

On June 8, Charles Pinckney proposed that the power to nullify state laws be extended to all such laws Congress should judge to be improper. Such an expansion would enslave the states, said Gerry, and the motion was rejected, seven states to three. Strong opposition now developed to any power to negate state laws. Madison continued to defend it as the most certain means of preserving the system, but Gouverneur Morris concluded that it would disgust all the states. On July 17 the Convention reversed its earlier action by voting seven to three against the power to negative. The problem of securing conformity of states to national law was finally resolved by adoption of a "supremacy" clause and the specific prohibition of certain state laws.

The Convention on July 17 also reconsidered the first of the Virginia resolutions. Sherman proposed as a substitute that Congress be empowered "to make laws binding on the people of the United States in all cases which may concern the common interests of the Union; but not to interfere with the Government of the individual States in any matters of internal police which respect the Government of such States only, and wherein the general welfare of the United States is not concerned." This formulation (in which the term "general welfare" made its first appearance in the Convention) seemed too restrictive to most delegates and it was rejected, eight to two. Then, by a vote of six states to four, the Convention inserted in the resolution approved May 31 the additional power to legislate "in all cases for the general interests of the Union."[60]

When this broad grant of legislative authority was examined by the Committee of Detail it seemed so vague and unlimited that the committee decided to replace it with an enumeration of specified powers. Eighteen of these powers were listed in the report of Aug. 6, which also contained, for the first time, lists of powers to be denied to Congress and to the states. The various lists formed the basis for the powers and prohibitions that were finally incorporated in Sections 8, 9 and 10 of Article I of the Constitution, of which the major provisions were developed as explained in the following pages.

Power to Tax

The committee's first proposal—that Congress "shall have the power to lay and collect taxes, duties, imposts and excises"—was adopted Aug. 16 without dissent. The Convention then became embroiled in the issue of paying off the public debt and soon amended the tax clause to provide that Congress "shall fulfill the engagements and discharge the debts of the United States and shall have the power to lay and collect taxes...." Pierce Butler objected that this provision would require Congress to redeem at face value all government paper, including that held by "bloodsuckers who had speculated on the distresses of others and bought up securities at heavy discounts."[61] They thought Congress should be free to buy up such holdings at less than full value.

As a result, the Convention dropped the language added to the tax clause and adopted in its place the declaration found in Article VI that "All debts contracted and engagements entered into before the adoption of this Constitution shall be as valid against the United States under this Constitution as under the Confederation." This declaration left open the question of full or partial redemption, which was to become a major issue in the First Congress.

But some delegates now thought that the power to tax should be linked explicitly to the purpose of paying the debt. Their position led to further amendment of the tax clause on Sept. 4 to provide that Congress "shall have power to lay and collect taxes, duties, imposts and excises, to pay the debts and provide for the common defense and general welfare of the United States." The further proviso in the first clause of Section 8 of Article I that "all duties, imposts and excises shall be uniform throughout the United States" had been approved earlier as a part of the effort to prevent Congress from discriminating against the commerce of any one state.

It was to be argued later that inclusion of the words "general welfare" was intended to confer an additional and unlimited power on Congress. The records of the Convention indicate, however, that when it was decided to qualify the power to tax "to pay the debts," it became necessary to make it clear that this was not the only purpose for which taxes could be levied. "To provide for the common defense and general welfare" was taken from the Articles of Confederation and used to encompass all of the other specific and limited powers vested by the Constitution in Congress.[62]

Direct Taxes. As already noted, in settling the basis for representation in the House, the Convention had linked the apportionment of "direct taxes" as well as representatives to a count of all whites and three-fifths of blacks. When this provision was reconsidered Aug. 20, King asked "what was the precise meaning of direct taxation" but, according to Madison, "no one answered."[63] The only direct taxes in use at that time were land taxes and capitation or poll taxes. Because southerners feared that Congress might seek to levy a special tax on slaves, the Committee of Detail recommended and the Convention later adopted a further provision, incorporated in Section 9 of Article I, that "No Capitation, or other direct, Tax shall be laid, unless in Proportion" to the count required by Section 2. Another limitation on the power to tax—also adopted as a concession to the South—prohibited levies on exports.

Power to Regulate Commerce

Trade among the states and with other countries was severely handicapped under the Confederation by a lack of uniformity in duties and commercial regulations. The states commonly discriminated against the products of neighboring states, incurring retaliation in kind that added to the divisiveness and suspicions of the times. To Madison and many others, it was as essential to the new plan of government that Congress have the power to regulate commerce as it was that it have the power to tax. It soon became clear, however, that the southern states would not accept a Constitution that failed to protect their vested interest in slave labor and agricultural exports from the burdensome restrictions that a Congress controlled by northerners might seek.

As a result, the Committee of Detail proposed that Congress have the power to regulate commerce with foreign nations and among the several states subject to two limitations—a ban on export taxes and a prohibition against any effort to tax or outlaw the slave trade. The general power to regulate commerce was approved on Aug. 16 without dissent. (The words "and with the Indian Tribes" were added Sept. 4.) But the proposed limitations met with considerable opposition.

In keeping with mercantilist doctrines, it was common practice at that time for governments to tax exports; the idea of prohibiting such action was novel. "To deny this power is to take from the common government half the regulation of trade," said Wilson.[64] It was also to deny Congress the power to menace the livelihood of the South by taxing the exports of rice, tobacco and indigo on which its economy was largely dependent. Other northerners considered this concession to the South as wise as it was necessary; Gerry said the Convention had already given Congress "more power than we know how will be exercised."[65] On Aug. 21, by a vote of seven states to four, the Convention agreed that "No Tax or Duty shall be laid on Articles exported from any State." This provision was placed in Section 9 of Article I in the final draft.

The second limitation on the power to regulate commerce provided that no tax or duty was to be laid on the migration or importation of such persons as the several States shall think proper to admit; nor shall such migration or importation be prohibited. The limitation was designed to meet the South's objection to any interference with the slave trade, although those words were carefully avoided. Luther Martin thought it was "inconsistent with the principles of the Revolution and dishonorable to the American character to have such a feature in the Constitution."[66] But most other delegates, including those opposed to slavery, argued that it was a political rather than a moral issue.

Some northerners, as well as southerners, agreed with Ellsworth that "the morality or wisdom of slavery" should be left to the states to determine. "Let us not intermeddle," he said, predicting that "slavery, in time, will not be a speck in our country."[67] Many others agreed with Mason that the "infernal traffic" in slaves was holding back the economic development of the country, and that for this reason the national government "should have power to prevent the increase of slavery."[68] Since the provision reported by the Committee of Detail was clearly unacceptable to many delegates, a committee was named to seek a compromise.

It now proposed that Congress be barred from prohibiting the slave trade until 1800, but that it have power to levy a duty on slaves as on other imports. Both provisions were approved Aug. 25, the first by a vote of seven states to four after the year 1800 had been changed to 1808, and the second after limiting the duty to $10. So the power of Congress to regulate commerce was further limited by these provisions respecting slaves, which became the first clause of Section 9 of Article I.

Still another limit on the commerce power, sought by the South and recommended by the Committee of Detail, would have required a two-thirds vote of both House and Senate to pass a navigation act. England had used such laws to channel colonial imports and exports into British ships and ports, and southerners now feared that the North, where shipping was a major interest, might try to monopolize the transport of their exports (then largely confined to English vessels) by a law requiring them to be carried aboard American ships.

Northern delegates were strongly opposed to the two-thirds proposal, and in working out the compromise on the slave trade succeeded in having it dropped. As a result, Charles Pinckney moved to require a two-thirds vote of both houses to enact any commercial regulation. This motion was rejected Aug. 29, seven states to four, and the Convention confirmed the decision to drop the proposed two-thirds rule for navigation acts. Mason (one of three who refused to sign the Constitution) later argued that a bare majority of Congress should not have the power to "enable a few rich merchants in Philadelphia, New York and Boston to monopolize the staples of the Southern States."[69]

A relatively minor limitation on the power to regulate commerce was adopted to allay the fear of Maryland that Congress might require ships traversing Chesapeake Bay to enter or clear at Norfolk or another Virginia port in order to simplify the collection of duties. As approved Aug. 31 and added to Section 9 of Article I, it provided that "No

Preference shall be given by any Regulation of Commerce or Revenue to the Ports of one State over those of another; nor shall Vessels bound to or from one State be obliged to enter, clear or pay Duties in another."

War and Treaty Power

The Articles of Confederation had given Congress the exclusive right and power of determining on peace and war. The Committee of Detail proposed giving to the new Congress as a whole the power to make war and to the Senate alone the power to make treaties. The treaty power was later divided between the President and the Senate. But in discussing the war power, Aug. 17, Charles Pinckney was for giving it to the Senate since "it would be singular for one authority to make war, and another peace." On the other hand, Butler thought the war power should rest with the President, "who will have all the requisite qualities and will not make war but when the Nation will support it." Neither view drew any support, and the Convention voted to give Congress the power "to declare war." The word "declare" had been substituted for "make" to leave the President free to repel a sudden attack. As Sherman put it, "The Executive should be able to repel, and not commence war."[70]

On Aug. 18, the Convention agreed to give Congress the power "to raise and support Armies," "to provide and maintain a Navy," and "to make Rules for the Government and Regulation of the land and naval Forces." All were taken from the Articles of Confederation. Gerry, voicing the old colonial fears of a standing army, wanted a proviso that "in time of peace" the army should consist of no more than two or three thousand men, but his motion was unanimously rejected.[71] On Sept. 5, however, the Convention added to the power to "raise and support Armies" the proviso "but no Appropriation of Money to that Use shall be for a longer Term than two Years."[72] This was intended to quiet fears similar to those that had led the British to require annual appropriations for the army.

The Convention approved without dissent the power, proposed by the Committee of Detail and included in Section 8 of Article I, "to provide for calling forth the Militia to execute the Laws of the Union, suppress Insurrections and repel Invasions." But a further proposal by Mason that

Congress have power to regulate the militia alarmed the defenders of state sovereignty. To Gerry, this was the last point remaining to be surrendered. Others argued that the states would never agree to let the militia out of their hands.

The shortcomings of the militia during the Revolutionary War were a bitter memory to most of the delegates, however, and they shared the practical view of Madison that "as the greatest danger to liberty is from large standing armies, it is best to prevent them by an effectual provision for a good militia."[73] So on Aug. 23 the Convention adopted the provision, as later incorporated in Section 8, giving Congress power "to provide for organizing, arming, and disciplining the Militia, and for governing such Part of them as may be employed in the Service of the United States...."

Special Case of Money Bills

The committee named to resolve the issue of equal or proportional representation in the Senate proposed as a compromise that each state have one vote in the Senate, but that the House originate all bills for raising and appropriating money and paying government salaries, and that the Senate be denied the right to amend such bills. Included in the proposal was the phrase that "No money shall be drawn from the public Treasury, but in pursuance of appropriations to be originated in the first branch." Seven states at this time required that money bills originate in the lower house, but only four of those states forbade amendment by the upper house. Some delegates objected that such a provision would be degrading to the Senate, but it was approved July 6, five states to three.

The Committee of Detail phrased the provision as follows: "All bills for raising or appropriating money, and for fixing the salaries of the officers of Government, shall originate in the House of Representatives, and shall not be altered or amended by the Senate." Madison was for striking the entire provision as likely to promote "injurious altercations" between House and Senate; others insisted that it was necessary because the people "will not agree that any but their immediate representatives shall meddle with their purse."[74] The Convention's division on the question reflected contrasting concepts of the Senate as likely to be the most responsible branch or the most aristocratic one, to be strengthened or checked accordingly.

On Aug. 8 the Convention reversed itself, voting seven states to four to drop the provision. Further debate, however, underscored the importance of reaching a compromise, and the one finally proposed was adopted Sept. 8, nine to two. It provided that "All bills for raising revenue shall originate in the House of Representatives, and shall be subject to alterations and amendments by the Senate; no money shall be drawn from the Treasury but in consequence of appropriations made by law." The first sentence, slightly revised, was incorporated in the final draft as the first clause of Section 7, while the second sentence was made one of the limitations on the powers of Congress listed in Section 9 of Article I.

The Constitution thus gave the House exclusive power to originate any bill involving taxes or tariffs of any kind, but it did not extend that power to appropriation bills. However, the House assumed the additional power, on the basis of the consideration it had received in the Convention, and it became the recognized prerogative of the House to originate spending as well as revenue bills.

Admission of New States

As early as 1780, the Continental Congress had resolved that lands ceded to the United States "shall be disposed of for the common benefit of the United States, and be settled and formed into distinct republican States, which shall become members of the Federal Union, and have the same rights of sovereignty, freedom and independence as the other States." By 1786 the Congress of the Confederation was in possession of all land south of Canada, north of the Ohio, west of the Alleghenies and east of the Mississippi. Provisions for governing this great territory were laid down by Congress in the Northwest Ordinance of July 13, 1787.

The Ordinance provided that, upon attaining a population of 5,000 free male inhabitants of voting age, the territory would be entitled to elect a legislature and send a nonvoting delegate to Congress. It provided also that no less than three nor more than five states were to be formed out of the territory. Each state was to have at least 60,000 free inhabitants to qualify for admission to the Union "on an equal footing with the original States in all respects whatever."

And the Ordinance declared that "there shall be neither slavery nor involuntary servitude in the said territory...."[75]

As this far-sighted plan was being approved in New York by the Congress of the Confederation, Gouverneur Morris and other eastern delegates to the Constitutional Convention in Philadelphia were arguing strongly against equality for the new states. "The busy haunts of men, not the remote wilderness, are the proper school of political talents," said Morris. "If the western people get the power into their hands, they will ruin the Atlantic interests. The back members are always most adverse to the best measures."[76]

Among those of an opposing view were the delegates of Virginia and North Carolina, whose western lands were to become Kentucky and Tennessee. Mason argued that the western territories "will either not unite with or will speedily revolt from the Union, if they are not in all respects placed on an equal footing." In time, he thought, they might well be "both more numerous and more wealthy" than the seaboard states. Madison was certain that "no unfavorable distinctions were admissible, either in point of justice or policy."[77]

In the light of this debate, the Committee of Detail proposed on Aug. 6 that Congress have the power to admit new states with the consent of two-thirds of the members present in each House (the Articles of Confederation required the consent of nine states) and, in the case of a state formed from an existing state, the consent of the legislature of that state. New states were to be admitted on the same terms with the original states. But when this proposal was considered Aug. 29, the Convention adopted a motion by Morris to strike out the provision for equality.

Morris and Dickinson then offered a new draft, eliminating the condition of a two-thirds vote, which was adopted and became the first clause of Section 3 of Article IV. It provided simply that new states could be admitted by Congress, subject to the consent of the state legislatures where concerned. Although this provision of the Constitution was silent as to the status of the new states, Congress was to adhere to the principle of equality in admitting them.

The Convention then adopted the provision governing territories set out in the second clause of Section 3 of Article IV. Madison had first proposed adding such a provision to the Constitution to give a legal foundation to the Northwest Ordinance, since the Articles of Confederation had given Congress no explicit power to legislate for territories. A proviso ruling out prejudice to any claims of the United States or of any particular state was added because some delegates feared that, without it, the terms on which new states were admitted might favor the claims of some state to vacant lands ceded by Britain.

Power of Impeachment

It was decided early in the Convention that the Executive should be "removable on impeachment and conviction of malpractice or neglect of duty."[78] Who should impeach and try him, however, depended on how he was to be chosen. So long as Congress was to elect the President—and that decision stood until Sept. 4—few delegates were willing to give Congress the additional power to remove him. The final decision to have the President chosen by presidential electors helped to resolve the problem.

The Virginia Plan called for the national judiciary to try "impeachments of any National officers," without specifying which branch of government would impeach. Because all the state constitutions vested that power in the lower house of the assembly, the Committee of Detail proposed removal of the President on impeachment by the House and conviction by the Supreme Court "of treason, bribery or corruption." No action was taken on this proposal until the special committee, in advancing the plan for presidential electors, suggested that the Senate try all impeachments and that conviction require the concurrence of two-thirds of the members present.

When this plan was debated Sept. 8, Charles Pinckney opposed trial by the Senate on the ground that if the President "opposes a favorite law, the two Houses will combine against him, and under the influence of heat and faction throw him out of office."[79] But the Convention adopted the formula for impeachment by the House, trial by the Senate, and conviction by a two-thirds vote. It also extended the grounds for impeachment from treason and bribery to "other high crimes and other misdemeanors" and made the Vice President and other civil officers similarly impeachable and removable.. These provisions were incorporated in Section 2 and 3 of Article I and in Section 4 of Article II.

Miscellaneous Powers

The Committee of Detail proposed that Congress retain the power granted in the Articles "to borrow money and emit bills on the credit of the United States." But state emissions of paper money in 1786 had contributed greatly to the alarms that had led to the calling of the Convention, and most delegates agreed with Ellsworth that this was a "favorable moment to shut and bar the door against paper money."[80] So the words "and emit bills" were struck out, with only two states dissenting, before this provision was approved Aug. 16.

Most of the other powers of Congress specified in Section 8 of Article I were derived from the Articles of Confederation or included as appropriate to the new plan of government, and were approved with little debate or dissent. This was true of provisions respecting naturalization and bankruptcy, coinage, counterfeiting, post offices, copyrights, inferior tribunals, piracies, and the seat of government. It was true also of the final provision of Section 8—proposed by the Committee of Detail and adopted Aug. 20 without debate—which was to be named the "sweeping clause" of the Constitution.

That clause authorized Congress "to make all Laws which shall be necessary and proper for carrying into Execution the foregoing Powers, and all other Powers vested by this Constitution in the Government of the United States, or in any Department or Officer thereof." The intent of this grant was simply to enable Congress to enact legislation giving effect to the specified powers. No member of the Convention suggested that it was meant to confer some power in addition to those previously specified. But the meaning of the clause and of the words "necessary and proper" was to become the focus of the continuing controversy between broad and strict constructionists of the Constitution that began with passage by the First Congress of a law to create a national bank.

Limits on Powers of Congress

Section 9 of Article I as finally adopted imposed eight specific limitations on the powers of Congress. Five of the limitations—those relating to the slave trade, capitation taxes, sport taxes, preference among ports, and appropriations—have been discussed in connection with the powers to tax, to regulate commerce and to originate money bills. The others were adopted as follows:

● On Aug. 28, Charles Pinckney moved to adopt a provision of the Massachusetts Constitution that barred suspension of the writ of habeas corpus except on the most urgent occasions and then for a period not to exceed one year. This was amended and adopted to provide that "the Privilege of the Writ of Habeas Corpus shall not be suspended, unless when in Cases of Rebellion or Invasion the public Safety may require it."

● On Aug. 22, Gerry proposed a prohibition on the passage of bills of attainder and ex post facto laws. Some delegates objected that such a provision would imply an improper suspicion of Congress and was an unnecessary guard. The Convention agreed, however, that "No Bill of Attainder or ex post facto Law shall be passed." A later motion by Mason to strike out ex post facto laws (on the ground that the ban might prevent Congress from redeeming the debt at less than face value) was unanimously rejected.

● On Aug. 23 the Convention adopted the two provisions that make up the final clause of Section 9 of Article I, both of which were taken from the Articles of Confederation. The bar to titles of nobility was proposed by the Committee of Detail. The bar to acceptance of emolument, office or title from foreign governments without the consent of Congress was urged by Pinckney to help keep American officials independent of external influence.

Pinckney and others proposed adding to the Constitution a number of provisions similar to those contained in the Bills of Rights of the various states. On Sept. 12, Gerry moved to appoint a committee to draft a Bill of Rights, but 10 states voted No. Anxious to complete their work and return home, the delegates were in no mood to spend additional time on something most of them believed to be unnecessary, since none of the powers to be vested in Congress seemed to countenance legislation that might violate individual rights. However, omission of a Bill of Rights became a major issue in seeking ratification of the Constitution and led to assurances that it would be amended promptly to include the missing guarantees.

Chapter 6

Executive and Judiciary

No question troubled the Convention more than the place to give the executive in the new plan of government. The office did not exist under the Articles of Confederation, which placed the executive function in Congress. A long-standing fear of executive authority had led Americans "to throw all power into the Legislative vortex," as Madison put it, and under most of the state constitutions the executives were indeed "little more than cyphers, the Legislatures omnipotent."[81] How much more authority and independence to give the National Executive remained in dispute until the very end of the Convention.

The Virginia Plan had in view a national executive chosen by the national legislature for a fixed term, ineligible for reappointment, and empowered with "a general authority to execute the National laws" as well as "the Executive rights vested in Congress by the Confederation." Debate on these proposals disclosed a spectrum of views ranging from that of Sherman, who thought the executive should be "nothing more than an institution for carrying the will of the Legislative into effect," to that of Gouverneur Morris, who felt the Executive should be "the guardian of the people" against legislative tyranny.[82]

Until September, the Convention favored a single executive chosen by Congress for one term of seven years, whose powers would be limited by the fact that Congress would appoint judges and ambassadors and make treaties. This plan for legislative supremacy was then abandoned for the more balanced one that was finally adopted and incorporated in Article II of the Constitution. The President would be chosen by electors for a four-year term without limit as to re-election, and he would have the power to make all appointments subject to confirmation by the Senate and to make treaties subject to approval by two-thirds of the Senate. Major provisions of Article II were developed as related below.

A Single Executive

Randolph, who presented the Virginia Plan, opposed a single executive as "the foetus of monarchy" and proposed three persons, who, Mason thought, should be chosen from the northern, middle and southern states. But Wilson foresaw "nothing but uncontrolled, continued and violent animosities" among three persons; a single executive, he said, would give "most energy, dispatch and responsibility to the office."[83] On June 4, the delegates voted for a single executive, seven states to four, and the Convention confirmed the decision July 17 without dissent.

The Committee of Detail then proposed that "the Executive Power of the United States shall be vested in a single person" to be called the President and to have the title of "His Excellency." These provisions were adopted Aug. 24 without debate, but in drafting the final document the Committee of Style dropped the title and provided simply that "the Executive Power shall be vested in a President of the United States of America." The omission from the Constitution of any title other than President helped to defeat a proposal in the First Congress that he be addressed as "His Highness."[84]

Method of Election, Term of Office

The method of election and term of office were closely related issues. If Congress were to choose the President, most delegates thought he should have a fairly long term and be ineligible for reappointment. For as Randolph put it, "if he should be reappointable by the Legislature, he will be no check on it."[85] But if the President was to be chosen in some other manner, a shorter term with re-eligibility was generally acceptable. Thus the method of election was the key question.

The Convention first decided that Congress should choose the President for a single seven-year term. On reflection, however, some delegates thought this would not leave him sufficiently independent. Wilson proposed election by electors chosen by the people, but Gerry considered the people "too little informed of personal characters" to choose electors, and the proposal was rejected, eight to two. Gerry himself proposed that the governors of the states pick the President to avoid the corruption he foresaw in having Congress choose him, but this plan also was rejected.[86]

Several other methods were proposed, and at one point the delegates agreed on choice by electors chosen by the state legislatures. But this decision was soon reversed. However, when Morris on Aug. 24 renewed Wilson's original proposal for electors chosen by the people, only six states were opposed and five were in favor. Three of the latter were smaller states that had opposed an earlier decision to have the Senate and the House ballot jointly when electing a President, thereby giving the large states a bigger voice in making the selection.

All of the questions concerning the President were then reconsidered by a special committee on postponed matters, whose report of Sept. 4 recommended most of the provisions that were finally adopted. According to Morris, the committee rejected choice of the President by Congress because of "the danger of intrigue and faction" and "the opportunity for cabal."[87] Instead, it proposed that he be chosen by electors equal in number to the senators and representatives from each state, who would be chosen as each state decided. They would vote by ballot for two persons, at least one of whom could not be an inhabitant of their state. The one receiving a majority of the electoral votes would become President, the one with the next largest vote would become Vice President. In the event of a tie, or if no one received a majority, the Senate would decide.

The plan provided for a four-year term with no restriction as to re-election; shifted from the Senate to the President the power to appoint ambassadors and judges and to make treaties subject to Senate approval, and gave the Senate instead of the Supreme Court the power to try impeachments. This realignment of powers between the President and the Senate appealed to the small states because it was generally assumed that the Senate (in which each state was to be represented equally) would have the final say in choosing the President in most cases.

For the same reason, however, some delegates now feared that the combination of powers to be vested in the Senate would (in Randolph's words) "convert that body into a real and dangerous aristocracy."[88] Sherman thereupon proposed moving the final election of the President from the Senate to the House, with the proviso that each state have one vote. The change, which preserved the influence of the small states while easing the fears expressed about the Senate, was quickly adopted, as was the rest of the electoral plan and the four-year term without limit as to re-eligibility.

Qualifications

The Committee of Detail first proposed that a President be at least 35 years of age, a citizen, and an inhabitant of the United States for 21 years, just as age, citizenship and minimum period of residence were the only qualifications stipulated for senators and representatives. The committee added the qualification that the President must be a natural born citizen or a citizen at the time of the adoption of the Constitution, and it reduced the time of residence within the United States to at least 14 years "in the whole." The phrase "in the whole" was dropped in drafting the final provision in Section 1 of Article II, which was also adjusted to make it clear that the qualifications for President applied equally to the Vice President.

The Vice President

The office of the vice presidency was not considered by the Convention until Sept. 4, when a special committee proposed that a Vice President, chosen for the same term as the President, serve as ex officio President of the Senate. (A Vice President or lieutenant governor served in a similar capacity in four of the 13 states.) The proposal was designed to provide a position for the runner-up in the electoral vote, and to give the Senate an impartial presiding officer without depriving any state of one of its two votes.

When this proposal was debated Sept. 7, Mason objected that "it mixed too much the Legislative and the Executive." Gerry thought it tantamount to putting the President himself at the head of the Senate because of "the close intimacy that must subsist between the President and the Vice President." But Sherman noted that "if the Vice President were not to be President of the Senate, he would be without employment."[89] The Convention then adopted the proposal with only Massachusetts opposed. The provision that the Vice President "shall be President of the Senate, but shall have no Vote unless they be equally divided," was placed in Section 3 of Article I.

The Convention never discussed the role of the Vice President as successor to the President in the event of the latter's removal by death or otherwise. It seems to have contemplated that he would merely perform the duties of President until another was elected. Thus the special committee proposed that in case of the President's removal (by impeachment), "death, absence, resignation or inability to discharge the powers or duties of his office, the Vice President shall exercise those powers and duties until another President be chosen, or until the inability of the President be removed."

This language was revised to provide that "in case of the removal of the President from office, or of his death, resignation, or inability to discharge the powers and duties of the said office, the same shall devolve on the Vice President." The revised wording, incorporated in Article II, left it unclear as to whether it was the "said office" or the "powers and duties" that were to "devolve" on the Vice President. The right of the Vice President to assume the office of President was first asserted by John Tyler in 1841 and became the established practice.[90]

There remained the question of providing for the office in the event both men were removed. Randolph proposed that Congress designate an officer to "act accordingly until the time of electing a President shall arrive." Madison objected that this would prevent an earlier election, so it was agreed to substitute "until such disability be removed, or a President shall be elected." The Committee of Style ignored this change, so the Convention voted on Sept. 15 to restore it. The final provision, authorizing Congress to designate by law an officer to "act as President" until "a President shall be elected," was joined to the earlier provision concerning the Vice President in Article II.[91]

Presidential Powers

Initially, the Convention conferred only three powers on the President—"to carry into effect the National laws," "to appoint to offices in cases not otherwise provided for," and to veto bills. The Committee of Detail proposed a number of additional powers drawn from the state constitutions, most of which were adopted with little discussion or change. This was true of provisions (placed in Section 3 of Article II) for informing Congress "of the State of the Union" and recommending legislation, for convening and adjourning Congress, for receiving ambassadors, and for seeing "that the Laws be faithfully executed."

The Convention also agreed without debate that "the President shall be Commander in Chief of the Army and Navy" and of the militia when called into national service; almost all of the state constitutions vested a similar power in the state executives. The power of the President "to grant reprieves and pardons except in cases of impeachment" was likewise approved, although Mason argued that Congress should have this power while Randolph wanted to bar pardons for treason as "too great a trust" to place in the President.[92] These two provisions were included in Section 2 of Article II.

Power to Appoint. The appointive powers of the President were limited until September to "cases not otherwise provided for." The Virginia Plan had proposed that judges be appointed by the legislature (a practice followed in all except three states), but the Convention voted to give the power to the Senate alone as the "less numerous and more select body." In July the delegates considered and rejected alternative proposals that judges be appointed by the President alone, by the President with the advice and consent of the Senate, and by the President unless two-thirds of the Senate should disagree.

All this was changed when, on Sept. 7, the Convention adopted the proposal of the special committee that the President appoint ambassadors and other public ministers, justices of the Supreme Court and all other officers of the United States "by and with the Advice and Consent of the Senate." This power (incorporated in Section 2) was further qualified Sept. 15 by requiring that offices not otherwise provided for "be established by law" and by authorizing Congress to vest appointment of inferior officers in the President, the courts or the heads of departments. Nothing was said of a power of removal from office—a power that was to become a much-argued issue.

Treaty Power. The proposal that the Senate alone have the power to make treaties (first put forward by the Committee of Detail) drew considerable opposition. Mason said it would enable the Senate to "sell the whole country by means of treaties." Madison thought the President, representing the whole people, should have the power. Morris argued for a provision that "no treaty shall be binding...which is not ratified by a law."[93] Southern delegates were especially concerned to prevent abandonment by treaty of free navigation of the Mississippi.

The issue was referred to a special committee on postponed matters, which recommended vesting the President with the power to make treaties subject to the advice and consent of two-thirds of the Senators present. The latter provision provoked extended debate. Motions were made and rejected to strike out the two-thirds requirement, to require consent of two-thirds of all members of the Senate, to require a majority of the whole number of senators, to provide that no treaty should be made without previous notice to the members and reasonable time for their attending.

On Sept. 7 the Convention voted to except peace treaties from the two-thirds rule. Madison then moved to authorize two-thirds of the Senate alone to make a peace treaty, arguing that the President "would necessarily derive so much power and importance from a state of war that he might be tempted, if authorized to impede a treaty of peace."[94] The motion was rejected, but after further debate on the advantages and disadvantages of permitting a majority of the Senate to approve a peace treaty, the Convention reversed itself and made all treaties subject to the concurrence of two-thirds of the Senators present.

Veto Power. The Virginia Plan had proposed joining the judiciary with the executive in exercising the power to veto acts of the legislature, subject to repassage. Because it was expected that the judiciary might have to pass on the constitutionality of legislation, most delegates thought it improper to give the judiciary a share of the veto power, and the proposal was rejected. Wilson and Hamilton favored giving the executive an absolute veto, but on June 4 the delegates voted, eight states to two, for Gerry's motion (based on the Massachusetts constitution) for an executive veto that could be overridden if two-thirds of each branch of the legislature so voted.

When this provision was reconsidered on Aug. 15, it was in the context of a plan to lodge in Congress the power to elect the President, to impeach him, and to appoint judges. Many delegates then agreed with Wilson that such an arrangement would not give "a sufficient self-defensive power either to the Executive or Judiciary Department," and the Convention voted to require a vote of three-fourths of each House to override a veto.[95] But on Sept. 12, after having adopted the presidential elector plan and other changes proposed by the special committee, the Convention restored the two-thirds provision.

The veto power was incorporated in Section 7 of Article I, setting out the procedure for the enactment of a bill with or without the President's signature. This section also made provision for the "pocket veto" of a bill when "the Congress by their Adjournment prevent its return, in which Case it shall not become Law." Although some delegates indicated a belief that the two-thirds provision was intended to apply to the entire membership of the House and Senate, a two-thirds vote of those present came to be accepted in practice.

The Judiciary

Article III of the Constitution, relating to "the judicial Power of the United States," was developed in the Convention with relative ease. The Virginia Plan called for "one or more supreme tribunals" and inferior tribunals to be appointed by the national legislature and to try all cases involving crimes at sea, foreigners and citizens of different states, "collection of the National revenue," impeachments, and "questions which may involve the national peace and harmony." The Convention went on to spell out the jurisdiction of these courts in greater detail, but the only basic changes made in the plan were to vest the Senate and finally the President with the power to appoint judges, and to transfer the trial of impeachments from the Supreme Court to the Senate.

Lower Courts and Appointment of Judges

The delegates agreed to one Supreme Court without debate, but some objected to establishing any lower courts. John Rutledge thought the state courts should hear all cases in the first instance, "the right of appeal to the Supreme National Tribunal being sufficient to secure the National rights and uniformity of judgments." Sherman deplored the expense. But Madison argued that without lower courts "dispersed throughout the Republic, with final jurisdiction in many cases, appeals would be multiplied to an oppressive degree." Randolph said the state courts "cannot be trusted with the administration of the National laws."[96] As a compromise, the Convention agreed to permit Congress to decide whether to "ordain and establish" inferior courts.

The proposal that the national legislature appoint the judiciary was based on similar provisions in most of the state constitutions. Wilson, arguing that "intrigue, partiality and concealment" would result from such a method, proposed appointment by the President. Madison urged appointment by the Senate as "a less numerous and more select body," and this plan was approved June 13.[97] A proposal that the President appoint judges "by and with the advice and consent of the Senate" was defeated by a tie vote July 18, but that was the method finally adopted in September as a part of the compromise that also moved the trial of impeachments from the Supreme Court to the Senate.

Tenure and Jurisdiction

Both the Virginia Plan and the New Jersey Plan provided that judges would hold office "during good behaviour"—a rule long considered essential to maintaining the independence of the judiciary. When this provision was considered Aug. 27, Dickinson proposed that judges "may be removed by the Executive on the application by the Senate and the House of Representatives." Others objected strongly, Wilson contending that "the Judges would be in a bad situation, if made to depend on every gust of faction which might prevail in two branches of our Government."[98] Only Connecticut voted for the proposal, and the Convention agreed to tenure during good behavior.

Most of the provisions embodied in Section 2 of Article III specifying the cases to which "the judicial Power shall extend," and in which cases the Supreme Court would have original and in which cases appellate jurisdiction, were set out in the Aug. 6 report of the Committee of Detail and adopted by the Convention on Aug. 27 with little change or debate. The most important change was made in the committee's first provision, extending jurisdiction to "all cases arising under the laws" of the United States, when the Convention voted to insert the words "the Constitution and" before "the laws." This made it clear that the Supreme Court was ultimately to decide all questions of constitutionality, whether arising in state or federal courts.

Article III did not explicitly authorize the court to pass on the constitutionality of acts of Congress, but the Convention clearly anticipated the exercise of that power as one of the acknowledged functions of the courts. Several delegates noted that state courts had "set aside" laws in conflict with the state constitutions. The Convention debated at great length (and rejected four times) a proposal to join the court with the President in the veto power; Wilson favored it because "laws may be unjust, may be unwise, may be dangerous, may be destructive, and yet may not be so unconstitutional as to justify the judges in refusing to give them effect." Mason agreed that the court "could declare an unconstitutional law void."[99]

Supremacy Clause

The role of the judiciary in determining the constitutionality of laws was also implicit in the provision, incorporated in Article VI, which asserted that the Constitution, the laws and the treaties of the United States "shall be the supreme Law of the Land." This provision first appeared on July 17 after the Convention had reversed itself and voted to deny Congress the proposed power. Anxious to place some restraint on the free-wheeling state legislatures, the Convention adopted instead and without dissent a substitute offered by Luther Martin and drawn directly from the New Jersey Plan of June 14.

The substitute provided that the laws and treaties of the United States "shall be the supreme law of the respective States, as far as those acts or treaties shall relate to the said States, or their citizens and inhabitants—and that the Judiciaries of the several States shall be bound thereby in their decisions, anything in the respective laws of the individual States to the contrary notwithstanding." In its report of Aug. 6, the Committee of Detail dropped the qualifying phrase "as far as those acts or treaties shall relate to the said States," substituted the word "Judges" for "Judiciaries" in the next clause and the words "Constitutions or laws" for "laws" in the final proviso, and made a few other word changes.

The Convention agreed to these changes Aug. 23 and to another prefacing the entire provision with "This Constitution." Further revision by the Committee of Style changed "supreme law of the several States" to "supreme law of the land," in what became the final phrasing of the provision in Article VI. The effect of the various changes was to make it clear that all judges, state and federal, were bound to uphold the supremacy of the Constitution over all other acts.

The "supremacy" clause was reinforced by the further provision in Article VI that all members of Congress and of the state legislatures, as well as all executive and judicial officers of the national and state governments "shall be bound by Oath or Affirmation to support this Constitution."[100]

Limits on Powers of the States

The "supremacy" clause was designed to prevent the states from passing laws contrary to the Constitution. Since the Constitution was also to specify the powers granted to Congress, those powers were denied by implication to the states. By the same reasoning, however, any powers not granted to Congress remained with the states. To eliminate any doubt of their intention to put an end to irresponsible acts of the individual states, the delegates decided to specify what the states could not or must do. Acts prohibited to the states were placed in Section 10 of Article I, while those required of them were placed in Sections 1 and 2 of Article IV.

Most of these provisions (many of which were taken from the Articles of Confederation) were proposed by the Committee of Detail and adopted by the Convention Aug. 28 with little debate or change. The committee had proposed that no state be allowed to make anything but gold or silver legal tender without the consent of Congress, but the Convention voted for an absolute prohibition on such laws, Sherman saying this was "a favorable crisis for crushing paper money."[101] The Convention also added a provision, drawn from the Northwest Ordinance, aimed at the welter of state laws favoring debtors over creditors: no state was to pass any ex post facto law or law impairing the obligation of contracts.

The provisions of Article IV requiring each state to give "full faith and credit" to the acts of other states, to respect "all Privileges and Immunities" of all citizens, and to deliver up fugitives from justice were derived from the Articles. To these the Convention added the provision, requested by southerners, that became known as the "fugitive slave" clause, requiring such persons to be "delivered up on Claim of the Party to whom such Service or Labour may be due." As with the rest of the Constitution, the enforcement of these provisions was assigned, by the "supremacy" clause, to the courts.

Chapter 7

Amendment and Ratification

A major reason for calling the Convention of 1787 had been the impossibility of obtaining the unanimous approval of the states that was required to amend the Articles of Confederation. So there was general agreement that it was better to provide for amending the Constitution "in an easy, regular and constitutional way, than to trust to chance and violence," as Mason put it.[102] But the method for doing so received little consideration until the final days of the Convention.

The Committee of Detail was the first to propose that the legislatures of two-thirds of the states have the sole power to initiate amendments by petitioning Congress to call a convention for that purpose. This provision was adopted Aug. 30 after a brief debate during which no one supported the argument of Gouverneur Morris that Congress also should have the power to call a convention on its own. But, on reconsideration Sept. 10, Hamilton asserted that Congress "will be the first to perceive and will be the most sensible to the necessity of amendments," and he proposed that two-thirds of the Senate and House also have the power to call a convention."[103]

Wilson moved that amendments be adopted when ratified by two-thirds of the states. When that proposal was defeated, six states to five, Wilson moved to substitute ratification by three-fourths of the states, which was approved without dissent. The Convention then adopted a new formula, providing that Congress "shall" propose amendments "whenever two-thirds of both Houses shall deem necessary or on the application of two-thirds" of the state legislatures, and that such amendments would become valid when ratified by the legislatures or conventions of three-fourths of the states as Congress might direct.

Under this formula, any amendment requested by two-thirds of the states would be submitted directly to the states for ratification. As modified Sept. 15, on the motion of Morris, the formula provided instead that on the application of two-thirds of the states, Congress "shall call a Convention for proposing Amendments." Thus, as finally drafted, Article V provided that, in proposing amendments to the Constitution, Congress would act directly while the states would act indirectly. In either case, however, amendments would take effect when approved by three-fourths of the states.

While working out these terms, the Convention also adopted two restrictions on the amending power. As a concession to the southern states, the Convention had already agreed (in Section 9 of Article I) to prohibit Congress from outlawing the slave trade before 1808 or levying any direct tax unless in proportion to a count of all whites and three-fifths of blacks. On Sept. 10, Rutledge noted that unless a similar limit were placed on the amending power, the provisions "relating to slaves might be altered by the States not interested in that property and prejudiced against them."[104] So it was agreed, without debate, to add the proviso that no amendment adopted before 1808 "shall in any manner affect" those two provisions of Article I.

Sherman now worried that "three fourths of the States might be brought to do things fatal to particular States, as abolishing them altogether or depriving them of their equality in the Senate." He proposed, as a further proviso to the amending power, that "No state shall without its consent be affected in its internal police, or deprived of its equal suffrage in the Senate."[105] The term "internal police" covered much more than most delegates were prepared to exclude, and only three states supported Sherman. But the more limited proviso that "no State, without its Consent, shall be deprived of its equal suffrage in the Senate" was accepted without debate and added to Article V.

Campaign for Ratification

According to the resolution of Congress, the Philadelphia Convention was to meet for the "sole and express purpose of revising the Articles of Confederation and reporting to Congress and the several legislatures" its recommendations. But the nationalists who organized the Convention and persuaded it to ignore these narrow instructions were determined that the fate of the new Constitution should not be entrusted to the state legislatures, but that the instrument should be ratified "by the supreme authority of the people themselves," as Madison put it. The legislatures, he pointed out, were in any event without power to consent to changes that "would make essential inroads on the State Constitutions."[106]

By "the people themselves" the nationalists meant special conventions elected for the purpose. Conventions would be more representative than the legislatures, which excluded "many of the ablest men," and they would be more likely to favor the Constitution than would be legislatures that (as King said) "being to lose power will be most likely to raise objections." Opposed to this view were delegates like Ellsworth, who thought conventions were "better fitted to pull down than to build up Constitutions," and Gerry, who said the people "would never agree on anything."[107] But the Convention rejected Ellsworth's motion for ratification by the legislatures and agreed July 23, nine states to one, that the Constitution should be submitted to popularly elected conventions.

This decision was followed, on Aug. 31, by the key decision that the Constitution should enter into force when approved by the conventions of no more than nine of the 13 states. By this time, only a few of the delegates still felt as Martin did that "unanimity was necessary to dissolve the existing Confederacy."[108] Seven and ten were also proposed as minimums, but nine was chosen as the more familiar figure, being the number required to act on important matters under the Articles. It was also clearly impractical to require (as the Committee of Detail had proposed) that the Constitution be submitted to the Congress "for their approbation," so it was agreed to strike out that provision.

Randolph and Mason (two of the three delegates who finally refused to sign the Constitution) continued to argue that it should be submitted to another General Convention, along with any amendments proposed by the state conventions, before it was finally acted on. Few others believed another such gathering could improve the product significantly, and their proposal was unanimously rejected Sept. 13. As finally drafted, Article VII provided simply that "the Ratifications of the Conventions of nine States shall be sufficient for the Establishment of this Constitution between the States so ratifying the Same."

By a separate resolution adopted Sept. 17, it was agreed that the Constitution should "be laid before the United States in Congress assembled," and that in the opinion of the Convention it should then be submitted to "a Convention of Delegates, chosen in each State by the People thereof." As soon as nine states had ratified, the resolution continued, the Congress should set a day for the election of Presidential electors, Senators and Representatives, and "the Time and Place for commencing Proceedings under this Constitution."[109]

Ten days after the Philadelphia Convention had adjourned on Sept. 17, 1787, the Congress of the Confederation submitted the Constitution to the states for their consideration and the struggle for ratification began. In that contest, ironically, those who had argued successfully in the Convention for a national rather than a merely federal plan and who now took the lead in urging ratification, called themselves Federalists (although there was no reference to anything federal in the Constitution). Those who opposed the Constitution became the Anti-Federalists.

These two factions, out of which the first political parties were formed, tended to reflect long-standing divisions among Americans between commercial and agrarian interests, creditors and debtors, men of great or little property, tidewater planters and the small farmers of the interior. But there were important and numerous exceptions to the tendency of Federalists and Anti-Federalists to divide along class, sectional and economic lines. Among the Anti-Federalists were some of the wealthiest and most influential men of the times, including George Mason, Patrick Henry, Richard Henry Lee, George Clinton, James Winthrop and many others.

As in drafting the Constitution, the Federalists seized the initiative in seeking speedy ratification. The ensuing campaign of political maneuver, persuasion and propaganda was intense and bitter. Both sides questioned the motives of the other and exaggerated the dire consequences of one or the other course. All Anti-Federalists, wrote Ellsworth, were either "men who have lucrative and influential State offices" or "tories, debtors in desperate circumstances, or insurgents."[110] To Luther Martin, the object of the Federalists was "the total abolition of all State Governments and the erection on their ruins of one great and extreme empire."[111]

All of the newspapers of the day published extensive correspondence on the virtues and vices of the new plan of government. The fullest and strongest case for the Constitution was put in a series of letters written by Madison, Hamilton and Jay under the name of "Publius." Seventy-seven of the letters were published in New York City newspapers between Oct. 27 and April 4, 1788, and in book form (along with eight additional letters) as *The Federalist* on May 28, 1788. These letters probably had only small influence on ratification, but *The Federalist* came to be regarded as the classic exposition of the Constitution.

Political maneuvers were common in both camps. In Pennsylvania, Federalists moved to call a convention before Congress had officially submitted the Constitution. Nineteen Anti-Federalists thereupon withdrew from the assembly, depriving it of a quorum until a mob seized two of them and dragged them back. When the Massachusetts Convention met, the Anti-Federalists were in the majority until John Hancock, the president, was won over to the Federalist side by promises of support for the new post of Vice President of the United States.

Among the major arguments advanced against the Constitution were the failure to include a Bill of Rights and the fear that the presidency would tend toward monarchy through endless re-election. Federalists met the first argument by pledging the early enactment of amendments, which Massachusetts and Virginia were particularly determined should be included. The fear of monarchy was mitigated by a widespread assumption (held also in the Convention) that George Washington would become the first President. This assumption, together with the fact that most Americans knew Washington and Benjamin Franklin supported the Constitution, contributed as much as anything to the success of the ratification campaign.

The Delaware Convention was the first to ratify, unanimously, on Dec. 7, 1787. Then came Pennsylvania, by a vote of 46 to 23, Dec. 12; New Jersey, unanimously, Dec. 19; Georgia, unanimously Jan. 2, 1788; Connecticut, 128 to 40, January 9; Massachusetts, 187 to 168, Feb. 6; Maryland, 63 to 11, April 26; South Carolina, 149 to 73, May 23; and New Hampshire, 57 to 46, June 21. This met the requirement for approval by nine states, but it was clear that without the approval of Virginia and New York the Constitution would stand on shaky ground.

In Virginia, according to Ellsworth, "the opposition wholly originated in two principles: the madness of Mason, and enmity of the Lee faction to Gen. Washington."[112] But Randolph, who had refused with Mason to sign the Constitution, was brought over to its support, and on June 25 the Federalists prevailed, by a vote of 89 to 79. New York, where Governor Clinton led the Anti-Federalists, finally ratified on July 26 by an even narrower margin of 30 to 27, after Hamilton and Jay had threatened that otherwise New York City would secede and join the Union as a separate state. North Carolina ratified on Nov. 21, 1789, and Rhode Island (which had not taken part in the Philadelphia Convention) became the last of the 13 states to ratify, on May 29, 1790.

In accord with the request of the Philadelphia Convention, the Congress of the Confederation on Sept. 13, 1788, fixed New York City (where it sat) as the seat of the new government, the first Wednesday of January 1789 as the day for choosing presidential electors, the first Wednesday of February for the meeting of electors, and the first Wednesday of March for the opening session of the new Congress.

The First Elections

The Constitution empowered the state legislatures to prescribe the method of choosing their presidential electors as well as the time, place and manner of electing their representatives and senators. Virginia and Maryland put the choice of electors directly to the people; in Massachusetts, two were chosen at large while the other eight were picked by the legislature from 24 names submitted by the voters of the eight congressional districts. Elsewhere, all electors were chosen by the legislature. But in New York, where Federalists controlled the senate and

Anti-Federalists dominated the assembly, the two houses became deadlocked on the question of acting by joint or concurrent vote, and the legislature adjourned without choosing electors.

Elections to the House also involved a number of spirited contests between Federalists and Anti-Federalists, although the total vote cast (estimated between 75,000 and 125,000) amounted to a small fraction of the free population of 3,200,000. In Massachusetts and Connecticut, several elections were required in some districts before one candidate obtained a majority. Elbridge Gerry, who had refused to sign the Constitution, finally beat Nathaniel Gorham (also a delegate to the Philadelphia Convention) after saying he no longer opposed it. In New Jersey the law did not fix a time for closing the polls and they stayed open for three weeks; the elections of all four New Jersey representatives were contested when the House was finally organized.

Although March 4, 1789, had been fixed as the day for commencing proceedings of the new government, only 13 of the 59 representatives and eight of the 22 senators had arrived in New York City by then. (Seats allotted to North Carolina and Rhode Island were not filled until 1790, after those states had ratified the Constitution.) It was not until April 1 that a 30th representative arrived to make a quorum of the House, while the Senate attained its quorum of 12 on April 6. The two houses then met jointly, for the first time, to count the electoral vote.

As everyone had assumed, each of the 69 electors had cast one vote for George Washington, who thus became President by unanimous choice. (Four additional electors—two from Maryland and two from Virginia—had failed to show up on Feb. 4 to vote.) Of 11 other men among whom the electors distributed their second vote, John Adams received the highest number—34—and was declared Vice President.

Adams arrived in New York on April 21, Washington on the 23rd, and the inaugural took place on the 30th. Washington took the oath of office prescribed by the Constitution on the balcony of Federal Hall (New York's former City Hall that housed the President and both houses of Congress until all moved to Philadelphia in 1790). The President then went to the Senate chamber to deliver a brief inaugural address, in the course of which he declined to accept whatever salary Congress might confer on the office. Thus, by April 30, 1789, the long task of designing and installing a new government had been completed.

PART II

History of the
House of Representatives

Chapter 8

Formative Years: 1789-1809

When the 30th of the 59 representatives elected to the First Congress reached New York on April 1, 1789, the assembled quorum promptly chose as Speaker of the House Frederick A. C. Muhlenberg of Pennsylvania. Next day, Muhlenberg named a committee of 11 to draw up the first rules of procedure, which the House adopted April 7. The first standing committee of the House—a seven-member Committee on Elections—was chosen April 13, and its report accepting the credentials of 49 members was approved April 18. By then, the House was already debating the first tariff bill.

By contrast, it took five years of study and negotiation to produce agreement in the 91st Congress on a limited revision of House rules. The House had long since become a highly structured institution governed by an elaborate set of rules, precedents and customs, all closely guarded by its most senior, privileged and influential members. Since its founding, however, the House had often adapted its procedures to the needs of the times, and its continuing ability to do so seemed to be confirmed by the passage of the Legislative Reorganization Act of 1970.

From the beginning, politics and personalities have played their part in influencing the timing and direction of changes in House procedure and organization. But it was the rapid increase in the size of its membership in the 19th century and of its workload in the 20th century that compelled development of what became the major features of the legislative process in the House—strict limitations on floor debate, a heavy reliance on the committee system, and the elaboration of techniques for channeling and maintaining the flow of House business.

It was Speaker Thomas B. Reed who told the House, in 1890, that "the object of a parliamentary body is action, and not stoppage of action."[1] But how to insure the right of a majority to work its will has been a perennial challenge in the House, conceived by George Mason in 1787 to become "the grand depository of the democratic principles of the government."[2] The men, parties and events that contributed to the evolution of the House as a legislative body are the focus of this account. *(Footnotes, p. 301)*

The great majority of the representatives elected to the First Congress had served in the Continental Congress or in their state legislatures, and the procedures followed in those bodies (which were derived in large part from English parliamentary practice) formed the basis for the first rules of the House. Those rules included provisions that:

● The Speaker was to preside over the House, preserve decorum and order, put questions and decide all points of order. He was to announce the results of votes and to vote in all cases of ballot by the House.

● Committees of three or fewer members were to be appointed by the Speaker, while larger ones were to be chosen by ballot.

● Members could not introduce bills or speak more than twice to the same question without leave of the House. They were required to vote if present, unless excused, and barred from voting if not present or if they had a direct personal interest in the outcome.

The first rules also set forth legislative procedure. As in the Continental Congress, the principal forum for considering and perfecting legislation was to be the Committee of the Whole House—the House itself under another name. When sitting in Committee of the Whole, a member other than the Speaker occupied the chair and certain motions permitted in the House—such as the previous question and the motion to adjourn—were not in order, nor were roll-call votes taken. Amendments rejected in committee could not be offered again in the House except as part of a motion to recommit. As in the House, it took a majority of the members to make a quorum in the Committee of the Whole.

Early House Procedure

In the early years of the House, it was the practice to begin discussion of all major legislative proposals in Committee of the Whole House on the State of the Union. After broad agreement had been reached on the principles involved, a select committee was named to draft a bill. When this committee reported back to the House, the bill itself was referred to a Committee of the Whole for section-by-section debate and approval or amendment. Its work completed, the committee rose, the Speaker resumed the chair, and the House either accepted or rejected the amendments agreed to in Committee of the Whole. This was followed by a third and final reading of the engrossed or complete bill and passage by the House.

Since there were no time limits as yet on the right of members to speak, even the small membership of the First and Second Congresses found this procedure cumbersome. Rep. James Madison blamed the "delays and perplexities" of the House on "the want of precedents."[3] But Rep. Fisher Ames of Massachusetts saw the problem as an excessive concern with detail in the "unwieldy" Committee of the Whole, for "a great, clumsy machine is applied to the slightest and most delicate operations—the hoof of an elephant to the strokes of mezzotinto."[4]

A small time-saver was introduced in 1790, when the House amended its rules to permit the Speaker to appoint all committees unless otherwise specially directed by the House. Similarly, in 1794, the House empowered the Speaker to name the chairman of the Committee of the Whole, who had been elected each time theretofore. But the practice of hammering out the broad terms of major legislation in Committee of the Whole before naming a select committee to draft a bill (more than 350 select committees were formed during the Third Congress) prevailed into the 1800s.

By confiding each proposal to a special committee that ceased to exist when a bill was reported, the House kept effective control over the legislation. But as its business multiplied and its membership increased (to 106 after the census of 1790 and to 142 after that of 1800), the House began to delegate increasing responsibility for initiating legislation to standing or permanent committees. Four were established by 1795; between 1802 and 1809, six were added. Among the more important were the Committees on Interstate and Foreign Commerce, created in 1795; Ways and Means, a select committee made permanent in 1802; and Public Lands, whose establishment in 1805 was prompted by the Louisiana Purchase.

Emergence of Parties

Neither the Constitution nor the first rules of the House envisioned a role for political parties in the legislative process. The triumph of Federalists over Anti-Federalists in winning ratification of the Constitution, the unanimous and nonpartisan choice of Washington as the first President, and the great preponderance of nominal Federalists elected to the First Congress tended to obscure the underlying economic, sectional and philosophic differences of the times. But these differences were not long in surfacing after Alexander Hamilton took office as the first Secretary of the Treasury. The statute creating the department required the Treasury "to digest and prepare plans for the improvement and management of the revenue and for the support of the public credit."[5]

Hamilton, a skilled financier, administrator and political organizer at 34, quickly responded with proposals for paying off the national and state debts at par and for creating a Bank of the United States. Designed to establish confidence in the new federal government, these proposals also appealed to the mercantile and moneyed interests to whom Hamilton looked for support in his desire to strengthen central authority. Since most of those elected to the First Congress shared his outlook (and some members stood to profit from his proposals), he soon emerged as the effective leader of a new Federalist party, meeting frequently with its adherents in caucus to plan legislative strategy.

Madison was the first to take issue with the substance of Hamilton's program as well as the dominance of the executive branch in guiding the decisions of the House. He was joined by his close friend and fellow Virginian, Thomas Jefferson, who became Secretary of State in 1790. Jefferson strongly opposed Hamilton from within the Cabinet. In a letter to President Washington, Jefferson criticized his colleague for attempting to exert undue influence upon Congress. He wrote that Hamilton's "system flowed from principles adverse to liberty, and was calculated to undermine and demolish the republic, by creating an influence of his department over the members of the legislature."[6] The cleavage was reinforced by the French Revolution and the wars that followed in its wake; Hamilton and the Federalists, with strong commercial and other ties to England, urged American neutrality, while Jefferson and his followers looked on the French as democratic allies to be helped.

By 1792, Madison and Jefferson were the recognized leaders of a nascent Republican Party of opposition, rooted in southern fears of Federalist economic policies and rising agrarian antagonism to the aristocratic views of Hamilton, Vice President John Adams and other prominent Federalists. In the Third through the Sixth Congresses, spanning Washington's second term and Adams' single term as President, the House was closely divided between Republicans and Federalists. But in 1800 Jefferson's party emerged with a clear majority, and during his two terms as President the Republicans outnumbered the Federalists in the House two and three to one.

Leadership in the House

With the early emergence of two parties, choice of a Speaker soon fell to the party with a majority in the House. Thus in 1799, Theodore Sedgwick of Massachusetts was elected Speaker over Nathaniel Macon of North Carolina by a vote of 44 to 38, a margin that approximated that of Federalists over Republicans in the Sixth Congress. Two years later, Macon was elected Speaker by the heavy Republican majority in the Seventh Congress.

As party choices, the early Speakers were not unwilling to use their powers in support of party policies. In 1796, when House Republicans mounted an attack on Jay's treaty with Britain, Speaker Jonathan Dayton, a Federalist, twice voted to produce ties that resulted in the defeat of anti-treaty motions. Republicans in the Sixth Congress found the rulings of Sedgwick so partisan that they refused to join in the by-then customary vote of thanks to the Speaker at adjournment.

But these early Speakers were not the actual political or legislative leaders of the House. Until he left the Treasury in 1795, Hamilton—operating through members of his own choice—dominated the Federalist majority—an "all-powerful" leader, according to one Republican, who "fails in nothing, he attempts."[7] As the leader of House Republicans until he left Congress in 1797, Madison was seen in much the same light by Federalist Fisher Ames, who wrote: "Virginia moves in a solid column and the discipline of the party is as severe as the Prussian. Deserters are not spared."[8]

As Republicans (or Democrats, as the Federalists soon took to calling them), Jefferson and Madison were opposed in principle to the concept of executive supremacy embraced by Hamilton and the early Federalists. When he became President in 1801, Jefferson promptly discarded a favored symbol of Federalist theory—the personal appearance of the President before a joint session of Congress to read his annual State of the Union message and instituted the practice (followed by all Presidents until Woodrow Wilson) of sending up the message to be read by a clerk. But Jefferson also took steps to assert his leadership over the new Republican majority in the House.

Jefferson's Secretary of the Treasury, Swiss-born Albert Gallatin (who had succeeded Madison as leader of House Republicans) soon became as adept as Hamilton had been in guiding administration measures through the party caucus and the House. Moreover, Jefferson picked his own floor leader, who was named chairman of the Committee on Ways and Means at the same time. The men who held the posts of floor leader and Ways and Means chairman during Jefferson's tenure were known as the President's spokesmen in establishing party policy. When one of these leaders, the tempestuous John Randolph, broke with Jefferson over a plan to acquire Florida, the President had him deposed as the committee chairman.

Randolph, meanwhile, had already affronted some members of the House by his conduct as Ways and Means chairman. Representative James Sloan complained in 1805 that he had tied up committee business "by going to Baltimore or elsewhere, without leave of absence" and by keeping appropriations' estimates "in his pockets or locked up in his drawer," and that he had rushed out important bills at the end of the session "when many members are gone home."[9] Sloan proposed that all standing committees be elected by ballot and choose their own chairmen. Committees were given the choice of selecting their own chairmen under a rule adopted in the Eighth Congress, but selection of chairmen (as well as committee members) reverted to the Speaker at the beginning of the 11th Congress.

In sum, the first 20 years of the House saw the beginnings of the standing committee system and the emergence of a floor leader and committee chairmen as key men in the legislative process. But that process was dominated, by and large, by the executive branch, and the effective decisions on legislative issues were reached behind the scenes in closed caucuses of the majority party. As Federalist Josiah Quincy lamented in 1809, the House "acts and reasons and votes, and performs all the operations of an animated being, and yet, judging from my own perceptions, I cannot refrain from concluding that all great political questions are settled somewhere else than on this floor."[10]

Chapter 9

Congressional Ascendancy: 1809-1829

The era of executive supremacy over Congress came to an end under Jefferson's successor, James Madison, whose strong performance in the Constitutional Convention, in the House and as Secretary of State for eight years was not matched in the presidency. Although he was nominally backed by Republican majorities during his two terms in office, Madison soon lost control of his party to a group of young "war hawks" (as John Randolph called them) first elected to the 12th Congress, who pushed the President into the War of 1812 against England. Led in the House by Henry Clay and John C. Calhoun, these men capitalized on Madison's weakness and a rising resistance to executive control to effect a shift of power to Congress that was not reversed until Jackson became President in 1829.

Clay as Speaker

Henry Clay first came to national attention while serving briefly as a senator from Kentucky in 1810-11. He then spoke eloquently of the need for "a new race of heroes" to preserve the achievements of America's founders. He proposed the conquest of Canada, asserting that "the militia of Kentucky are alone competent to place Montreal and Upper Canada at your feet."[11] It was as spokesman for a new nationalism, affronted by British interference with

American trade and shipping, that Clay entered the House in 1811 and—although only 34 and a newcomer—was promptly elected Speaker by like-minded Republicans. Using to the full his power to appoint committees and their chairmen, Clay put his fellow war hawks in all of the key positions. Together they took control of the House.

Clay greatly enhanced the power and prestige of the Speaker. In addition to presiding over the House as his predecessors had, he took over leadership of the majority party. This made him the leader of the House in fact as well as name. A forceful presiding officer, Clay was also an accomplished debater who frequently used his right to speak in the House as in Committee of the Whole. Gifted with great charm and tact, Clay remained Speaker as long as he was in the House. Although he resigned his seat twice—in 1814 (to help negotiate an end to the War of 1812) and in 1820—he was again elected Speaker as soon as he returned to the House in 1815 and in 1823.

It was the job of the Speaker, Clay said in his 1823 inaugural speech, to be prompt and impartial in deciding questions of order, to display "patience, good temper, and courtesy" to every member, and to make "the best arrangement and distribution of the talent of the House" for the dispatch of public business. Above all, he said, the Speaker must "remain cool and unshaken amidst all the storms of debate, carefully guarding the preservation of the permanent laws and rules of the House from being sacrificed to temporary passions, prejudices or interests."[12]

This was no easy job in Clay's time, when political passions were strong, the size of House membership continued to increase (to 186 after the census of 1810 and to 213 after that of 1820), and the right of debate was essentially unlimited. It is true that the House (after becoming exasperated with the unyielding tactics of Barent Gardenier, a New Yorker who once held the floor for 24 hours) had decided in 1811 that a majority could shut off further debate by calling for the previous question—the device which in time became the normal means of closing debate in the House. But in this period John Randolph was not alone in regarding this as a gag rule, and it was not easily invoked. Under the existing rules, moreover, those skilled in parliamentary tactics (as Randolph was) could and frequently did succeed in tying up House proceedings.

Clay once outwitted Randolph. It was after the House in 1820 had finally passed the hotly disputed Missouri Compromise bill to admit Missouri as a slave state but to bar slavery in any future state north of 36°30' north latitude. When Randolph, who opposed the bill, moved the next day to reconsider the vote, the Speaker held the motion to be out of order pending completion of the prescribed order of business. Clay then proceeded to sign the bill and send it to the Senate before Randolph could renew his motion. The Speaker's action was upheld, in effect, when the House refused, 61-71, to consider Randolph's subsequent motion to censure the clerk for having removed the bill.

Growth of Standing Committees

Efforts to refine House procedures continued in the period 1809-1829. The first rule to establish a daily order of business was adopted in 1811. In 1812 the Committee on Enrolled Bills was given leave to report at any time—a privilege later granted to certain other committees in order to expedite consideration of important bills. A rule adopted in 1817 enabled the House to protect itself against business it did not wish to consider. In 1820 the House created by rule the first calendars of the Committee of the Whole. And in 1822 it was decided that no rule should be suspended except by a two-thirds vote.

But the chief development in House procedures during this period was the proliferation of standing committees and their emergence as the principal forums for the initial consideration of proposed legislation—a practice recognized in 1822 by a rule giving standing committees leave to report by bill or otherwise. The number of select committees created to draft bills had dropped from 350 in the Third Congress (1793-95) to 70 in the 13th Congress (1813-15). And the number of standing committees grew from 10 in 1809 to 28 in 1825.

Among the standing committees were the Committee on the Judiciary, made permanent in 1813, and the Committees on Military Affairs, Naval Affairs and Foreign Affairs, all created in 1822. Six Committees on Expenditures in as many executive departments were established by Clay in 1816 to check up on economy and efficiency in the administration. Between 1816 and 1826 these and other House committees conducted at least 20 major investigations. The inquiries included such matters as the conduct of General Andrew Jackson in the Seminole War, charges against Secretary of the Treasury William Crawford, and the conduct of John Calhoun as Secretary of War.

Decline of King Caucus

In Clay's time as Speaker, the party caucus still afforded House Republicans an important means of reaching legislative decisions. It took Federalist Daniel Webster less than two weeks after being seated in 1813 to conclude that "the time for us to be put on the stage and moved by the wires has not yet come," since "before anything is attempted to be done here, it must be arranged elsewhere."[13] And Webster soon noted that the caucus worked "because it was attended with a severe and efficacious discipline, by which those who went astray were to be brought to repentance."[14] But the extent of party unity among Republicans had already started to decline under Jefferson as a result of sectional rivalries, and while the Federalists continued to lose ground as a national party, factionalism increased among the Republicans in Congress.

The change was reflected also in the rise and fall of the congressional caucus as the agency for selecting party nominees for President and Vice President. The practice began in 1800, when both Federalist and Republican members of the House and Senate met secretly to pick running mates for Jefferson and Adams. In 1804, Jefferson was renominated unanimously and openly by a caucus of 108 Republican senators and representatives. Four years later, a caucus of 94 Republicans nominated Madison for President over the protests of others who preferred James Monroe. But only 83 of the 133 Republicans in Congress attended the caucus that renominated Madison in 1812, just before he asked Congress for the declaration of war against England that Clay and others had been urging.

The Republican caucus of 1816 drew 119 of the party's 141 members in the House and Senate. Madison favored the nomination of Secretary of State Monroe for President, but there was rising opposition to continuation of the Virginia "dynasty" in the White House, and Monroe was nominated by only 65 votes to 54 for Secretary of War William Crawford of Georgia. By 1820, however, there was no real opposition in either party to Monroe, who was credited with bringing about "the era of good feelings" and had kept clear of the controversy over the Missouri Compromise. Fewer than 50 members showed up for the caucus that found it inexpedient to make any nomination, and Monroe was re-elected with every electoral vote but one.

The race to succeed Monroe began almost at once and included three members of his Cabinet—Crawford, Calhoun and John Quincy Adams—as well as Henry Clay and Andrew Jackson, hero of the Battle of New Orleans. When it appeared that Crawford would get a majority in a caucus, supporters of the other candidates began to denounce the caucus system. As a result, only 66 of the 261 senators and representatives then seated in Congress attended the caucus that nominated Crawford early in 1824. The election that fall gave Jackson a plurality but not a majority of the popular and electoral votes, and the choice went to the House, which picked Adams.

The presidential contest of 1824 marked the end of the old party system and the congressional nominating caucus. Helping to kill the caucus were changes in voting procedures and an expansion of the suffrage. Between 1800 and 1824. the number of states in which the electors were chosen by popular vote instead of by the legislature increased from five out of 16 to 18 out of 24. Four years later, in 1828, the electors were popularly chosen in all except two of the 24 states, and the popular vote jumped from less than 400,000 in 1824 to more than 1.1 million. With the emergence of a mass electorate, aspirants for the presidency were forced to seek a much broader base of support than the congressional caucus.

Chapter 10

A House Divided: 1829-1861

National politics entered a period of increasing turmoil, lasting until the Civil War, during the presidency of Andrew Jackson. Jackson made unprecedented use of the veto and of the removal and patronage powers of his office to establish primacy over Congress. Two new parties emerged during his presidency (1829-37): the Jacksonian Democrats, heirs to the agrarian and states' rights philosophy of the Jeffersonian Republicans, and the Whigs, spokesmen for the commercial and industrial interests once represented by the Federalists. But the Democrats now embraced the Federalist principle of executive leadership, while the Whigs extolled the Republican doctrine of legislative supremacy and tried thereafter to weaken the presidency.

The power and influence of the House began to decline under Jackson, when the size of the membership was increased to 242. Such former luminaries of the House as Henry Clay, Daniel Webster and John Calhoun moved to the Senate, which now became the major arena of debate on national policy. Party control of the presidency, the House and the Senate fluctuated considerably after Jackson. Increasingly, however, both Democrats and Whigs found themselves divided by the issue of slavery and its extension to the new territories and states beyond the Mississippi. The issue was reflected in the bitter election battles for the speakership that occurred in 1839, 1849, 1855 and 1859.

Contests to Elect the Speaker

Intra-party contests for Speaker were not new in the House. In 1805, when Republicans outnumbered Federalists almost four to one, it took four ballots to re-elect Macon, a southerner, over Joseph B. Varnum, the northern candidate. Two years later, when there were five candidates, Varnum won on the second ballot after Macon withdrew. By 1820—the year of the Missouri Compromise—the issue of slavery was an explicit part of the sectional contest for Speaker; to replace Clay, who had resigned, the House cast 22 ballots before electing John W. Taylor of New York, the antislavery candidate, over William Lowndes of South Carolina, a compromiser.

Next year, Taylor was one of five candidates in a contest that underscored the breakup of the Republicans and foreshadowed the presidential race of 1824. Taylor lost on the 12th ballot to Philip C. Barbour of Virginia, a Crawford supporter. And in 1834, when Andrew Stevenson resigned in his fourth term as Speaker (only to see the Senate reject his nomination as Minister to Great Britain), it took 10 ballots to elect John Bell over his fellow Tennessean, James K. Polk.

Contest of 1839. Martin Van Buren, Jackson's handpicked successor, was elected President in 1836, but Democrats barely won control of the House in the 25th Congress (1837-39). When it adjourned, Whigs deplored the "most partial and unjust rulings" of Speaker Polk, who then left the House to become Governor of Tennessee. At the opening of the 26th Congress on Dec. 2, 1839, the House found itself with 120 Democrats, 118 Whigs, and five contested seats in New Jersey. Control of the House rested on the decision of these contests, but the clerk (who presided under House practice pending election of a Speaker) refused to choose between the claimants until the House was organized.

After four days of bitter debate, the members elected a temporary chairman—the venerable John Quincy Adams, who had returned to the House in 1831. But it was Dec. 14 before it was decided to elect a Speaker without the New Jersey votes. There were six candidates to start, and John W. Jones of Virginia led on the first five ballots. But Robert M. T. Hunter—also of Virginia—was elected Dec. 16 on the 11th ballot (when there were 13 candidates) because he "finally united all the Whig votes and all the malcontents of the administration," according to Adams.[15]

Contest of 1849. Control of the House passed to the Whigs in the 27th Congress (1841-43), then to the Democrats in the 28th and 29th, then back to the Whigs in the 30th (1847-49) during the last two years of the Polk administration. Zachary Taylor, the Whig candidate, was elected President in 1848, but neither party had a majority in the House when the 31st Congress met on Dec. 3, 1849, because a number of Free-Soil Whigs and Democrats refused to support the leading candidates for Speaker—Robert C. Winthrop of Massachusetts, Whig Speaker in the previous Congress, and Howell Cobb, a Democrat from Georgia. The pending issue was what to do about slavery in the territory won in the war against Mexico, and the Free Soilers were determined to prevent the election of a Speaker who would appoint pro-slavery majorities to the Committees on Territories and the District of Columbia.

Cobb led 11 candidates on the first ballot with 103 votes. But there were five recognized factions in the House—Whigs, Democrats, Free Soilers, Native Americans and Taylor Democrats—and neither Cobb nor Winthrop, who alternated in the lead for 60 ballots, could get a majority. Finally, on Dec. 22, the House voted, 113 to 106, to elect a Speaker by a plurality, so long as it was a majority of a quorum. Cobb, the pro-slavery candidate, was elected on the 63rd ballot when he received 102 votes to 100 for Winthrop, with 20 votes spread among eight other candidates. This decision was then confirmed by a majority vote of the House.

Contest of 1855. Pro-slavery Democrats held firm control of the House in the 32nd and 33rd Congresses (1851-55), when Linn Boyd of Kentucky was Speaker. But their attempt to extend slavery into the Kansas and Nebraska Territories produced a large turnout of anti-slavery forces in the elections of 1854—the first in which a new Republican party, successor to the Whigs, participated. When the 34th Congress convened on Dec. 3, 1855, the House membership was divided among 108 Republicans or Whigs, 83 Democrats and 43 members of minor parties that sprang up in the 1850s. Although the so-called "Anti-Nebraska men" were in the majority, they were unable to unite behind any candidate for Speaker; two months passed and 133 ballots were taken before a choice was made.

The 21 candidates on the first ballot were led by William A. Richardson of Illinois with 74 votes. As in previous contests, various motions to help resolve the deadlock—including one to drop the low man on each ballot until only two remained—were made and tabled as the voting continued. After a series of votes in which Nathaniel P. Banks of Massachusetts fell only a few votes short of a majority, the House finally agreed to follow the plurality rule of 1849. On Feb. 2, 1856, Banks was declared Speaker. On the 133rd ballot he had received 103 votes to 100 for William Aiken of South Carolina. Banks, who had been elected to the 33rd Congress as a Coalition Democrat and to the 34th as a candidate of the nativist American Party of Know Nothings, fulfilled the expectations of the anti-slavery forces by his committee appointments.

Contest of 1859. Democrats won the presidency in 1856 with James Buchanan, last of the "northern men with southern principles." They also gained control of the House in the 35th Congress (1857-59). But the 36th opened on Dec. 5, 1859, with no party in control of the House, which was composed of 109 Republicans, 101 Democrats and 27 Know Nothings. Pro- and anti-slavery blocs were again deadlocked over the choice of a Speaker. With passions running high and debate unchecked by a presiding clerk who refused to decide any points of order, the struggle continued for two months.

John Sherman of Ohio, the Republican choice, led the early balloting, receiving at one point 110 votes, just six short of a majority. But Sherman had become anathema to the pro-slavery camp, and the Republicans finally concluded that he couldn't be elected. So Sherman withdrew on the 39th ballot, and the Republicans switched their support to William Pennington of New Jersey, a new member of the House and politically unknown. Pennington received 115 votes on the 40th ballot (compared to one on the 38th) and was elected on the 44th, on Feb. 1, 1860, by a bare majority of 117 votes out of 233. Pennington's distinction (shared with Clay) of being Speaker in his first term ended there, for he was defeated at the polls the next year and served only the one term in the House.

Changes in House Rules

Agitation over the issue of slavery was not confined to the contests over the choice of a Speaker. In 1836, John Quincy Adams challenged a House practice (begun in 1792) of refusing to receive petitions and memorials on the subject of slavery. Adams offered a petition from citizens of Massachusetts for the abolition of slavery in the District of Columbia. His action led to protracted debate and the adoption of a resolution (by a vote of 117 to 68) that any papers dealing with slavery "shall, without being either printed or referred, be laid upon the table and that no further action whatever shall be had thereon."[16]

Adams, who considered adoption of the resolution to be a violation of the Constitution and of the rules of the House reopened the issue in 1837 by asking the Speaker how to dispose of a petition he had received from 22 slaves. Southerners moved at once to censure Adams. The move failed, but the House agreed, 163-18, that "slaves do not possess the right of petition secured to the people of the United States by the Constitution."[17] Further agitation led the House in 1840 to adopt (by a vote of 114-108) a rule that no papers "praying the abolition of slavery...shall be received by this House or entertained in any way whatever."[18] Four years later, however, the rule was rescinded by a vote of 108-80.

Other rules adopted in this period were more significant to the long-range development of House procedures. In 1837, for example, precedence was given to floor consideration of revenue and appropriation bills, and the inclusion of legislation in an appropriation bill (which had led the Senate to kill a number of such bills) was barred. In 1841, the House finally agreed to limit to one hour the time allowed any member in a debate—a proposal made first in 1820 after John Randolph had spoken for more than four hours against the Missouri Compromise. At the same time, to prevent indefinite debate in Committee of the Whole, a rule was adopted providing that the House by majority vote could discharge the committee from consideration of a bill after pending amendments were disposed of without debate.

Objection to the latter provision led in 1847 to adoption of the five-minute rule, giving any member that much time to explain his amendment. But this rule encouraged a practice of offering and then withdrawing scores of amendments in an effort to delay action on controversial bills. So the rule was amended in 1850 to prohibit the withdrawal of any amendment without unanimous consent. But the House was still at the mercy of a determined minority; during debate on the Kansas-Nebraska bill in 1854, according to Asher Hinds (R Maine), opponents engaged in "prolonged dilatory operations, such as the alternation of the motions to lay on the table, for a call of the House, to excuse individual members from voting, to adjourn, to reconsider votes whereby individual members were excluded from voting, to adjourn, to fix the day to which the House should adjourn, and, after calls of the House had been ordered, to excuse individual absentees,"[19] all of which required 109 roll calls and consumed many days.

In 1858, the House agreed to set up a select committee to revise the accumulation of more than 150 rules. The committee included the Speaker—the first time that officer had served on any committee of the House. While its report was not acted on, most of its recommendations were repeated in 1860 by another committee named the day Pennington was finally chosen Speaker. As approved by the House in March, this first general revision of the rules was largely of a technical nature, although it included important changes affecting use of the previous question and the motion to strike the enacting clause. On balance, however, the revised rules of 1860 left ample opportunity for a resolute minority to keep a closely divided House tied up in parliamentary knots for days at a time.

Apart from the adoption of the first limitations on debate—the Hour Rule and the Five-Minute Rule in the 1840s—there was little significant change in House procedures in the period 1829-1860. The system of standing committees that had been established by 1825 (when there were 28) was expanded by the addition of eight more. The Committee on Ways and Means continued to handle both appropriations and revenue bills, and while its chairman was not always the designated floor leader of the majority party, he was always among the most influential members. The Speaker continued to appoint members to committees and to designate their chairmen.

But none of the Speakers who followed Clay achieved his stature or influence. Of the 14 who were elected between 1825 and 1860, only three—Stevenson, Polk and

Boyd—served for more than one Congress. In only one respect was the job of leading the House made, not easier, but at least no more difficult: the size of the membership increased to 242 in 1833 and was kept about the same for the next 40 years. Otherwise, the rising passions of the country doomed the House to increasing turmoil as America moved toward internecine conflict.

Chapter 11

New Complexities: 1861-1890

The Civil War all but eliminated the South from national politics and representation in Congress for eight years. Most of the 66 House seats held by the 11 secessionist states in 1860 remained vacant from 1861 to 1869. The war also greatly weakened the Democratic Party outside the South; as in the War of 1812, when the Federalists were criticized for their pro-British sympathies, the Democrats suffered from their identification with the southern cause. And Democratic weakness helped the Republicans to keep control of the presidency until 1885, of the Senate until 1879, and of the House until 1875.

At the same time, the war and its aftermath gave rise to bitter conflict between Congress and the President leading to the impeachment of Andrew Johnson in 1868 and to a prolonged period of legislative dominance thereafter. The years from 1860 to 1890 saw a further expansion of House membership, an intensification of House efforts to control government spending, an increase in the number and power of House committees, and a continuing struggle to adapt the rules of the House to its legislative purposes.

Congress is Paramount

President Lincoln assumed unprecedented powers during the Civil War, at a time when the Republican majorities in Congress were dominated by Radicals committed to the

Whig doctrine of legislative supremacy. The conflict between Lincoln and Congress was sharpest over the issue of Reconstruction. Lincoln, who held that the Confederate states had never left the Union, was prepared to restore their political rights as quickly as possible. But the Radicals were determined to reshape the power structure of the South before readmitting the secessionists and insisted that the decision rested with Congress.

When Lincoln set up new governments in Louisiana and Arkansas in 1863, the Radicals passed a bill to place all Reconstruction authority under the direct control of Congress. Lincoln pocket-vetoed the bill after Congress had adjourned in 1864, whereupon the Radicals issued the Wade-David Manifesto asserting that "the authority of Congress is paramount and must be respected." If the President wanted their support, said the Radicals, "he must confine himself to his executive duties—to obey and execute, not make the laws—to suppress by arms armed rebellion, and leave political reorganization to Congress."[20]

The Radicals proceeded to put their views into effect with a vengeance under Andrew Johnson, the Tennessee Democrat who became President when Lincoln was assassinated in 1865 and whose views were openly sympathetic to the established order in the South. Passed over Johnson's veto were numerous bills the effects of which were to give Congress full control over Reconstruction and to strip the President of much of his authority.

One of these measures was the Tenure of Office Act of 1867, passed on the suspicion that Johnson intended to fire Secretary of War Edwin Stanton. The law made it a high misdemeanor to remove without the Senate's approval any official whose nomination had been confirmed by the Senate. After Johnson—holding the law to be unconstitutional—had suspended Stanton from office, the House voted, 126-47, to impeach him. Tried by the Senate, Johnson was acquitted May 16, 1868, when a vote of 35 to 19 for conviction fell one short of the two-thirds required by the Constitution.

Power of the Purse

The Civil War led to renewed efforts by the House to control federal expenditures (which climbed from $63 million in 1860 to $1.3 billion in 1865) by a more careful exercise of its power over appropriations. Until then, the Committee on Ways and Means had handled all supply as well as revenue bills, in addition to bills on monetary matters. But in 1865 the House agreed with little opposition to transfer some of these responsibilities to two new standing committees—a Committee on Appropriations and a Committee on Banking and Currency. Speaking of the former, the sponsor of the change declared that "we require of this new committee their whole labor in the restraint of extravagant and illegal appropriations."[21]

Congress now began to tighten controls on spending. Wartime authority to transfer funds from one account to another was repealed, agencies were required to return unexpended funds to the Treasury, and obligation of funds in excess of appropriations was prohibited. Although Congress continued to make lump-sum appropriations to the Army and the Navy, it specified in great detail the amounts and purposes for which money could be spent by the civilian departments and agencies. These efforts helped to keep federal expenditures below $300 million in every year except one from 1871 to 1890

The House's "power of the purse" was exercised to another end during the administration of Rutherford B. Hayes (1877-81), the Republican successor to Ulysses S. Grant (1869-77). Democrats were again in the majority in the House in the 45th Congress (1877-79) and won control of both chambers in the 46th, but by margins too small to be able to override a veto. So in their attempts to repeal certain Reconstruction laws, the Democrats revived the practice of adding legislative riders to appropriation bills in the hope of forcing the President to accept them. But Hayes vetoed a series of such bills, rejecting the tactic as an attempt at coercive dictation by the House. When they were unable to override his vetoes, the Democrats finally passed the appropriation bills without the riders.

During the height of the dispute in 1879, Hayes wrote in his diary: "This is a controversy which cannot and ought not to be compromised. The Revolutionists claim that a bare majority in the House of Representatives shall control all legislation, by tacking the measures they can't pass through the Senate, or over the President's objections, to the appropriation bills which are required to carry on the government.... [I]t is idle to talk of compromises as to the particular measures which are used as riders on the appropriation bills. These measures may be wise or unwise. It is easy enough to say in regard to them, that used as they are to establish a doctrine which overthrows the Constitutional distribution of power between the different departments of the government, and consolidates in the House of Representatives, the whole law making power of the government...we will not discuss or consider them when they are so presented....

"To tack political legislation to appropriation bills and to threaten that no appropriations will be made unless the political measures are approved is not in my judgment constitutional conduct."[22]

Meanwhile, House members of both parties were becoming concerned over a concentration of power in the Appropriations Committee itself. In 1877, the committee was deprived of its jurisdiction over appropriations for rivers and harbors—the "pork barrel" on which members relied to finance projects of interest to their districts. The agriculture appropriation was taken from the committee in 1880, and in 1885, it was stripped of authority over six other supply bills—Army, Navy, Military Academy, Consular and Diplomatic Affairs, Post Office and Post Roads, and Indian Affairs—all of which were transferred to the appropriate legislative committees.

In taking from the Appropriations Committee control over bills comprising almost one-half of the federal budget, the House was apparently moved by hostility to Chairman Samuel J. Randall (D Pa.) and what was considered to be the committee's excessive concern for economy under his leadership. The feeling was widespread and bipartisan; three-fourths of the Democrats and of the Republicans joined in the vote of 227 to 70 to strip the committee of a giant share of its jurisdiction. They were led, moreover, by the senior members of most of the other important committees, underscoring the rivalry that had developed among House committees.

The effect of this decision in 1885 was to reinforce the decentralization of power in the House and to give added weight to the criticism of Congress voiced by Woodrow Wilson that year in his book *Congressional Government.* According to Wilson, power in the House was scattered among "47 seigniories, in each of which a standing committee is the court-baron and its chairman lord-proprietor."[23] Wilson noted that, "by custom, seniority in congressional service determines the bestowal of the principal chairmanships," and that on the House floor "chairman fights against chairman for use of the time of the assembly."[24]

Wilson attributed the lack of strong party control in the House to the fact that committees were not composed entirely of members of the majority, as he believed they should be. "The legislation of a session does not represent the policy of either [party]," he wrote; "it is simply an aggregate of the bills recommended by committees composed of members from both sides of the House, and it is known to be usually, not the work of the majority men upon the committees, but compromise conclusions...of the committeemen of both parties."[25]

Speakers and the Rules

If power in the House was not dispersed among the standing committees and their chairmen, it was also true (as Wilson noted) that "he who appoints those committees is an autocrat of the first magnitude."[26] While Speakers had held that authority since the earliest days of the House, its exercise had assumed new importance with the broadening legislative interests of the country and of the House.

Schuyler Colfax, first elected to the House from Indiana in 1854, served as Republican Speaker from 1863 to 1869, when he left the House to become Vice President during the first term of President Grant. Although Colfax enjoyed as much personal popularity as had Henry Clay, he was not a forceful Speaker and was regarded as a figurehead in a House dominated by Thaddeus Stevens (R Pa.), who became chairman of the Ways and Means Committee in 1861 and of the newly created Appropriations Committee in 1865. Stevens, who engineered the impeachment of President Johnson, was described by George Boutwell, a fellow Republican, as "a tyrant" in his rule as leader of the House who was "at once able, bold and unscrupulous."[27]

Colfax's successor as Speaker was James G. Blaine of Maine, one of the founders of the Republican Party, who entered the House in 1863. As Speaker from 1869 to 1875, Blaine was an avowed partisan of Republican principles and successfully manipulated committee assignments to produce majorities favorable to legislation he desired. Like Clay, Blaine aspired to become President. But after losing the Republican nomination to Rutherford B. Hayes in 1876 and to James A. Garfield in 1880, he was nominated in 1884 only to lose the election to Democrat Grover Cleveland.

Democrats won control of the House in 1875. After the death in 1876 of their first choice for Speaker, Michael C. Kerr of Indiana, they elected Samuel J. Randall of Pennsylvania, who had entered the House with Blaine and Garfield in 1863. Randall, who was Speaker until 1881, initiated a thorough revision of House rules in 1880 designed "to secure accuracy in business, economy in time, order, uniformity and impartiality."[28] The net effect of these changes was to increase to some extent the ability of floor leaders and committee chairmen to expedite legislation on the floor. The Committee on Rules, which had been a select committee since 1789 and had been chaired by the Speaker since 1858, was made a standing committee, and it soon began to make systematic use of special orders or rules which, when adopted by majority vote of the House, governed the amount of time to be allowed for debate on major bills and the extent to which members might offer amendments.

The Democrats lost control of the House in the 47th Congress (1881-83) but regained it in the 48th Congress (1883-85). They then passed over Randall (because he had opposed the party's low-tariff policy) and elected John G. Carlisle of Kentucky as Speaker. Carlisle, a member since 1877 who remained Speaker from 1883 to 1889, made notable use of his power of recognition to forestall motions he opposed. By the device of asking "For what purpose does the gentleman rise?"[29] Carlisle was able to withhold recognition from any member whose purpose he did not share. But Carlisle did not lead a united party; in 1884, for example, the Democrats lost a tariff reduction bill through the defection of Randall and 40 other party members.

Blaine, Randall and Carlisle all contributed importantly to the body of precedents by which Speakers were guided under the House rules. But none was able or willing to prevent determined minorities from obstructing the business of the House. Under Carlisle, in particular, the House was frequently subjected to organized filibusters and such dilatory tactics as the "disappearing quorum" which was likely to result in endless roll calls to no purpose but delay. These displays, coupled with a disappointing legislative output, led to increasing public criticism of the House and to demands that the rules be modified "to permit the majority to control the business for which it is responsible," as the *New York Tribune* put it.[30]

The Reed Rules

The opportunity for reform came when Republicans took control of the House in 1889 and elected Thomas B. Reed of Maine as Speaker. First elected to the House in 1876, Reed had been a leader of House Republicans since 1882 when he became a member of the Rules Committee and an increasingly outspoken critic of the rules. He once said, "The only way to do business inside the rules is to suspend the rules."[31]

When the 51st Congress convened on Dec. 2, 1889, the House was composed of 330 members, with Republicans in a small majority. Reed was elected Speaker over Carlisle on a party-line vote, and in keeping with long-standing practice the rules of the 50th Congress were referred to the five-member Rules Committee (of which the Speaker was chairman) while the House proceeded under general parliamentary procedure. With several election contests pending, it was expected that the Republicans would settle them in their favor (as party majorities had always done) in order to increase their majority, before adopting new rules.

On Jan. 29, 1890, the Republicans called up the West Virginia election case of Smith vs. Jackson. Charles F. Crisp of Georgia, the Democratic leader, immediately raised the question of consideration, to be decided by majority vote. The roll call produced 161 "yeas," two "nays" and 165 not voting—mostly Democrats who, although present, were using the device of the "disappearing quorum" to block action. But when the point of "no quorum" was made (since less than one-half of the members had voted), Speaker Reed ordered the clerk to enter the names of those present and refusing to vote; he then ruled that a quorum was present and consideration in order.[32]

In the ensuing uproar, Reed was denounced as a "tyrant" and a "czar" but held to his ground. An appeal from his ruling was tabled by a majority of a quorum. When next day, in order to make a quorum, he again counted nonvoting Democrats who were present, he refused to allow another appeal on the ground that the House had already decided the question. Reed went on to declare that he would refuse to recognize any member rising to make a dilatory motion, saying:

"There is no possible way by which the orderly methods of parliamentary procedure can be used to stop legislation. The object of a parliamentary body is action, and not stoppage of action. Hence, if any member or set of members undertakes to oppose the orderly progress of business, even by the use of the ordinarily recognized parliamentary motions, it is the right of the majority to refuse to have those motions entertained...."[33]

Reed's rulings on dilatory motions and the counting of a quorum were incorporated in the revised rules reported by the Rules Committee, Feb. 6, 1890, and adopted by the House after four days of debate by a vote of 161 to 144. Of the rule that "no dilatory motion shall be entertained by the speaker," the committee report said: "There are no words which can be framed which will limit members to the proper use of proper motions. Any motion the most conducive to progress in the public business...may be used for purposes of unjust and oppressive delay.... Why should an assembly be kept from its work by motions made only to delay and to weary, even if the original design of the motion was salutary and sensible?"[34]

In addition to these changes in the rules, the revision of 1890 reduced the size of the quorum required in the Committee of the Whole from one-half of the membership of the House to 100 members—a change that facilitated floor action as the size of the House continued to grow. The revised rules also took account of the fact that the House had long since abandoned its original requirement that members obtain leave to introduce bills; the practice of introducing bills simply by filing them with the clerk was now made a rule.

Coincidentally, the number of bills introduced, which had first passed the 1,000 mark in the 24th Congress (1835-37) and had not exceeded 2,000 until the 40th Congress (1867-69), reached a new peak of more than 19,000 in the 51st Congress (1889-91). But the fate of most of these bills continued to be as described by Woodrow Wilson in 1885: "As a rule, a bill committed [to committee] is a bill doomed. When it goes from the clerk's desk to a committee room, it crosses a parliamentary bridge of sighs to dim dungeons of silence whence it will never return."[35]

Under the Reed Rules of 1890, the Speaker was enabled to take effective command of the House. By his authority to name the members and chairmen of all committees, he had the power to reward or to punish his fellow members. As chairman of the Rules Committee (which now shared with Ways and Means and Appropriations the right to report at any time and thereby get immediate access to the floor), he could control the timing and content of bills to be brought before the House. And now, with unlimited power of recognition, he could determine in large measure what was to be taken up on the floor.

Chapter 12

Tyranny and Reaction: 1890-1919

Although the Democrats dropped the rule against the "disappearing quorum" when they took control of the House in the 52nd Congress (1891-93), they restored it in the 53rd (1893-95), and Charles F. Crisp of Georgia, the Democratic Speaker in both Congresses, made just as full use of his powers as had Reed in the 51st. Crisp (who persuaded two rivals to withdraw from the party contest for Speaker by promising them the chairmanships of Appropriations and Ways and Means) once refused to entertain an appeal by Reed from a ruling, refused to let Reed speak any further, and directed the Sergeant at Arms to see that he took his seat.

Reed, who served as minority leader during these four years and as Speaker again for the next two Congresses (1895-99), was able by his forceful leadership of House Republicans to restore the concept of party responsibility within the House. His chief aides in the 51st Congress included William McKinley (R Ohio), as chairman of the Ways and Means Committee, and Joseph G. Cannon (R Ill.), as chairman of the Appropriations Committee. McKinley left the House in 1891 (to become governor, then President in 1897), and when Reed resumed the speakership in 1895 he named Nelson Dingley (R Maine) to head Ways and Means. Cannon again became chairman of the Appropriations Committee in 1897, when Reed also named

James A. Tawney (R Minn.) as the first Republican whip, charged with keeping party members on the floor and voting with the leadership. Under Reed, House Republicans achieved an exceptional degree of party unity during the 1890s, occasionally voting solidly for measures on which they had been sharply divided in caucus.

The centralization of power in the House during this period coincided with another, less visible change of significance. Until the Civil War, few members had chosen—or had been enabled by the voters—to make a career of service in the House. As late as the 1870s, more than half of the 293 Representatives then elected to the House every two years were freshmen, and the mean length of service for all members was barely two terms. Thus, although Speakers for some time had followed seniority to a degree in appointing members to committees of their choice and in advancing them to chairmanships, it was not a matter of great importance to most members when they failed to do so.

By 1899, however, the proportion of newcomers among the 357 members entering the House had fallen to 30 per cent, while the mean period of service had increased to more than three terms. As more members sought to stay in the House for longer periods, it became of increasing importance to them that they have the opportunity to gain political recognition through specialization and rising influence within the committee structure. There was thus a growing demand among members of both parties for assurance that their seniority would be respected in assigning them rank on committees of their choice. The resulting new expectations contributed to the reaction against centralization that began under Speaker Cannon.

Revolt Against 'Cannonism'

Speaker Reed resigned from the House in 1899, having broken with President McKinley over American intervention in Cuba and the annexation of Hawaii. The Republican majority in the 56th Congress (1899-1901) replaced Reed with David B. Henderson of Iowa, who served two ineffective terms as Speaker (1899-1903) before retiring from the House. In 1903, when Joseph G. Cannon was finally elected Speaker by the Republicans (having been an unsuccessful candidate in 1881, 1889 and 1899), he was the oldest representative in age (67) and service (28 years) ever to have headed the House.

Like Reed, Cannon set out to rule the House and its Republican majority through his control of the Rules Committee and the key chairmen. He kept Sereno E. Payne (R N.Y.) as majority leader and chairman of the Ways and Means Committee (positions to which Payne was first appointed by Henderson in 1899). He also retained Tawney as majority whip until 1905, when he named him chairman of Appropriations. Cannon turned over the committee assignments of Democrats to their leader, John Sharp Williams of Mississippi, subject to his veto. But Williams used his authority to build party unity among the Democrats, and Cannon took back the privilege in 1908 when James Beauchamp (Champ) Clark (D Mo.) succeeded Williams as minority leader.

As a strong conservative, Cannon was out of sympathy with much of the progressive legislation sought by President Theodore Roosevelt (1901-1909) and by a growing number of liberal Republicans and Democrats in the House. To maintain control, therefore, he made increasing use of his powers as Speaker to block legislation that he opposed and to thwart and punish members who opposed him. In a period of rising public interest in political reform, "Cannonism" came to be a synonym for the arbitrary use of the Speaker's powers to obstruct the legislative will, not of the majority party, but of a new majority of House members of both parties.

The movement to curb Cannon got under way during the last session of the 60th Congress when, just before final adjournment on March 3, 1909, the House adopted the Calendar Wednesday rule. This set aside Wednesday of each week for calling the roll of committees, whose chairmen or other authorized members could then call up bills that their committees had reported without getting clearance from the Rules Committee. At the time, progressives considered this a major reform because it seemed to insure the House a chance to act on measures favored in committee but opposed by the leadership. In practice, however, the procedure proved ineffective and in later years the House commonly agreed to dispense with Calendar Wednesday by unanimous consent.

When the 61st Congress first met, in special session, on March 15, 1909, the House was composed of 219

Republicans and 172 Democrats. But the Republicans included about 30 insurgents led by George W. Norris of Nebraska and John M. Nelson of Wisconsin. After helping to elect Cannon to a fourth term as Speaker, the Republican insurgents joined with the Democrats to defeat the usual motion to adopt the rules of the preceding Congress. Clark, the Democratic leader, then offered a resolution to take from the Speaker his existing authority to appoint all committees, to limit that authority to only five committees (of which the only important one would be Ways and Means), to remove the Speaker from the Rules Committee, and to enlarge that body from five to 15 members.

Although 28 Republicans joined in supporting the Clark resolution, 22 Democrats led by Rep. John J. Fitzgerald (N.Y.) voted with the majority of Republicans to defeat it. The House thereupon adopted a compromise resolution, offered by Fitzgerald, which passed over the principal abuses complained of and only slightly curtailed the Speaker's authority. The main change was to establish a Consent Calendar for minor bills of particular interest to individual members and to set aside two days each month when bills on this Calendar could be called up without the prior approval of the Speaker and passed by unanimous consent. (Adoption of this rule led both parties to designate certain members as official "objectors," to prevent passage of bills opposed for any reason within the party. But the Consent Calendar became a useful device for processing minor bills.)

Agitation against "Cannonism" nevertheless continued, and the coalition of Democrats and progressive Republicans finally prevailed in 1910. Taking advantage of a parliamentary opening on March 16, Rep. Norris asked for immediate consideration of a reform resolution modeled on Clark's that had been bottled up in the Rules Committee. When Cannon held the motion out of order, the House overruled him by a decisive vote. Debate then began on the Norris resolution, which stripped the Speaker of all authority to appoint committees and their chairmen, removed him from the Rules Committee, and expanded that committee to 10 members who would choose their own chairman.

Rep. Nelson expressed the feelings of the insurgents in these terms: "Have we not been punished by every means at the disposal of the powerful House organization? Members long chairmen of important committees, others holding high rank—all with records of faithful and efficient party service to their credit—have been ruthlessly removed, deposed and humiliated before their constituents and the country because, forsooth, they would not cringe or crawl before the arbitrary power of the Speaker and his House machine.... We are fighting with our Democratic brethren for the common right of equal representation in this House, and for the right of way of progressive legislation in Congress."[36]

The House finally adopted the Norris resolution on March 19, by a vote of 191 to 156, after a continuous session of 29 hours during which Cannon had done his best to round up absentees among his supporters. Recognizing the nature of his defeat, Cannon invited a motion to declare the chair vacant so that the House might elect a new Speaker. Rep. A. S. Burleson (D Texas) made the motion, but it was quickly tabled; Cannon, known to the House as "Uncle Joe," was personally popular with many members, and the Republican insurgents were unwilling to help elect a Democrat. Cannon remained Speaker until the end of the 61st Congress in 1911 and a member of the House (except in the 63rd Congress) until 1923, by which time he had completed 46 years of service.

The revolt against "Cannonism" was consolidated in 1911, when the Democrats took control of the House, elected Champ Clark as Speaker, and adopted a revised body of rules that incorporated most of the changes agreed to in 1909-10. The new rules provided that all members of the standing committees, including their chairmen, would be "elected by the House, at the commencement of each Congress."[37] The rules of 1911 included the Calendar Wednesday and Consent Calendar innovations of 1909, as well as a discharge rule (adopted in 1910) by which a petition signed by a majority of House members could be used to free a bill locked up in any committee. Also established at this time was a special calendar for private bills, which could be called up two days each month.

Return of the Caucus

No less important than the rules of 1911 were the procedures adopted by the Democratic majority for organizing their control of the House. At the party caucus of Jan. 19 that nominated Clark for Speaker, it was also agreed that

113

Oscar W. Underwood of Alabama would be majority leader and chairman of the Ways and Means Committee. And it was decided that the Democratic members of Ways and Means would constitute the party's Committee on Committees to draw up the committee assignments of all Democrats, leaving to the Republicans (who first established their own Committee on Committees in 1917) the selection of their own committeemen. In practice, therefore, the election of committees and their chairmen now took the form of a perfunctory vote to approve the slates drawn up by key members of the majority and minority parties and endorsed by the party caucus.

Underwood rather than Speaker Clark became the recognized leader of House Democrats from 1911 to 1915 (when he moved to the Senate), and he made frequent use of the party caucus to develop unity on legislative issues. Democratic caucus rules at this time provided that "in deciding upon action in the House involving party policy or principle, a two-thirds vote of those present and voting at a caucus meeting shall bind all members of the caucus" so long as the vote represented a majority of the Democrats in the House. But no member could be bound "upon questions involving a construction of the Constitution of the United States or upon which he made contrary pledges to his constituents prior to his election or received contrary instructions by resolution or platform from his nominating authority."[38]

A typical caucus resolution of 1911 bound Democrats to vote for certain bills reported by the Ways and Means Committee and "to vote against all amendments, except formal committee amendments, to said bills and motions to recommit, changing their text from the language agreed upon in this conference."[39] Underwood also used the caucus to develop legislative proposals which would then be referred to committees for formal approval, to instruct committees as to which bills they might or might not report, and to instruct the Rules Committee on the terms to be included in its special orders governing floor consideration of major bills.

Thus the power once concentrated in the hands of Speaker Cannon and now passed to the Democratic Caucus, which was dominated by Underwood as majority leader. Historian George B. Galloway described Underwood's power: "As floor leader, Underwood was supreme, the Speaker a figurehead. The main cogs in the machine were the caucus, the floor leadership, the Rules Committee, the standing committees, and special rules. Oscar Underwood became the real leader of the House. He dominated the party caucus, influenced the rules, and as chairman of Ways and Means chose the committees. Clark was given the shadow, Underwood the substance of power. As floor leader, he could ask and obtain recognition at any time to make motions, restrict debate or preclude amendments or both."[40]

Wilson and Congress

As President, Wilson revived the custom of Washington and Adams (abandoned since the Jefferson presidency) of addressing Congress in person. He worked closely with the Democratic leaders in both houses and conferred frequently with committees and individual members to solicit support for his legislative program. With Wilson's help, Underwood and the Democrats were able to effect House passage of four major pieces of legislation in the 63rd Congress—the Underwood Tariff Act, the Federal Reserve Act, the Clayton Antitrust Act, and the Federal Trade Commission Act.

The Democrats were not so united on foreign policy, however. Both Speaker Clark and Majority Leader Underwood disagreed with Wilson over repeal of the exemption from Panama Canal tolls originally accorded to American coastal shipping. Claude Kitchin (D N.C.), who had become second-ranking Democrat on Ways and Means in 1913 and who succeeded Underwood as chairman and majority leader in 1915, openly challenged the President on several issues, notably when Wilson asked for a declaration of war against Germany in 1917. Clark later denounced the President's military conscription program.

Reflecting these disagreements, the strong party unity displayed by House Democrats during Wilson's first term began to fracture in his second. When the party lost control of the House at the mid-term elections of 1918, the binding party caucus had ceased to be an effective instrument in the hands of the leadership. The Republican minority, meanwhile, had all but abandoned use of the binding caucus in 1911, erecting in its place a non-binding "conference" used for little more than to choose the party's nominee for Speaker and to ratify committee slates. By

1919, the House was no longer willing to accept the centralization of power that had developed under Speakers Reed, Crisp and Cannon and Majority Leader Underwood. Party leaders thus were faced with the task of finding new ways to build and maintain consensus.

Accompanying this change—and helping to account for it—was a hardening of the unwritten rule of seniority that virtually guaranteed succession to committee chairmanships by the next-ranking majority members on the committees. Democrats violated the rule three times in 1911 and on a few occasions thereafter, as did the Republicans. But representatives could now fairly count on rising in the ranks of their committees (so long as they were re-elected) upon the retirement or death of the more senior members of those committees. Such assurance gave to sitting chairmen and ranking members a degree of independence from dictation that put a new premium on the persuasive skills of party leaders.

Recognition of seniority in the advancement of committee members still left the party committees on committees with the job of assigning vacancies to newcomers and to representatives seeking to switch from one committee to another. The task of filling vacancies was complicated by keen competition among individuals and among state and regional delegations for the right to places on such choice committees as Ways and Means and Appropriations; in the inevitable bargaining, the political loyalties of the competitors weighed as much as their interests and capabilities. The filling of important committee vacancies was to remain a significant tool in the hands of party leaders.

Chapter 13

Republican Years: 1919-1931

By the end of the First World War in 1918, a majority of American voters were already anxious for the return to normalcy promised to them two years later by Warren G. Harding as the Republican nominee for President. The midterm elections of 1918 replaced Democratic with Republican majorities in both houses of the 66th Congress (1919-21), during which President Wilson lost his historic battle with the Senate over the Treaty of Versailles. With the election of Harding in 1920 began a decade of undivided Republican control of the executive and legislative branches of the federal government, lasting until Democrats recaptured the House in 1931.

These were not years of presidential leadership or strong party government. Harding's administration was marked by widespread corruption, brought to light by Senate investigators after his death in 1923. As Harding's successor, Calvin Coolidge (1923-29) did little to push his legislative program through Congress. President Herbert Hoover (1929-33) was unable to deal effectively with the economic depression that began soon after he took office. Meanwhile, Republican control of the Senate was occasionally nominal, and a minority of party progressives often held the balance of power. Party conservatives were more successful in keeping control of the House during the 1920s, and legislative conflicts between the Senate and the

House were common. A notable case in point involved the Senate-approved "lame duck" amendment to the Constitution, which House leaders managed to block until 1932.

There were some important changes in the organization and procedures of the House in this period. Full authority over money bills was reconcentrated in the Appropriations Committee in 1920, and some minor committees were abolished in 1927. Republican leaders introduced, then abandoned, use of a party Steering Committee to guide their legislative program. Under pressure from progressives, House rules were modified in 1924, but the Rules Committee continued to exercise tight control over the legislative options of members. Meanwhile, the representative nature of the chamber declined as the House put off until 1931 the reapportionment of seats that should have followed the census of 1920.

New Budget System

Until 1920, there was no central system for drawing up the federal budget or for its consideration in Congress. The Secretary of the Treasury did no more than compile the estimates of the various departments, which in the House were referred to eight different committees, each of which would report an appropriation bill with no reference to total expenditures or revenues. Nor were all of the requests of a department considered by one committee and appropriated in one bill; other committees commonly reported bills that included appropriations. This process, which was repeated in the Senate, led to rising criticism; as Rep. Alvan T. Fuller (R Mass.) put it in 1918: "The President is asking our business men to economize and become more efficient while we continue to be the most inefficient and expensive barnacle that ever attached itself to the ship of state."[41]

To improve control over expenditures within the executive branch, President Wilson in 1919 proposed a new budget system. Although he vetoed the first bill passed by Congress in 1920 (because it placed the comptroller general beyond his power of removal), a second bill, signed by President Harding, became the Budget and Accounting Act of 1921. This measure directed the President to prepare and transmit to Congress each year a budget showing federal revenues and expenditures for the previous and current years and estimated for the ensuing year. It set up a Bureau of the Budget as his agency to do the work, and it created a General Accounting Office under the comptroller general to assist Congress in exercising oversight of the administration of federal funds.

Anticipating the passage of this bill, the House on June 1, 1920, voted to restore to the Committee on Appropriations the jurisdiction over all supply bills granted to it originally in 1865. A sizable number of senior House Republicans and Democrats opposed the move, and the House barely agreed to the special rule bringing the resolution to the floor, which was adopted by a vote of 158 to 154. The resolution, which was then approved by a vote of 200 to 117, provided for an increase in the size of the Appropriations Committee from 21 to 35 members. At the same time, the House barred its conferees on appropriation bills from accepting Senate amendments that contravened the rules of the House unless so authorized by a separate House vote on each such amendment.

Most of the responsibility for reviewing budget estimates was now lodged in 10 five-member subcommittees of the House Appropriations Committee, each of which passed on the requests of one or more agencies. Parallel subcommittees were set up by the Senate Appropriations Committee, and in 1922 it, like the House, was given exclusive authority over money bills. These steps toward a more systematic approach to federal expenditures came at a time of general concern for greater economy in government and helped to hold outgo to little more than $3 billion a year from 1922 to 1930. With revenues of close to $4 billion each year, the public debt was reduced from $25 billion in 1919 to $16 billion in 1930.

Additional House Changes

When the Republicans regained control of the House in 1919, their leading contender for Speaker was Rep. James R. Mann (R Ill.), who had been minority leader since 1911. But Mann had offended many of his party colleagues by objecting to passage of their private bills, while others feared that he would seek to recentralize power in the manner of his mentor and close friend, former Speaker Cannon. So the Republican conference, looking for more of a figurehead as Speaker, nominated the respected but less forceful Frederick H. Gillett (R Mass.), a member of the House since

119

1893. Mann refused the title of majority leader, which went to Frank W. Mondell (R Wyo.), and for the first time this position was divorced from the chairmanship of the Ways and Means Committee.

In a further effort to decentralize power, the Republicans created a five-member Steering Committee chaired by the majority leader and barred both the Speaker and the chairman of the Rules Committee from sitting on it. Complaints about the narrow range of views and states represented on the Steering Committee led to expansion of its membership to eight in the 67th Congress (1921-23), when Mondell also took to inviting the Speaker, the chairman of Rules and others to sit with the committee, which met almost daily and served as the major organ of party leadership from 1919 to 1925.

With a Republican majority of 300 in the 67th Congress, party leaders nevertheless came in for growing criticism for blocking action on measures with wide support in the House. Rules Chairman Philip P. Campbell (R Kan.), for one, simply refused to report a number of resolutions approved by a majority of his committee to authorize certain investigations. He once told the committee: "You can go to hell. It makes no difference what a majority of you decide. If it meets with my disapproval, it shall not be done. I am the committee. In me repose absolute obstructive powers."[42] And Campbell's right to pocket a resolution was upheld by Speaker Gillett and, on appeal, by the House.

But Campbell and many other Republicans were defeated in the elections of 1922, and when the 68th Congress met in December of 1923 the House consisted of 225 Republicans and 207 Democrats. Lack of a larger majority enabled a group of about 20 reform-minded Republican progressives to hold up the election of a Speaker in an effort to bring about some liberalization of the rules. For two days and eight ballots the two party nominees—Speaker Gillett and Minority Leader Finis J. Garrett (D Tenn.)—received about 195 votes each, while the progressives cast 17 votes for Rep. Henry A. Cooper (R Wis.).

Then Nicholas Longworth (R Ohio), who had succeeded Mondell as majority leader, persuaded the insurgents to support the election of Gillett in return for a promise to allow full debate on revision of the rules in January; Gillett was re-elected Speaker on the ninth ballot. Democrat Henry T. Rainey (Ill.) congratulated Longworth for having steered safely "between the Scylla of progressive Republicanism...and the Charybdis of conservative Republicanism.... There is not a scratch on the ship. The paint is absolutely intact."[43]

The promised debate lasted five days and led to a number of changes in House rules. One, designed to outlaw the "pocket veto" exercised by Chairman Campbell, required the Rules Committee to "present to the House reports concerning rules, joint rules, and order of business within three legislative days of the time when ordered reported by the Committee."[44] The new rule provided also that if the member making the report failed to call it up within the next nine days, any other member designated by the Committee could do so.

The House also agreed at this time, by a vote of 253 to 114, to amend the discharge rule first adopted in 1910. The amended rule reduced from 218 (or a majority of members) to 150 the number required to sign a motion to discharge a committee from further consideration of a bill. Once signed, however, such a motion could be called up only on the first and third Mondays of the month and was subject to other constraints. The single attempt (led by Democrats) to use the new rule in the 68th Congress was successfully thwarted by the Republican leadership.

Disciplining of Progressives

President Coolidge won an easy victory in the election of 1924, when he received 15.7 million votes to 8.4 million for Democrat John W. Davis and 4.8 million for the Progressive candidate, Sen. Robert M. LaFollette (R Wis.). At the same time, the Republican majority of 225 in the House was increased to 247 in the 69th Congress. This gain wiped out the leverage that Republican Party Progressives had been able to exert at the beginning of the 68th Congress and opened the way for party leaders to discipline those—including most of the Wisconsin delegation—who had supported La Follette in the 1924 campaign.

By the time the new Congress met on Dec. 7, 1925, the Republican Conference had agreed to nominate Majority Leader Longworth for Speaker (Gillett having been elected to the Senate), to oust Progressive leaders, John M. Nelson and Florian Lampert, both of Wisconsin, from their positions as chairmen of the Committee of Elections and the Committee on Patents, and to let the other insurgents know that their committee assignments would depend on how they voted for Speaker and for a new and tougher discharge rule. The insurgents responded by again nominating and voting for Cooper. As Progressive James A. Frear put it:

"The Wisconsin delegation in Congress today finds itself challenged by those assuming to be in control of the Republican party by threats and intimidation on the one hand and by the offer of party recognition with its favors and patronage on the other. We refuse to compromise, or to bargain with Mr. Longworth or with any other Member of the House on an issue affecting our rights as Representatives in Congress to vote our convictions.... Neither flattery nor suggestions concerning committee assignments nor threats will cause the Wisconsin delegation in the House to deviate...."[45]

Longworth was easily elected Speaker on the first ballot, receiving 229 votes to 173 for Democratic Leader Garrett and 13 for Cooper. By a vote of 210 to 192, the House then agreed to substitute for the discharge rule of 1924 a new rule described by Rep. Charles R. Crisp (D Ga. and son of the one-time Speaker) as one that "hermetically seals the door against any bill ever coming out of a committee when the Steering Committee or the majority leaders desire to kill the bill without putting the members of this House on record on the measure."[46]

The new rule to instruct committees not only required that a majority of the membership (or 218 instead of 150) sign the motion to discharge, but also stipulated that a similar majority second its consideration by a teller vote, for which most members would rarely show up. Moreover, the motion could be called up only on the third Monday of the month, and if it then failed to be seconded as prescribed, it could not be brought up again during the same Congress. (Not surprisingly, the rule was never invoked during its life, which ended when Democrats revived the old discharge rule in 1931.)

Ten days later, when the Republican slate of committee assignments was submitted to the House, those Progressives who had voted for Cooper and against the new rule found themselves demoted to the bottom of their committees. (Senate Progressives who had supported La Follette were also dropped to the foot of their committees.) Other Republicans had apparently been brought into line by threats of similar action, according to Minority Leader Garrett, who said "it was demanded that 71 gentlemen who at the beginning of the 68th Congress thought a discharge rule was proper should change their votes, demanded that they should eat the bravest word that many of them ever spoke in order to maintain their standing with the party."[47]

These developments at the beginning of the 69th Congress reflected Longworth's determination to play the role of party leader in the House. He had already stated his belief that it was the duty of the Speaker, "standing squarely on the platform of his party, to assist in so far as he properly can the enactment of legislation in accordance with the declared principles and policies of his party and by the same token resist the enactment of legislation in violation thereof...."[48] As Speaker, Longworth ignored the party Steering Committee and for six years (1925-31) personally took charge of the House with the aid of Majority Leader John Q. Tilson (R Conn.) and Rules Committee Chairman Bertrand H. Snell (R N.Y.).

Norris Amendment Blocked

The power of House Republican leaders during the 1920s was illustrated by their success in blocking an amendment to the Constitution designed to abolish the regular "short" session of every Congress by advancing from March to January the time when the life of the previous Congress would expire and that of the new one begin. House leaders liked the short session because its automatic termination on March 3 strengthened their ability to control the legislative output of the House. Sponsored by Sen. George W. Norris (R Neb.), the progressive who had helped to curb the powers of Speaker Cannon in 1910, the proposed abolition of the short session was approved six times by the Senate before the House in 1932, finally consented to what became the Twentieth Amendment.

The effort to adopt what was popularly called the "lame duck" amendment began during the 67th Congress in 1922. Sen. Thaddeus H. Caraway (D Ark.) offered a resolution "that all members defeated at the recent polls abstain from voting on any but routine legislation." When his request that the resolution be referred to the Agriculture Committee, chaired by Sen. Norris, was greeted by laughter from his colleagues, he explained: "I presume that by ordinary parliamentary procedure the concurrent resolution would go to the Committee on the Judiciary but...I have every reason to believe that it will slumber there, as some other resolutions that I introduced found a morgue there; and I should like to have the Senate itself pass upon this one."[49]

The Agriculture Committee reported instead a joint resolution embodying the "lame duck" amendment, and the Senate endorsed it on Feb. 13 by a vote of 63 to 6—well over the two-thirds majority required by the Constitution.

The Norris resolution was approved a week later by the House Election Committee, and a special rule for its consideration was ordered reported by majority vote of the Rules Committee. But the chairman of the Rules Committee, Rep. Philip P. Campbell, pocketed the rule, refusing to report it. Then, while sitting as Speaker for the ailing Gillett during the last few days of the session, Campbell (who was himself a "lame duck," having been defeated the previous November) refused to recognize members who were seeking recognition for the purpose of appealing to the House to override his refusal to report the rule.

On March 18, 1924, in the first session of the 68th Congress, the Senate again adopted the Norris resolution, by a vote of 63 to 7, and three days later it was again reported to the House by the Election Committee. This time, however, it was blocked in the Rules Committee, leading Norris to accuse House leaders of "killing it, not directly but smothering it without giving the House of Representatives an opportunity to vote." Norris added that the resolution was "being held up because machine politicans can get more out of this [legislative] jam than the people's representatives can get."[50] The resolution died with the adjournment of the 68th Congress on March 3, 1925.

The Senate approved the proposed amendment for a third time on Feb. 15, 1926, in the first session of the 69th Congress, by a vote of 73 to 2, and on Feb. 24 it was again reported to the House by a unanimous vote of the Election Committee. Chairman Hays B. White (R Kan.) then discussed the problem he faced under the rules: "Gentlemen, realize how meager is the chance to reach the resolution under the Calendar Wednesday rule. That is the logical and proper rule under which it should be considered.... I cannot get unanimous consent...nor can I hope to pass a measure fundamental as this under a motion to suspend the rules.... The last alternative is for the Rules Committee to grant a special rule for its early consideration."[51] But the rule was not forthcoming before the final adjournment of the 69th Congress on March 3, 1927.

On Jan. 4, 1928, in the first session of the 70th Congress, the Senate again adopted the Norris resolution, by a vote of 65 to 6, and this time its supporters in the House brought it to the floor. Rep. Ole J. Kvale (Farmer-Labor Minn.), said the leaders who had kept the House from voting on it for so long "did not dare block it any longer."[52] Rules Committee Chairman Snell acknowledged that "if it had not been for the significant application of these two words, lame duck, the propaganda that has been spread throughout this country would never have been one-half as effective as it has been, and if it had not been for that propaganda I doubt whether this proposition would be on the floor at this time."[53] The amendment was endorsed by a majority on March 9, 1928, but the vote of 209 to 157 fell 35 short of the two-thirds required for approval.

The Senate approved the Norris resolution for a fifth time on June 7, 1929, by a vote of 64 to 9. A slightly amended version was reported in the House on April 8, 1930, but was not taken up on the floor until Feb. 24, 1931, a week before adjournment. Speaker Longworth then offered a further amendment, to provide that the second session of each Congress should expire automatically on May 4. The Longworth amendment was adopted by a vote of 230 to 148 before the resolution itself was approved, 290 to 93. But the measure was locked in conference when Congress adjourned on March 3.

When the 72nd Congress convened in December 1931, however, Democrats took control of the House, and after the Senate had adopted the resolution for the sixth time on Jan. 6, 1932, 63 to 7, the House quickly followed suit by a vote of 335 to 56 on Feb. 16. Within less than a year, the Twentieth Amendment had been ratified by three-fourths of the states.

125

Struggle Over Reapportionment

By 1920, no state had lost a seat in the House through reapportionment since Maine and New Hampshire were deprived of one each after the census of 1880. The reason was that Congress had regularly agreed to increase the total membership by a sufficient number to prevent such a loss. Thus the House was enlarged to 357 members after the census of 1890, to 391 after that of 1900 and to 435 after that of 1910.

The 1920 census showed that unless the size of the House were again increased, 11 states would lose seats through reapportionment while eight would gain. One argument against such a shift was that voiced by Rep. John E. Rankin (D Miss.) in 1921: "The census was taken at a time when we were just emerging from the World War, and when so many thousands of people had left the farms and the small towns temporarily and gone to the large cities of the North and East that a reapportionment under that census would necessarily take from Mississippi and other agricultural states their just representation and place it to the credit of the congested centers."[54]

Limit on Size of House. To avoid reducing the representation of any state, the House Census Committee early in 1921 reported a bill that would have increased the membership to 483, with the additional seats going to 25 states whose population relative to that of the others had grown the most. But the House proceeded to reverse the committee, voting 267 to 76 to keep the membership at 435. Proponents of that limit argued that the great size of the membership had already resulted in serious limitations on the right to debate and an overconcentration of power in the hands of the leadership. Much was also made of the increased costs of a larger membership.

The bill passed by the House on Jan. 19, 1921, therefore, provided for reapportionment on the basis of the existing membership and would have taken 12 seats from 11 states. But the Senate failed to act on the measure before the 66th Congress adjourned on March 3. When the 67th Congress was called into special session a month later, the House Census Committee, by a vote of 9 to 7, reported a new bill that would have fixed the membership at 460 and cost only two states—Maine and Missouri—one seat each. But on Oct. 14, 1921, the House voted 146 to 142 to recommit the bill to committee, and no further action was taken.

By 1925, it was clear that the wartime shift of population from rural to urban areas was not to be reversed. Such rapidly growing cities as Los Angeles and Detroit began to clamor for the increased representation in the House to which they were entitled. When the House Census Committee still refused to report a new bill, Rep. Henry E. Barbour (R Calif.) moved, April 8, 1926, to discharge the committee from further consideration of a bill similar to that passed in 1921. Barbour argued that the bill was privileged under the Constitution, while Rules Committee Chairman Snell, raising a point of order, denied that reapportionment was mandatory under the Constitution.

Speaker Longworth found that three of his predecessors—Keifer, Reed and Henderson had ruled, to the contrary, that Congress was required to order a new apportionment after each census. But Longworth said he doubted whether such a ruling was correct, and he put to the House this question: "Is the consideration of the bill called up by the motion of the gentleman from California in order as a question of constitutional privilege, the rule prescribing the order of business to the contrary notwithstanding?"[55] By a vote of 87 yeas to 265 nays, the House decided the question in the negative.

Coolidge for Reapportionment. In January 1927, President Coolidge made it known for the first time that he favored enactment of a reapportionment bill. When the House Census Committee refused to act, its chairman, E. Hart Fenn (R Conn.), moved on March 2, the day before adjournment, to suspend the rules and pass his bill to authorize a reapportionment of the House by the Secretary of Commerce on the basis of the 1930 census. With only 40 minutes of debate allowed under the rule (which also required a two-thirds vote) and a filibuster under way in the Senate, the House rejected the Fenn motion by a vote of 183 to 197.

The Fenn bill was rewritten early in the 70th Congress, but on May 18, 1928, the House voted 186 to 165 to recommit it to committee. After further revision, the measure was passed by voice vote on Jan. 11, 1929. Reported to the Senate four days later, it was finally abandoned by its supporters on Feb. 27—five days before the end of the session—in the face of a threatened filibuster by senators from states that were destined to lose seats in the House.

President Hoover called the 71st Congress into special session on April 15, 1929, and listed provision for the 1930 census and for reapportionment as matters of emergency legislation. On June 13, 1929, the Senate passed, 48 to 37, a combined census-reapportionment bill that had been approved by voice vote of the House two days earlier.

Automatic Reapportionment. The 1929 law established a permanent system for reapportioning the 435 seats in the House following each census. It provided that immediately after the convening of the 71st Congress in December 1930, the President should transmit to Congress a statement of the apportionment of representatives to each state according to the existing size of the House. Failing enactment of new apportionment legislation by Congress, that apportionment would go into effect for ensuing elections without further action and would remain in effect until another census had been taken. Reapportionment would be effected in the same manner after each decennial count of the population.

The reapportionment based on the 1930 census resulted in a major reshuffling of House seats in the 73rd Congress, which was elected in 1932. Twenty-one states lost a total of 27 seats; Missouri alone lost three, and Georgia, Iowa, Kentucky and Pennsylvania two each. Among the 11 states to which these seats were transferred, California alone gained nine, increasing the size of its delegation from 11 to 20. Other states to win more than one additional seat were Michigan (four), Texas (three), and New Jersey, New York and Ohio (two each).

Chapter 14

Democratic Years: 1931-1945

The Great Depression that began in 1929 foreshadowed the end of Republican rule in Washington. The party's majority of 267 in the House of the 71st Congress (1929-31) evaporated in the mid-term elections of 1930, when the returns indicated that the next House would be composed of 218 Republicans, 216 Democrats and one independent. By the time the 72nd Congress met on Dec. 7, 1931, however, 14 representatives-elect (including Speaker Longworth) had died, and special elections to fill the vacancies had resulted in a net gain of four seats for the Democrats, giving them control of the House.

With 12 million Americans unemployed by 1932, Democrat Franklin D. Roosevelt was elected President along with commanding Democratic majorities in both houses of Congress. A strong party leader, Roosevelt in his first term (1933-37) obtained the enactment of a broad range of New Deal economic and social measures. He was less successful in dealing with Congress in his second term (1937-41), when he came into conflict with a conservative coalition opposed to his domestic programs. Germany's attack on Poland in 1939, followed by the fall of France in 1940, helped to re-elect Roosevelt to an unprecedented third term (1941-45) that was largely devoted to waging and winning World War II. But legislative-executive relations deteriorated during the war and when Roosevelt died at the beginning of a fourth term in 1945, Congress was in open rebellion against his plans for postwar reconstruction.

The Democrats who led the House during these years worked closely with the President and did their best, by and large, to marshal support for administration requests. But their power to shape the legislative output of the House was sharply curtailed after 1937, when a coalition of southern Democrats and Republicans gained effective control of the Rules Committee, which had been a key arm of House leaders since 1880. The focus of reformers became much broader during the war, however, when the capacity of Congress as a whole to function effectively as a co-equal branch came under attack. This situation led to passage of the Legislative Reorganization Act of 1946.

Party Leaders

The long tenure of southern Democrats commenced when the party took control of the House in 1931. John Nance Garner of Texas, who had become minority leader on the retirement of Rep. Finis J. Garrett of Tennessee in 1929, was elected Speaker. A member since 1903, Garner was then the second-ranking Democrat in the House. Third-ranking Henry T. Rainey (Ill.) was named majority leader. But southerners became chairmen of 28 of the 47 standing committees of the House. Among them were Edward W. Pou (N.C., since 1901), chairman of Rules; Joseph W. Byrns (Tenn., since 1909), Appropriations; James W. Collier (Miss., since 1909), Ways and Means; and Sam Rayburn (Texas, since 1913), Interstate and Foreign Commerce.

When Garner became Vice President in 1933, House Democrats elevated Rainey to Speaker and made Byrns the new majority leader. Rainey died in 1934 and Byrns was elected Speaker at the beginning of the 74th Congress in 1935, to be succeeded as majority leader by William B. Bankhead (Ala.), who had become chairman of the Rules Committee on the death of Pou in 1934. When Byrns died in 1936, Bankhead became Speaker and the Democrats chose Rayburn as majority leader. Bankhead remained Speaker until his death in 1940, when he was succeeded by Rayburn, and a northern Democrat—John W. McCormack of Massachusetts—became majority leader. Rayburn and McCormack remained in these posts until Republicans took control of the House in 1947.

While the Democrats had been in the minority during the 1920s, southerners had constituted more than one-half of their ranks and there was little occasion for complaint about an unwarranted influence in party councils. But when the party won control of the House in 1931, northern and western Democrats pressed for a larger voice in committee assignments. They proposed entrusting the assignments to a new committee on committees (in place of the one composed of Democratic members of the Ways and Means Committee) to be made up of one member from each state having Democratic representation in the House. This committee would also choose a nine-member steering committee to be in charge of the legislative program.

Steering Committee. These steps were not agreed to in 1931, although additions to the Ways and Means Committee (including McCormack) brought about a better balance of geographical representation. By 1933, however, the Democratic majority in the House had been increased to 313 members, nearly two-thirds of whom were from states outside the South. So it was agreed to set up a Steering Committee composed of the Speaker, majority leader and whip, chairmen of the Appropriations, Ways and Means and Rules Committees and of the party caucus, plus 15 representatives from as many zones to be chosen by Democratic members within those areas. The Steering Committee operated with some success during the 73rd Congress (1933-35), but fell into disuse thereafter.

Gag Rules. The Rules Committee itself was the major tool of House Democratic leaders during the 73rd Congress, which was called into special session by President Roosevelt on March 9, 1933, and asked to pass a series of emergency recovery measures almost sight unseen. Ten of the measures were brought to the House floor under special "closed" rules—drafted by the Rules Committee and adopted by majority vote—that barred all except committee amendments, waived points of order, and sharply limited debate. Among the laws enacted at this session of 100 days with the help of these "gag" rules were the Emergency Banking Act, the Economy Act, the Emergency Relief Act, the first Agricultural Adjustment Act, the Tennessee Valley Authority Act, and the National Industrial Recovery Act.

Faced with mounting opposition to cuts in veterans' benefits and government salaries ordered under the

131

Economy Act, the Rules Committee at the opening of the second session on Jan. 3, 1934, brought in a rule to bar amendments to any appropriation bill for the remainder of the session that would conflict with the economy program of 1933. The purpose, said Rep. Bankhead, was to have the House "deliberately determine for today and hereafter...whether they are going to follow the President's recommendations or not."[56]

Minority Leader Bertrand H. Snell (R N.Y.), saying that he had never been opposed to special rules so long as they were "fairly fair," called this "the most vicious, the most far-reaching special rule" ever proposed. No majority, he said, had "ever dared bring in a rule that not only hog-tied and prohibited the members from expressing themselves on the legislation in hand but even extended through the entire session of Congress." The real purpose, said Snell, was that "you think it will be easier to hog-tie your own men today than it will after we have been in session for five months."[57] Snell was joined by all of the Republicans, 84 Democrats and five Farmer-Labor members in voting against the rule, which was barely adopted, 197 to 192.

The only major change in the standing rules of the House in this period involved the discharge rule. When the Democrats took control of the House in 1931, they replaced the unworkable rule of 1925 with that of 1924, which was altered slightly to reduce from 150 to 145 the number of signatures needed to place a discharge motion on the calendar. But that number was increased to 218 or a majority of the House (as it had been from 1910 to 1924) at the beginning of the 74th Congress in 1935, when Democrats in the House numbered 322 and the leadership was finding it difficult to maintain party unity.

The Conservative Coalition

Party unity was badly shaken at the beginning of the 75th Congress in 1937 when President Roosevelt submitted a plan to reorganize the Supreme Court, through the appointment of additional justices, in order to get a majority that could be counted on to uphold the constitutionality of New Deal measures, of which several had been overturned. This plan to "pack" the Court (which died in the

Senate) created a furor in the country and led to a new align-
ment of conservative Democrats and Republicans in
Congress generally and on the House Rules Committee in
particular.

The "conservative coalition" first appeared in August
of 1937, when the Rules Committee voted 10 to 4 against
granting a special rule for floor consideration of an administration bill that eventually became the Fair Labor
Standards Act. The committee was then chaired by Rep.
John O'Connor (D N.Y.) and was composed of five northern
Democrats, five southern Democrats, and four Republicans.
After its refusal to grant the special rule, House leaders obtained 218 signatures on a discharge petition, but when they
brought the bill to the floor in December the House voted
216 to 198 to recommit it to the Labor Committee.

When the Rules Committee in 1938 again refused to
clear the wage-hour bill, House leaders once more resorted
to the discharge rule to bring the bill to a vote, obtaining
passage this time by a margin of 314 to 97. (Although the
House had occasionally passed a bill by use of the discharge
rule, the Fair Labor Standards Act of 1938 was the first such
measure to become law.) Chairman O'Connor's defection in
this case made him one of the targets of President
Roosevelt's attempted purge of anti-New Deal Democrats in
the 1938 primaries. At a press conference, Aug. 16, 1938, Mr.
Roosevelt denounced the Rules chairman as "one of the
most effective obstructionists in the lower house."[58] O'Connor, unlike other prominent targets of the purge effort, lost
his bid for renomination.

O'Connor was succeeded as chairman of the Rules
Committee in 1939 by Rep. Adolph J. Sabath of Illinois, the
senior House Democrat by then and an ardent New Dealer.
But Sabath continued to be outvoted in the committee by a
coalition of Republicans and southern Democrats led by
Reps. E. E. Cox (D Ga.) and Howard W. Smith (D Va.).
During the 76th Congress (1939-40), the committee began
the practice of demanding, as the price of sending administration bills to the floor, substantive changes in these
bills to accord with the views of conservatives.

Not only did the coalition use its power on the Rules
Committee to block or water down administration
measures; it was also in a position to clear measures opposed by the administration. Thus the committee in 1939

authorized an investigation of the National Labor Relations Board; in 1943, an investigation of activities of executive agencies; and in 1944, an investigation of the government's seizure of properties of Montgomery Ward & Co. All were intended to embarrass the administration. Also in 1944, the committee reported a rule to bring to the floor a price control bill that had been rejected by the Banking and Currency Committee and never reported to the House. Speaker Rayburn took the floor to denounce the rule, saying the Rules Committee "was never set up to be a legislative committee," and the House voted it down.[59]

At the beginning of the 79th Congress in 1945, the size of the Rules Committee was reduced from 14 to 12 members consisting of eight Democrats and four Republicans. Sabath was still chairman, but whenever Reps. Cox and Smith decided to vote with the Republicans they could produce a tie that would block committee action. In 1945, for example, the committee by a vote of six to six refused a direct request by President Truman for a rule that would permit the House to vote on a bill to establish a permanent Fair Employment Practices Commission. The coalition also blocked a rule to permit consideration of an administration bill to raise the minimum wage from 40 to 65 cents an hour.

In 1946, when the Rules Committee was asked to clear an administration-backed labor relations bill reported by the House Labor Committee, it reported instead a rule to permit substitution of a more drastic measure sponsored by Francis H. Case (R S.D.), which had just been introduced. Chairman Sabath denounced the action as arbitrary and undemocratic, but in this case a majority of House members upheld the committee majority by adopting the rule and passing the Case substitute. which was later vetoed.

The Rules Committee thus ceased to be a dependable arm of the Democratic leadership after 1937, when the coalition of conservative Democrats and Republicans took control. While the views of members of the coalition on social and economic issues were in conflict with those of most Democrats in the House, they frequently reflected the legislative preferences of a bipartisan majority, and it was the support of this broader conservative coalition that enabled those who controlled the Rules Committee to make the most effective use of its powers.

1946 Legislative Reorganization Act

Talk of the need for congressional reform mounted during World War II, when the powers of the executive branch were vastly enlarged. A report of the American Political Science Association asserted in 1945: "Congress must modernize its machinery and methods to fit modern conditions if it is to keep pace with a greatly enlarged and active executive branch. This is a better approach than that which seeks to meet the problem by reducing and hamstringing the executive. A strong and more representative legislature, in closer touch with and better informed about the administration, is the antidote to bureaucracy."[60]

Responding to such criticisms, the House and Senate agreed early in 1945 to establish a Joint Committee on the Organization of Congress composed of six members from each house equally divided among Democrats and Republicans. Sen. Robert M. La Follette Jr. (Prog Wis.) was named chairman with Rep. A. S. Mike Monroney (D Okla.) as vice chairman. From March 13 through June 29, 1945, the group took extensive testimony from more than 100 witnesses, including many members of Congress.

Among the proposals heard were several to restrict the power of the House Rules Committee. Rep. Christian A. Herter (R Mass.) thought the committee should be required to grant, within a specified time, requests for special orders on bills favorably reported by the legislative committees. Herter said: "The House Committee on Rules should not have the power of deciding which committee reports shall be considered by the whole House, but should be confined merely to determining the order of their consideration. The Rules Committee ought not to be permitted to prevent the submission of favorable committee reports to the whole House."[61] Rep. Sherman Adams (R N.H.) thought a unanimous report from a legislative committee should automatically give a bill the right of way without reference to Rules.

But in its final report on March 4, 1946, the La Follette-Monroney committee made no recommendations concerning Rules "because of a lack of agreement within the committee as to workable changes in existing practices."[62] Nor did the committee recommend any of the various proposals it had received to select committee chairmen on some other basis than seniority, or proposals to make it easier to limit debate in the Senate. The report nevertheless included a broad range of proposals designed to streamline the committee structure, strengthen congressional control over the budget, reduce the workload of Congress, and improve staff assistance, and most of these reforms were incorporated in the Legislative Reorganization Act of 1946 that was signed by President Truman on Aug. 2. The major provisions of the act dealt with committees, the legislative budget, the congressional workload, staff and salaries.

Committees. The law reduced the number of standing committees from 33 to 15 in the Senate and from 48 to 19 in the House, dropping inactive committees and merging others with related functions. The House committees were: Agriculture, Appropriations, Armed Services, Banking and Currency, District of Columbia, Education and Labor, Expenditures in the Executive Departments (name changed to Government Operations in 1952), Foreign Affairs, House Administration, Interior and Insular Affairs, Interstate and Foreign Commerce, Judiciary, Merchant Marine and Fisheries, Post Office and Civil Service, Public Works, Rules, Un-American Activities (name changed to Internal Security in 1969), Veterans' Affairs, and Ways and Means. (Un-American Activities, a select committee before and during World War II, had been made a standing committee by a 208-186 vote of the House on Jan. 3, 1945.)

All standing committees (except Appropriations) were directed to fix regular days for meeting, keep complete records of committee action including votes, and open all hearings to the public except executive sessions for marking up the bills or for voting, or where the committee by a majority vote orders an executive session. The act made it the duty of each committee chairman to report or cause to be reported promptly to the House any measure approved by his committee and to take or cause to be taken necessary steps to bring the matter to a vote. But no measure was to be reported from any committee unless a majority of the members were actually present.

Legislative Budget. The act directed the House Ways and Means, the Senate Finance, and the Appropriations Committees of both houses, acting as a Joint Budget Committee, to prepare each year a legislative budget, including estimates of total receipts and expenditures. The Budget Committee's report was to be accompanied by a concurrent resolution for adopting the budget and fixing the amount to be appropriated. Congress was prohibited from appropriating more than estimated receipts without at the same time authorizing an increase in the public debt. The act did not include a proposal that the President be required to reduce all appropriations by a uniform percentage if expenditures were later found to be exceeding receipts.

Workload. The act prohibited the introduction of private bills for the payment of pensions or tort claims, the construction of bridges, or the correction of military records—categories of legislation that at one time consumed much time. But Congress did not accept the Joint Committee's proposal that the District of Columbia be given home rule, a step that would have eliminated the District Committees in both houses and a considerable amount of legislative work.

Staff. The act authorized each standing committee to appoint four professional and six clerical staff members, although no limit was placed on the number that could be hired by the Appropriations Committees. It also made the Legislative Reference Service, which provided information for committees and members requesting it, a separate department of the Library of Congress. The Joint Committee had recommended the appointment of a director of personnel, authorized to establish the equivalent of a Civil Service for legislative employees, but this proposal was eliminated in the Senate.

Salaries. The act increased the salaries of senators and representatives from $10,000 to $12,500, effective in 1947, and retained an existing $2,500 non-taxable expense allowance for all members. The salaries of the Vice President and the Speaker were raised to $20,000. The Act also brought members of Congress under the Civil Service Retirement Act and made them eligible for benefits at age 62 after at least six years of service.

The Legislative Reorganization Act also included, as Title III, the Federal Regulation of Lobbying Act which for the first time required lobbyists to register with and report their expenditures to the clerk of the House. But it did not include a provision, recommended by the La Follette-Monroney committee, that both parties establish seven-member policy committees in each chamber, with the majority policy committees to "serve as a formal council to meet regularly with the executive, to facilitate the formulation and carrying out of national policy and to improve relationships between the executive and legislative branches of government."[63] (The Senate, but not the House, agreed later in 1946 to set up party Policy Committees.)

Despite its shortcomings, the 1946 act was regarded at the time as a major achievement. But its provisions for a legislative budget soon proved to be unworkable, while the Regulation of Lobbying Act was too weak to shed much light on the purposes and activities of pressure groups. In reducing the number of standing committees, it was hoped to limit representatives to serving on one committee (and senators on two) in order to make more efficient use of their time. But this practice broke down in later years with the establishment in both chambers of numerous subcommittees and several select committees. The reform of 1946 skirted the issue of the distribution of power within Congress and did not resolve the question of the balance of power between Congress and the executive; these remained troublesome issues throughout the postwar years.

Chapter 15

Postwar Developments: 1945-1969

The Democrats lost control of the House and Senate to the Republicans in the 80th Congress (1947-48) and the 83rd (1953-54) but won majorities in all of the other Congresses from 1949 through 1975. Meanwhile, the presidency passed from Democrat Harry S Truman (1945-52) to Republican Dwight D. Eisenhower (1953-60), who was followed by Democrats John F. Kennedy (1961-63) and Lyndon B. Johnson (1963-68) and Republicans Richard M. Nixon (1969-74) and Gerald R. Ford (1974—). Thus during two years under Truman, six under Eisenhower, five under Nixon and the first two years of the Ford administration, the President was faced with a Congress controlled by the other party.

These periods of divided government tended to emphasize the partisan aspects of conflict between the President and Congress over public policy. But none of the postwar Presidents was in full command of his own party in Congress, whether it was in the majority or minority, and all were forced at times to seek bipartisan support to get their programs enacted. House Democrats always included 60 or more southern conservatives who were opposed to many of their party's economic and social programs, while a score of moderate to liberal Republicans were frequently at odds with the party's conservative majority.

Leadership in the House was relatively stable in this period. As after the Civil War and World War I, the control of federal expenditures became a central issue after World War II, and attempts by Congress generally and the House Appropriations Committee in particular to exercise the power of the purse were matters of controversy. There was continuing agitation over the power of the House Rules Committee to block or reshape major legislation, leading to several efforts to restrict the powers of the committee. Talk of the need for broad-scale congressional reform increased in the 1960s, and in 1970 the House finally agreed to a reorganization bill that had cleared the Senate in 1967.

Party Leaders

Sam Rayburn of Texas was the unrivaled leader of House Democrats from 1940 until his death in 1961, serving as Speaker in all but the Republican-controlled 80th and 83rd Congresses, when he acted as minority leader. Rayburn was a strong Speaker whose influence was enhanced by his veneration of the House as an institution and his high personal standing with most of his colleagues. Faced with a divided party on many issues, he relied heavily on his personal friendships with key members on both sides of the aisle to attain his ends. And younger Democrats who followed his advice—"to get along, go along"—could expect to be rewarded with preferment of some kind, especially if they could demonstrate talent and a capacity for hard work.[64]

Rayburn's preferences were controlling when it came to Democratic committee assignments. In 1948 he obtained the removal from the Un-American Activities Committee of three Democrats who had supported Dixiecrat Strom Thurmond in the 1948 presidential campaign. He saw to it that Democrats named to vacancies on the Ways and Means Committee were favorable to reciprocal trade bills and opposed to reductions in the oil depletion allowance. And he turned the Education and Labor Committee from a predominantly conservative into a liberal body during the 1950s by an infusion of younger Democrats. But Rayburn resisted pressure from party liberals to restructure the Rules Committee until 1961, when he reluctantly agreed to go along.

When Rayburn died late that year after 49 years in the House, Democrats chose John W. McCormack of Massachusetts, who had served as majority leader during

Rayburn's entire tenure as Speaker. Carl Albert (D Okla.) was named majority leader at the same time. McCormack's performance as Speaker suffered by comparison with that of Rayburn. Criticism of his weakness as a party leader culminated at the beginning of the 91st Congress in 1969, when 58 Democrats voted for Morris K. Udall (D Ariz.) for Speaker in the party caucus. Although easily re-elected Speaker, McCormack decided in 1970 to retire at the end of his term, after 42 years in the House, and Carl Albert was designated to succeed him as Speaker. Hale Boggs (D La.) became majority leader when Albert moved up. Albert was re-elected Speaker for the 93rd and 94th Congresses. Thomas P. O'Neill Jr. (D Mass.) succeeded Boggs, who died in an airplane accident, as majority leader in 1972.

House Republicans were led from 1939 to 1959 by Joseph W. Martin Jr. (R Mass.), who also served as Speaker in the 80th and 83rd Congresses, when Charles A. Halleck (R Ind.) held the post of majority leader. Martin, a close friend of Rayburn's, was considered by more conservative House Republicans to be too accommodating to the Democratic leadership during the 1950s, and in 1959 he lost his post as minority leader to Halleck, an outspoken partisan. In time, Halleck incurred the opposition of younger Republicans seeking a more forceful and positive style of leadership, and in 1965 he was himself ousted when the Republican Conference, by a 73-67 vote, named Gerald R. Ford (R Mich.) as minority leader. John J. Rhodes (R Ariz.) became minority leader in 1973 when Ford assumed the vice presidency.

Efforts to Control Spending

In 1947, pursuant to the requirement of the Legislative Reorganization Act of 1946, the Republican-controlled 80th Congress formed a Joint Committee on the Legislative Budget which quickly agreed to ceilings on appropriations and expenditures that were substantially under the amounts projected in President Truman's budget. The House approved these ceilings, but the Senate increased them and insisted that any budget surplus be used to reduce the public debt rather than to provide a tax cut desired by House leaders. As a result, the resolution embodying the legislative budget died in conference.

In 1948, both chambers reached quick agreement on a legislative budget that projected a surplus of $10 billion (or more than twice the President's estimate) and paved the way for passage of a tax cut over the President's veto. But Republican leaders expressed doubt about the efficacy of the legislative budget as a device for reducing expenditures. Rep. John Taber (N.Y.), then chairman of the House Appropriations Committee, called it "a stab in the dark."[65] His Senate counterpart, H. Styles Bridges (N.H.) said it was "a pre-game guess at the final score."[66] In fact, the projected surplus vanished in fiscal 1949, which ended with a deficit of $1.8 billion.

When the Democrats took control of the 81st Congress, Rep. Clarence Cannon (D Mo.) again became chairman of the House Appropriations Committee. In his view, the legislative budget was "unworkable and impracticable." He told the House: "We have tried it [legislative budget]. We gave it every opportunity. It cannot be made effective. We can no more expect success...with this well-meant but hopeless proposal than we can expect a verdict from the jury before it has heard the evidence."[67] Congress put off a decision by voting to postpone until May 1 the deadline for the Joint Committee's recommendations, but these were never forthcoming. The provisions of the 1946 act for a legislative budget remained a part of the law, but Congress made no further effort to comply with them.

In 1950 Cannon tried another approach to expenditure control by having his committee draft a single omnibus appropriations bill that carried almost $37 billion in spending authority as finally enacted. But this bill was quickly outdated by the Korean War and the need for large supplemental appropriations. More important, the omnibus approach had the effect of reducing the authority of the Appropriations Committee's subcommittees and their chairmen. Cannon asserted that "every predatory lobbyist, every pressure group seeking to get its hands into the U.S. Treasury, every bureaucrat seeking to extend his empire downtown is opposed to the consolidated bill."[68] But in 1951 the committee voted 31 to 18 to return to the traditional method of separate appropriation bills.

Cannon and his committee were in full agreement, however, in opposing the concept of a Joint Budget Committee, to be composed of several members of the Senate and House Appropriations Committees. Bills to create such a group were passed by the Senate eight times between 1952 and 1967 but were never accepted by the House. Rep. George H. Mahon (D Texas), who succeeded Cannon as chairman of the House Committee in 1964, summed up the prevailing view of the House on this proposal in 1965 when he said that "every key provision of the bill...is, in my judgment, either unsound, unworkable, or unnecessary."[69]

House-Senate Feud. Behind Mahon's statement lay a long history of resentment over the Senate's claim to co-equal status in the appropriations process, where the House had always asserted its primacy. The issue boiled over in 1962 when the House Appropriations Committee demanded that conference meetings (traditionally held on the Senate side) be rotated between the Senate and House sides of the Capitol. The Senate Appropriations Committee countered by proposing that it initiate one-half of all appropriation bills. The ensuing deadlock froze action on pending bills for months.

The House committee complained at one point that "in the past 10 years the Senate conferees have been able to retain $22 billion of the $32 billion in increases which the Senate added to House appropriations—a 2 to 1 ratio in favor of the body consistently advocating larger appropriations, increased spending, and corresponding deficits."[70] Sen. A. Willis Robertson (D Va.) called the communication in which this complaint was voiced "the most insulting document that one body has ever sent to another."[71] When the Senate adopted a continuing resolution (to let federal agencies keep on spending at the old rate until appropriations for the new fiscal year had been approved), the House went on record, 245-1, that the Senate action was "an infringement on the privileges" of the House.[72] The Senate resolved, in turn, that "the acquiescence of the Senate in permitting the House to first consider appropriation bills cannot change the clear language of the Constitution nor affect the Senate's co-equal power to originate any bill not expressly 'raising revenue.' "[73]

The feud was allowed to die without resolution. While it was true that the Senate had consistently voted for larger expenditures than the House, it was also true that Congress had managed generally to authorize less spending than was proposed by the postwar Presidents. Yet the amounts authorized grew more or less steadily after 1947, and it became increasingly apparent that the capacity of Congress to control expenditures through its power of the purse was quite limited. Congress did not pass legislation to reform its budget procedures until 1974.

Checking the Rules Committee

The negative power of the House Rules Committee was forcefully displayed during the Republican 80th Congress in connection with efforts to enact a major housing bill. The committee insisted that the Banking and Currency Committee delete provisions for public housing and slum clearance before it would agree to release the bill. The committee also refused to allow the House to vote on a universal military training bill reported by the Armed Services Committee, and it was only under strong pressure from Speaker Martin that the committee cleared a bill to revive the lapsed Selective Service System.

Liberals dominated the Democratic majority of 263 elected to the House in 1948, but they were again faced with the prospect that the 12-member Rules Committee would be controlled by a conservative coalition of four Republicans and three southern Democrats—Reps. E. E. Cox (Ga.), Howard W. Smith (Va.) and William M. Colmer (Miss.). So with the backing of Speaker Rayburn the party caucus voted 176 to 48 for a "21-day rule" proposed by Rules Committee Chairman Adolph J. Sabath (D Ill.). The rule authorized the chairman of any legislative committee which had reported a bill favorably, and requested a special rule from the Rules Committee, to bring the matter to the House floor if the committee failed to act within 21 calendar days of the request.

Adopted by the House on Jan. 3, 1949, by a procedural vote of 275 to 143, the 21-day rule was used eight times during the 81st Congress to obtain House passage of bills blocked in the Rules Committee, such as an anti-poll tax bill and statehood measures for Alaska and Hawaii. An effort to repeal the new rule in 1950, led by Rep. Cox, was rejected by the House by a vote of 183 to 236.

The Democrats lost 29 seats in the 1950 elections and when the 82nd Congress met on Jan. 3, 1951, Cox again moved to drop the rule. It had been adopted in 1949, he said, because the Rules Committee had "refused to stampede under the lash of the whip applied by strong unofficial minority groups."[74] Rep. Charles A. Halleck (R Ind.) supported repeal because it was the job of the Rules Committee to screen "unwise, unsound, ill-timed, spendthrift and socialistic measures."[75] Sabath protested that repeal would permit an "unholy alliance" of southern Democrats and Republicans to "tear down the rights of every member of the House."[76] But 91 Democrats joined 152 Republicans to repeal the 21-day rule by a vote of 243 to 180.

Smith's Reign. Control of the Rules Committee by a conservative coalition was virtually unchallenged for the next decade. Rep. Smith, who became chairman in 1955, made the most of his power to censor the legislative program of the House. Because the committee had no regular meeting day and could be called together only by the chairman, it was sometimes unable to clear any bills during the final days of a session when Smith simply disappeared to his Virginia farm.

In 1958, 283 Democrats were elected to the House—their largest majority since 1936—and party liberals again talked of curbing the Rules Committee. They proposed changing the ratio of Democrats to Republicans on the committee from 8-4 to 9-3 and reinstituting the 21-day rule. Speaker Rayburn was opposed to any changes, however, and the liberals called off their drive when he "offered his personal assurance" that housing, civil rights, labor and other social welfare legislation "would not be bottled up in the committee."[77]

Rayburn however, was unable to fulfill his pledge during the 86th Congress (1959-60). When Democrat John F. Kennedy was elected President in 1960 (along with a reduced Democratic majority of 263 in the House), it was clear that much of his program might be stymied unless administration Democrats gained control of the Rules Committee when the 87th Congress convened in 1961. Rayburn decided to try to enlarge the committee from 12 to 15 members to make room for the addition of two loyal Democrats and thus create an 8 to 7 majority that would act favorably on administration bills. But his plan was stoutly opposed by Chairman Smith and Republican Leader Halleck, and it took Rayburn and his lieutenants a month of maneuvering and lobbying to round up enough votes to win.

Enlargment of the Rules Committee. The House finally adopted the rule to increase the size of the committee from 12 to 15 on Jan. 31, 1961, by a vote of 217 to 212. Voting for the change were 195 Democrats, including 47 southerners led by Rep. Carl Vinson (Ga.), and 22 Republicans, including former Speaker Martin. Opposed were 64 Democrats—all except one of them southerners—and 148 Republicans. The new balance thus achieved on the Rules Committee proved to be precarious. A major school aid bill was effectively killed by the committee in 1961 when James J. Delaney (D N.Y.), a Catholic from a heavily Catholic district, joined the conservative coalition in voting against it because no provision was made for aid to parochial schools. Two pro-administration southern Democrats on the committee helped to kill a bill to create a department of urban affairs in 1962, after Robert C. Weaver, a black, was designated to become the new secretary.

Terms of the resolution adopted in 1961 limited the enlargement of the committee to the life of the 87th Congress. But the House on Jan. 9, 1963, at the beginning of the 88th Congress, agreed by a vote of 235 to 196 to make the change permanent. Although party ratios had scarcely changed, the resolution was supported this time by 207 Democrats, 59 of them southerners, and 28 Republicans, and opposed by 148 Republicans and 48 Democrats, all except three of them southerners.

New Rules. Democratic leaders nevertheless continued to have problems with the Rules Committee. But the election of President Johnson in 1964, together with a Democratic majority of 295 in the House, paved the way for three further changes in the House rules at the beginning of the 89th Congress in 1965, again over the opposition of a bipartisan coalition. The new rules were adopted Jan. 4 by voice vote after a motion for the previous question ending all debate had been approved by a roll-call vote of 224 to 202. Only 16 Republicans voted with 208 Democrats for the motion, while 79 Democrats (all except four of them southerners) and 123 Republicans were opposed.

The first of the new rules revived, with one change, was the 21-day rule that had been in force during the 81st Congress. Under the 1949 rule the Speaker had been required to recognize the chairman or other member of the committee seeking to bring before the House a bill that had been denied a rule by the Rules Committee for 21 days. The 1965 rule left the question of recognition to the discretion of the Speaker, thereby ensuring that no bill opposed by the leadership could be brought up under the rule.

The second new rule permitted the Speaker to recognize a member to offer a motion that would permit the House to send a bill to conference with the Senate by majority vote, provided that this action was approved by the committee with jurisdiction over the bill. Previously, it had been necessary to obtain unanimous consent or approval of a special rule from the Rules Committee to send a bill to conference, or to suspend the rules by a two-thirds vote.

The third change agreed to in 1965 repealed a rule dating from 1789 that had permitted any member to demand the reading in full of the engrossed (or final) copy of a House bill. Members opposed to legislation had frequently used this privilege to delay final passage of a bill until it could be printed.

The 21-day rule was employed successfully eight times during the 89th Congress, and the threat of its use persuaded the Rules Committee to send several other controversial measures to the floor. As in 1951, however, Republican gains in the 1966 elections opened the way to repeal of the rule at the beginning of the 90th Congress; the vote on Jan. 10, 1967, was 233 to 185. The prevailing coalition included 157 Republicans and 69 southern Democrats. The two other rules adopted in 1965 were retained.

Repeal of the 21-day rule in 1967 proved to be of little consequence during the 90th Congress, largely because of two other developments affecting the Rules Committee. Chairman Smith had been defeated in a primary election in 1966, as had another committee Democrat, and these vacancies were filled by administration supporters. Smith's successor as chairman, Rep. Colmer of Mississippi, was no less strong a conservative, but he was now outvoted on the committee. This became apparent on Feb. 28, 1967, when for the first time in its history the committee adopted a set of rules to govern its procedures. These rules took from the chairman his exclusive power to set meeting dates, required the consent of a committee majority to table a bill, and set limits on proxy voting by members. The net effect of these changes was substantial cooperation with the Democratic leadership in 1967-68 and the end of a decade of agitation for reform of the committee. The situation remained substantially the same during the 91st Congress (1969-70).

Pressures for Reform

Efforts to modify the organization and procedures of the House after 1946 were not confined to the protracted struggle for control of the Rules Committee. Both the Senate and the House came under pressure to curb the free-wheeling activities of their investigating committees in the early 1950s. The questionable conduct of some senators and representatives raised new doubts about congressional ethics in the 1960s to which both chambers were forced to respond. Mounting criticism of the methods and operations of Congress as a whole led both chambers to begin a re-examination in 1965 that finally produced a second reorganization act in 1970. These developments are discussed below.

Fair Play for Committee Witnesses. The efforts of the House Un-American Activities Committee to expose subversion and disloyalty through public hearings became a subject of great controversy in the early 1950s. The committee's access to television was cut off in 1952 when Speaker Rayburn effectively banned radio, television or film coverage of any House committee hearings by holding that there was no authority for such coverage in the rules of the House. But criticism increased in the Republican-controlled 83rd Congress when Chairman Harold H. Velde (R Ill.) of the Un-American Activities Committee and Sen. Joseph R. McCarthy (R Wis.), head of the Senate Permanent Investigations Subcommittee, were accused of conducting one-man investigations and mistreating witnesses. McCarthy was eventually censured by the Senate in 1954 for contemptuous treatment of two Senate committees.

The Rules Committees of both chambers held hearings in 1954 on proposals to reform committee procedures. On March 23, 1955, the House adopted 10 new rules respecting committee conduct which—

● Required a quorum of not less than two committee members for taking testimony and receiving evidence.

● Allowed witnesses at investigative hearings to be accompanied by counsel for the purpose of advising them concerning their constitutional rights.

● Stipulated that if a committee found that evidence may tend to defame, degrade, or incriminate any person, it receive such evidence in executive (closed) session and allow such person to appear as a witness and request the subpoena of others.

● Barred the release or use in public sessions of evidence or testimony received in executive session without the consent of the committee.

The Senate Rules Committee recommended a similar set of standards in 1955, but the Senate left it to individual committees to draw up their own rules of conduct. Those adopted by the Permanent Investigations Subcommittee in 1955, when Sen. John L. McClellan (D Ark.) became chairman, incorporated provisions similar to those approved by the House. Although the investigative practices of congressional committees continued to vary considerably thereafter, the question of the fair treatment of witnesses declined in importance as a public issue.

Congressional Ethics. Although members of Congress were never immune to the temptations of using public office for private gain, the ethics of Congress as a whole did not begin to stir broad public interest until the years following World War II. Contributing to this interest were the rising costs of political campaigns and an increasing concern with conflicts of interest at all levels of government. The fact that some members of Congress continued to engage in private law practice or other business activities, and to hold a financial interest in such government-regulated businesses as banks and television stations, added to the concern.

Pressure to do something about congressional ethics was intensified in 1963 by charges that Robert G. (Bobby) Baker had used his office as secretary to the Senate majority to promote his outside business interests. The Senate responded by establishing in 1964 a six-member bipartisan Select Committee on Standards and Conduct empowered to investigate allegations of improper conduct by senators and Senate employees, to recommend disciplinary action, and to draw up a code of ethical conduct. Its first inquiry led to the Senate's censure of Sen. Thomas J. Dodd (D Conn.) in 1967 by a vote of 92 to 5, for misuse of political campaign contributions.

In 1968 the Select Committee recommended and the Senate adopted new rules aimed at the practices disclosed in the Baker and Dodd cases. Included were provisions to regulate the outside employment of Senate employees, to require a full accounting of campaign contributions and limit the uses to which they could be put, and to require senators and higher-ranking employees to file copies of their tax returns and some other financial data with the comptroller general each year. But this information was to remain confidential (although accessible to the Select Committee) and the only public accounting required under the new rules was of gifts of $50 or more and honoraria of $300 or more. The Senate, by a vote of 40 to 44, had rejected a proposal for full public disclosure of the finances of its members.

The House, meanwhile, had become embroiled in attempts to discipline Rep. Adam Clayton Powell (D N.Y.), a member since 1945, chairman of the Education and Labor Committee since 1961, and one of the few blacks in the House. Powell was indicted for tax evasion in 1958 and eventually paid $28,000 in back taxes and penalties. He was sued for libel in 1960 and held in contempt of court in the case on several occasions. He kept his wife on his payroll at $20,000 a year although she lived in Puerto Rico. But it was his extensive travels at public expense, his prolonged absences from Congress and his high-handed actions as a committee chairman that turned most of his colleagues against him.

At the beginning of the 90th Congress in 1967, the Democratic Caucus removed Powell as chairman of the Education and Labor Committee, and the House voted 365-65 to deny him his seat pending an investigation by a special committee. Its report recommended that Powell be seated but that he be censured for "gross misconduct," stripped of his seniority and fined $40,000 for misuse of public funds."[78] But on March 1 the House rejected these proposals and voted instead to exclude Powell from the 90th Congress and declare his seat vacant.

Powell promptly filed suit in a federal court to regain his seat on the grounds that he met the constitutional qualifications for membership and that the House had no authority to exclude him. A district court dismissed the case for lack of jurisdiction, and the court of appeals affirmed the finding, noting that the case involved a political question which, if decided by the courts, would constitute a violation of the separation of power. On June 16, 1969, however, the

Supreme Court reversed the lower courts by a vote of 7 to 1; the opinion by Chief Justice Earl Warren held that Powell had been improperly excluded by the House.

Powell had been overwhelmingly re-elected following his exclusion in 1967, but he had made no effort to take his seat during the remainder of the 90th Congress. Re-elected in 1968, he presented himself at the opening of the 91st Congress in 1969. By this time tempers had cooled. The House by a vote of 254-158 adopted a resolution that permitted him to take his seat but fined him $25,000 as punishment and "stripped him of his seniority."[79] Powell accepted the judgment, but his career in the House was ended in 1970 when he was defeated in the primary election.

The Powell case, together with the Senate's actions, helped to persuade the House in 1967 to establish its own 12-member, bipartisan Committee on Standards of Official Conduct. In 1968 the committee recommended and the House adopted (as Rule 43) a Code of Official Conduct which included provisions that—

● Forbade a member or employee to use his official position improperly to receive compensation.

● Prohibited the acceptance of gifts of substantial value from an individual or group with a direct interest in legislation before Congress.

● Prohibited acceptance of honoraria of more than the usual and customary value for speeches and articles.

● Required representatives to keep campaign funds separate from personal funds and not to convert campaign funds to personal use.

● Required that, unless some other purpose was made clear in advance, all funds raised at testimonial events must be treated as campaign contributions subject to the reporting requirements and spending limits of the Corrupt Practices Act of 1925.

● Required that employees of a member perform the work for which they were paid.

The House also adopted at the same time a new rule (Rule 44) that required members and officers of the House, their principal assistants, and professional staff members of committees to file with the Committee on Standards of Official Conduct each year a report disclosing certain financial interests—which were to be available to the public—and a sealed report on the amount of income from those interests.

As under the Senate rules, the sealed report could be opened by the committee only if it determined that it was essential to an investigation, while the data that might be made public were extremely limited.

The new rules adopted by the Senate and House in 1968 did not put an end to the questioning of congressional ethics. The practice of certain senators in introducing hundreds of private immigration bills for Chinese ship-jumpers came under fire in 1969 and an aide to Speaker McCormack was indicted for influence peddling in 1970. When Supreme Court Justice Abe Fortas resigned in 1969 following disclosures of certain financial activities, Sen. Clifford P. Case (R N.J.) renewed his argument that public confidence in the government would not be restored until Congress made it mandatory for Supreme Court justices and all other members of the federal judiciary, as well as members of Congress and high officials in the executive branch, to make full, regular and, most importantly, public reports of their income and financial activities.[80] But when or whether a majority of senators and representatives would agree to make a full public disclosure of their finances was left an open question until the 1970s.

Reorganization Bill. The efficiency and equity of congressional procedures also were questioned with increasing frequency in the 1960s, and in 1965 the Senate and the House agreed to set up a new Joint Committee on the Organization of the Congress modeled on the committee headed by Sen. Robert M. La Follette Jr. (Prog. Wis.) and Rep. A. S. Mike Monroney (D Okla.) that had put through the Legislative Reorganization Act of 1946. A senator since 1951, Monroney was named co-chairman of the new committee along with Rep. Ray J. Madden (D Ind.). After extensive hearings in 1965, the committee in 1966 issued a long list of recommendations most of which were incorporated in a bill passed by the Senate in 1967. But the bill met with strong opposition from committee chairmen and other senior members of the House and remained bottled up in the Rules Committee until the end of the 90th Congress.

Chapter 16

Sweeping Reforms: 1970-1976

Over a six-year period from 1970 to 1976, Congress ended or revised long-established practices that critics claimed made it the most ossified of the nation's governmental institutions.

The changes were made in the rules and procedures of the Senate and House under the unremitting pressure of middle- and low-ranking members. They produced a Congress that was much different in early 1976 than at the beginning of the decade.

The changes, which reached a peak in 1975, produced a basic upheaval in the manner that power is held and exercised in Congress. Almost absolute authority had been vested through the seniority system and rarely was challenged successfully.

The 1970-75 revisions overturned these traditional power preserves. By the end of the first session of the 94th Congress in December 1975, the rigid seniority system was in shambles as the sole method by which members rose to power. The system still functioned as a useful device for ordering the hierarchy on committees, but it no longer was the dominant force. Both chambers had created methods by which committee chairmen had to stand for election by their colleagues, and in the House three chairmen were removed at the beginning of 1975.

By instituting internal changes, Congress gave itself new tools that reformers deemed necessary for improved operations in the last quarter of the 20th century for stricter accountability of members and for re-establishment of Congress as an equal with the presidency under the Constitution.

Foreign Policy, Watergate

The Indochina crisis presented Congress with a unique challenge to participate in foreign policy. Congress was initially criticized for being slow to act, but ultimately it did respond. Over presidential veto, Congress enacted the War Powers Act of 1973, marking the first time in history that Congress had defined and limited the President's power to make war.

After the withdrawal of all U.S. combat forces from Indochina, Congress in 1975 refused President Ford further military aid for South Vietnam and Cambodia. Members expressed fears that more aid might mean a never-ending U.S. involvement.

Elsewhere in foreign affairs, Congress clashed with the Ford administration over arms to Turkey in the wake of that country's invasion of Cyprus in July 1974. Turkey had used U.S.-supplied weapons in that invasion in violation of U.S. foreign aid laws. In opposition to President Ford in February 1975, Congress put an embargo on arms aid to Turkey. In October, the lawmakers partially lifted the ban as a result of intensive White House lobbying.

In another clash with the President, the House on Jan. 27, 1976, approved a Senate-sponsored amendment to the defense appropriations bill which barred all further U.S. aid to factions fighting Communist groups in the civil war in Angola. President Ford had publicly called upon the House to reject the amendment, passed by the Senate Dec. 19, 1975, but the House approved it 323-99. President Ford did not veto the bill, and the ban on aid to Angola became law.

The second crisis, the Watergate scandal began with the burglary of the Democratic National Party headquarters in the Watergate building on June 17, 1972. It ended Aug. 9, 1974, when President Nixon resigned in the face of certain impeachment by the House.

In between those dates, Congress investigated the Nixon presidency. The Senate Watergate committee uncovered the existence of the incriminating White House tape recordings. Nixon's struggle to deny access to the tapes to Special

Prosecutor Archibald Cox resulted in the President firing Cox Oct. 20, 1973. Attorney General Elliot Richardson resigned rather than carry out the White House order to dismiss Cox; and Deputy Attorney General William D. Ruckelshaus was fired after he refused to execute the order.

Responding to an enormous outcry over these events, the "Saturday night massacre," House Democratic leaders met Oct. 22 with Speaker Carl Albert (Okla.) and agreed to have the House Judiciary Committee begin an inquiry into the grounds for impeachment. Ten months later, after the committee had voted three articles of impeachment, Nixon became the first President to resign from office.[81]

Reorganization Act of 1970

The legislative reorganization bill, proposed in 1966 by the joint committee chaired by Sen. A. S. Mike Monroney (D Okla.) and Ray J. Madden (D Ind.) died in the House Rules Committee in 1968. The reform effort was renewed in the 91st Congress. In the final weeks of the Congress, the House acted on a bill of its own, a more modest reform bill than that recommended by the 1966 report of the joint committee. The House passed its bill Sept. 17, 1970, and the Senate approved it Oct. 6.

The Legislative Reorganization Act of 1970, the first such law passed since 1946, ignored the seniority system, the power of the House Rules Committee and the two-thirds rule for cutting off Senate debate. But it did include a number of important provisions designed to give both chambers more information on government finances, to guarantee minority party rights and to maintain a continuing review of legislative needs through a Joint Committee on Congressional Operations.

One of the act's most important items affecting the House required that teller votes on the floor be recorded. Previously, teller votes had only been tabulated in total without recording members' votes. Thus, members had often employed the teller method to elude accountability. The reform put voting in the House on a par with the Senate where teller votes did not exist and where all important floor votes are usually recorded by name.

The 1970 Act required committees to have written rules, a check on the arbitrary use of power by committee chairmen, and to make public roll-call votes taken in closed committee sessions, a step toward holding members accountable for their actions in committee as well as on the floor. Other features were designed to give members more information and expedite congressional business. For example, committee reports had to be available at least three days before floor consideration and House quorum calls were shortened.[82]

New Leadership

House Democratic liberals hoped that the retirement of 79-year-old Speaker John W. McCormack (Mass.) in 1971 would result in a new leadership team supportive of their cause. The House chose Carl Albert (Okla.), who had served as majority leader since 1962. In 24 years in the House, Albert had traveled a careful political road along which he had made few enemies. He was acceptable to most factions of the Democratic Party. He was elected Speaker with only token, last-minute opposition.

By contrast, Hale Boggs (La.) had to overcome strong reformist opposition to advance from Democratic whip to majority leader. Boggs rankled the liberals because he made no commitment during the leadership race to a reform of procedures or a new distribution of power. But traditionalists prevailed in the Democratic Caucus, giving Boggs 140 votes to 88 for Morris K. Udall (Ariz.), principal candidate of the reformers, and 17 for B. F. Sisk (Calif.). After Boggs died in an Alaskan airplane crash, the Democrats chose Thomas P. O'Neill Jr. (Mass.) for majority leader in January 1973. Although he was representative of the traditional system of promotion up the leadership ladder (he had been whip under Boggs), O'Neill sided sometimes with the reformers.

Albert's passive style as Speaker drew mounting criticism, especially in the 94th Congress where the Democrats held a 2-to-1 majority in the House with the election of 75 freshmen in November 1974. That largely liberal class, disdaining the backbencher-role expected of freshmen, joined in the outcry against the leadership's inability to muster the two-thirds vote needed to override much Democratic legislation vetoed by President Ford. For example, the House on June 4, 1975, sustained the veto of a

Democratic-sponsored appropriations bill aimed at creating more than one million jobs in the public and private sectors. Consideration of the bill came as the national unemployment level was climbing to the May high of 9.2 per cent. Ford held the measure to be inflationary.

On the Republican side, Rep. John J. Rhodes (Ariz.) was elected minority leader in December 1973 when Gerald Ford was appointed vice president by Nixon. Rhodes, a conservative, generally supported Republican White House foreign and domestic policies, and enjoyed the conservative coalition votes of Southern Democrats in sustaining many presidential vetoes.[83]

Democratic Caucus

A major instrument of reform during the 1970s was a rejuvenated House Democratic Caucus. Once a powerful instrument in implementing Woodrow Wilson's domestic program, the caucus had fallen into disuse, meeting only at the beginning of a new Congress for the pro forma election of House Democratic leaders.

The move to revitalize the caucus was led by the House Democratic Study Group (DSG), an organization of moderate and liberal Democrats forming the largest reform bloc in the House. The opening came in 1969 when Speaker McCormack, in a move to appease the reformers, agreed to regular monthly meetings of the caucus.

In 1970, the caucus created the Committee on Study, Organization and Review, chaired by Rep. Julia Butler Hansen (Wash.), to study the seniority system. Its report was a prelude to change.

Reforms of 1973

Directed by the 150-member DSG with outside help from Common Cause, the public interest lobby, and Americans for Democratic Action, reform forces pushed through three new policies at the beginning of the 93rd Congress.

In a move toward more open government, the House adopted a caucus-inspired reform to curb committee secrecy. All committees and subcommittees were required to open to the public most bill-drafting sessions and other business meetings unless a majority voted at an open session to bar the public. Hearings had been open, but sessions where bills were marked up were usually closed. The reform allowed reporters and the public to witness the performance of committee members in shaping bills.

Two years later, first the House, then the Senate adopted rules opening conference committees to the press and public. Conferences, called to iron out differences in each chamber's version of a bill, were one of the last and most traditional vestiges of secrecy in Congress. Conferences had become the quiet preserves of senior members who exercised great powers over the final form of bills as compromises were worked out behind closed doors.

But a chief advocate of institutional reform in the House, Rep. Richard Bolling (D Mo.) was skeptical about the effectiveness of the new conference rules, saying, "Sunshine laws kid the public. They imply a total openness and there never will be." He cautioned that some accommodations and compromises would still have to be made in secret.

A second major 1973 reform was aimed at the Ways and Means Committee, which held jurisdiction over key legislative areas—taxes, foreign trade, Social Security, Medicare and others. Chairman Wilbur D. Mills (D Ark.) had long been successful in bringing Ways and Means legislation to the House floor under a closed rule, making amendments impossible. Mills, a skilled parliamentarian and an authoritarian chairman, argued that his legislation was so complex that amendments by individual members would twist the bills out of shape and the broader goals would be lost.

The caucus struck a compromise between the Mills position and unlimited floor amendments: a minimum of 50 Democrats could propose an amendment to the caucus, and if a majority of the caucus approved the amendment, Democratic members of the Rules Committee would be instructed to write a rule allowing the amendment to be taken up on the House floor. The author of the plan, Rep. Phillip Burton (D Calif.), explained that he was not trying to load every bill down with amendments. Mills, not present during the caucus action, did not oppose the Burton proposal.

Finally in 1973, the caucus created a new Democratic Steering and Policy Committee to assist the Speaker in developing party and legislative priorities.

Subcommittees Strengthened

The caucus-led attack on the seniority system struck out at the dominance of subcommittees by the full committee chairman. Through rigid control of all levels of major committees, a few chairmen, operating individually and collectively, held much House business in their grip during the 1950s and 1960s.

In 1971, the caucus adopted a rule that no Democratic committee member could be chairman of more than one legislative subcommittee. Two years later, the Democratic Caucus instituted a series of changes, known as the "bill of rights," which gave the subcommittees greater autonomy from control by the chairmen of the full committees. The changes, which affected the Democrats alone and were not made part of the House rules, included:

● Establishment of a Democratic Caucus on each full committee, forcing chairmen to share authority with other Democrats. The committee caucus was granted authority to select subcommittee chairmen, to establish subcommittee jurisdictions, to provide adequate subcommittee budgets, and to guarantee all members a major subcommittee assignment as vacancies opened up.

● Requirement that committee chairmen refer legislation to appropriate subcommittees within two weeks, thus preventing chairmen from killing bills by not scheduling them for committee action.

● The right of subcommittee chairmen and ranking minority members to hire one staff member each to work for them on the subcommittee. The purpose of this staff assistance was to help keep the subcommittees independent of the chairman of the full committee.

The diffusion of power to the subcommittees was solidified in 1975 when the Democratic Caucus voted to require all committees having more than 20 members to establish at least four subcommittees and to restrict committee members to positions on no more than two subcommittees. These requirements were designed to correct what the caucus regarded as abuses in the running of the two most powerful committees in the House—Ways and Means and Appropriations.

Ways and Means Chairman Wilbur D. Mills (D Ark.) had operated without subcommittees during most of his 16-

year reign (1958-74). In the Appropriations Committee, senior conservative Democrats had dominated important subcommittees handling defense, agriculture, health, education and welfare funding.

In another move designed to curb the Appropriations Committee, the caucus decided that starting with the 94th Congress in 1975, all subcommittee chairmen of the Appropriations Committee had to be approved by the caucus.

Committee Assignments

In 1973, House Democrats adopted a party rule guaranteeing each Democrat a major committee assignment, ending the old system of assigning newcomers to one or more minor committees.

At the December 1974 caucus another blow was struck at Ways and Means which had served since 1911 as the Democratic Committee on Committees. That power to assign Democrats to committees was switched to the party's Steering and Policy Committee, composed of House leaders, their nominees and members elected by the caucus on a regional basis.

Beginning in 1975, a new rule allowed each member of a full committee to choose a subcommittee position before any member could select a second subcommittee slot—a further step in breaking up the conservative monopoly over Appropriations subcommittees.

Seniority System Crippled

Although reforms had rolled on at a rapid pace, the same chairmen—though with reduced powers—were presiding over the same committees in 1974 as at the opening of the decade, unless their House service had been ended by voluntary retirement, re-election defeat or death.

But the Democratic Caucus was at work on its challenge to the seniority system. It began readying itself in 1971 with a modest policy change which allowed 10 or more Democrats to demand a separate vote on any chairman nominee. It was known as the "kamikaze rule" because challengers had to stand up publicly in caucus to demand the vote, risking retribution from unforgiving chairmen. The caucus also stated that seniority need not be considered in recommendations for chairmen, underlining the fact that advancement on the basis of congressional longevity was a custom, not a rule.

In 1973, the caucus passed a rule requiring that each Democratic committee chairman be elected by mandatory secret ballot, but then the caucus went on to award all chairmanships, on 21 separate votes, to the same members who would have received them if the seniority system had gone untouched.

When the 94th Congress convened in January 1975, the 2-to-1 House Democratic majority included the newly elected freshmen who owed no favors to the chamber's senior establishment. When the caucus had finished its work, the seniority system was no longer the sole route by which members became chairmen.

Three chairmen were deposed: Wright Patman (Texas) of the Banking, Currency and Housing Committee; F. Edward Hebert (La.) of the Armed Services Committee; and W. R. Poage (Texas) of the Agriculture Committee. Various reasons were given for their ouster, but there was little doubt the trio made a poor impression on the freshmen Democrats who had interviewed all three before deciding whom they would support in caucus. In addition, each of the three was accused of autocratic actions denying equitable treatment to their committee members. Ideology was thought to have played a role, but not a major one. Hebert was identified as a conservative who gave unflinching support to the military and who voted with Republicans on many issues. Patman, was a Southern populist with a long record of opposing tight money policies and high bank interest rates. At the age of 82, he had had trouble controlling his fractious committee colleagues.

The deposing of the three chairmen encompassed several maneuvers in the Democratic Steering Committee, which recommended chairmen nominees, and the caucus. In Patman's case, the independent-minded caucus ousted him in spite of Steering Committee support. The three chairmen were replaced with a senior member of each committee. The caucus also refined the method of nominating chairmen by allowing competitive contests and nominations from the caucus floor.

The removal of the three broke the system that for decades had governed representatives' progression to House power. In 1967, Rep. Adam Clayton Powell (D N.Y.) was removed from the chairmanship of the Education and Labor Committee following allegations of misconduct, including payroll padding, extensive travels at public expense and tax evasion. Before Powell, the last time the House had ousted a chairman was in 1925 when two Republican chairmen were removed for campaigning in 1924 for Progressive presidential candidate Robert LaFollette.

Budget Control

For years the House and Senate were plagued by a disjointed appropriations process that gave no overall control of funding to any congressional unit, nor even to the entire Congress itself. To remedy the chaotic situation, the Congressional Budget and Impoundment Control Act was passed in 1974, setting up House and Senate Budget Committees and a Congressional Budget Office. The act's goals were to focus congressional attention in a systematic way on two broad budgetary concerns: national fiscal policy and national priorities.

The sweeping reform required Congress to vote for the first time on a budget deficit. The process forced Congress to compare total spending and total receipts, instead of treating appropriations and tax measures as mutually-exclusive budget items. In doing so, Congress was required to confront such fiscal policy issues as the effect of the budget on inflation, unemployment and economic growth.

Congress also had to decide on budget priorities. For example, if Congress called for more spending for health purposes, it had to increase revenues through higher taxes, accept a large deficit or balance the addition by cutting other programs.

The law also created a complicated set of deadlines for congressional action on the budget. The key dates each year are May 15, when Congress was supposed to complete action on a first concurrent resolution containing budget targets to guide committees as they process fiscal legislation during the summer months, and Sept. 15, when Congress was to replace the targets with spending ceilings and a floor on revenues in a second concurrent resolution. If the amounts adopted in the fall differ from those adopted during the summer in actual spending and tax bills, Congress must reconcile the amounts before adjourning. Once this reconciliation process is completed, the limits in the second resolution become binding. Accordingly, the date of the beginning of the fiscal year was pushed back from July 1 to Oct. 1 to allow Congress time to complete the entire budget process before the fiscal year began.

Moving quickly, Congress in 1975 implemented some of the budget act mechanisms as a trial run during the new fiscal year 1976 (Oct. 1, 1975 to Oct. 1, 1976). The timetable proved difficult. Congress did not complete action on the second resolution until three months after the Sept. 15 deadline, which indicated trouble on the full set of deadlines which were to be operating in 1976.

The limited implementation of the Budget Act in 1975 did give the new system some credibility. For one thing, the positions of the House and Senate budget committees on the child nutrition and education appropriations bills did help both chambers override vetoes by President Ford in 1975. In the education measure, the spending ceiling was well below the first resolution target, but higher than the amount Ford had requested. The Budget Committees prevailed when they argued that, if the veto were allowed to stand, the priorities set by Congress in the first resolution would be repealed.

Other Reforms

During the first half of the 1970s other changes were instituted aimed at making the operation of the House more open, accountable and efficient. The steps included:

● **Rules Committee.** In a move to strengthen the party's leadership, the caucus gave the Speaker power to nominate Democratic members of Rules, subject to caucus ratification.

● **Proxy voting.** The practice of proxy voting in committee was banned in 1974 and partially restored in 1975 by allowing committees to decide if proxy voting could be used. If proxies were allowed, they could be used only on a specific amendment or on procedural matters, and they had to be in writing and given to a specific person. The practice of one member giving a proxy to another for use as the recipient saw fit was banned.

● **Electronic Voting.** The House in January 1973 started using an electronic system making the recording of the 435 members on roll call and teller votes and quorum calls easier and speedier. Members had 15 minutes to answer calls, and could vote at any of 48 consoles in the House chamber. As they voted, boards installed on the walls showed how they voted and provided a running breakdown of the votes cast.

● **Oversight Function.** Over the years, Congress has usually paid scant attention to the operations of agencies it has created or the administration of programs it had enacted. In 1974, the House approved a plan requiring committees with more than 20 members to set up oversight subcommittees and defining jurisdictional lines for investigations.

Televised Hearings

Although the Senate had a long tradition of permitting television and radio to cover committee hearings, the House did not amend its rules to permit the broadcast coverage of committee hearings until 1970. While the Senate left broadcast decisions to its committees, the House adopted a stringent set of standards for use by committees that did admit television cameras. Among them were requirements that broadcast coverage not distort the purposes of hearings, or cast discredit upon the House, committee or any member.

Television or radio were seldom allowed in the Ways and Means Committee and Rules Committees. The Armed Services Committee flatly prohibited broadcast coverage, a staff member said, simply "because the committee doesn't want it."

In general, House committees seemed to be moving toward more open acceptance of broadcasting. In 1974, in order to permit television coverage of the Judiciary Committee sessions on impeachment, including discussion and vote on the articles of impeachment, the House amended its rules to allow broadcasting of mark-up meetings as well as hearings. The Appropriations Committee, which in the past had permitted telecasting only of its formal budget hearings at the beginning of each year, opened its doors early in 1975 for coverage of testimony on Central Intelligence Agency activities by Defense Secretary James R. Schlesinger and CIA Director William E. Colby.

In 1975, the Joint Committee on Congressional Operations held hearings on the feasibility of live television coverage of Senate and House floor deliberations. The issue sparked lively discussion, and was continued into the 1976 session. In an interim report the committee noted the conclusion of pollster George Gallup that telecasts of the impeachment hearings were largely responsible for the improved public rating of Congress after they ended.

Campaign Finance

In 1971 Congress passed a campaign spending law tightening disclosure requirements on sources of campaign contributions and other income, strengthening reporting requirements of a candidate's expenditures and defining more strictly the roles unions and corporations could play in political campaigns.

The 1971 campaign act played a role in Watergate when the General Accounting Office (GAO), charged with administering the act, investigated press reports of a $25,000 contribution to President Nixon's re-election finance committee. The GAO uncovered key violations which it reported on Aug. 26, 1972. This discovery was a crucial link in the chain of events that opened up the whole Watergate scandal.

Congress followed up with another campaign reform act in 1974, setting political contributions and spending limits for candidates in federal elections and providing for public financing of presidential elections. The act contained no provisions for public financing of House or Senate campaigns.

Ethics

At the end of 1975, the House Committee on Standards of Official Conduct had made no formal investigation of any House member although several members had been convicted of crimes in court during the committee's nine-year existence. The committee did start one limited probe of a member in 1975, but halted it on a technicality, and was initiating an inquiry on conflict-of-interest charges against Rep. Robert L. F. Sikes (D Fla.) in April 1976.

Legislative Strategy

Although the House Democratic Caucus was credited with accomplishing significant reforms of procedures, its role as a vehicle of legislative strategy remained questionable. And in 1975 a quiet debate took place in the caucus as to its role setting party policy on legislation, an area of limited success since caucus revival.

In 1975, the caucus did instruct Democratic members of the Rules Committee to bring to the House floor two amendments relating to oil depletion, and passed a "sense of the caucus" resolution opposing more U.S. military aid to Indochina.

These actions caused a furor among some Democrats who felt the caucus was usurping the powers of the committees. The caucus was more restrained from then on until later in the year when conservatives attempted to have it order the Judiciary Committee report a constitutional amendment to prevent court-ordered school busing—exactly the sort of legislative involvement that many conservatives had complained about at the beginning of the year. But the caucus rejected the proposal even though it was done on a public, recorded vote on a volatile issue.

The anti-busing action was on the record because conservatives had persuaded the caucus to open its meetings to the public. This was one part of the effort by some Democrats, mostly conservatives, to make the caucus less active. "We don't really like sunshine for the caucus, but we've got to stop this damn caucus from legislating," said Rep. Joe D. Waggonner Jr. (La.), a leader of the conservative faction. [84]

Committee Jurisdiction

In 1974, the House defeated an ambitious plan for reorganization of its committees. The rejected plan had been drafted and unanimously approved by a bipartisan select committee headed by Rep. Richard Bolling (D Mo.). By proposing a wholesale realignment of committee jurisdictions and a limitation of one major committee per member, the Bolling Committee alienated many chairmen and other senior members whose power centers would have been diminished—a sign that veteran members still wielded considerable weight in blocking liberal reformers.

Instead of the Bolling plan, the House passed on Oct. 8, 1974, a much less drastic proposal that left committee jurisdictions largely unchanged. That plan, adopting some Bolling proposals, was drawn up by the Democratic Committee on Organization, Study and Review, chaired by Rep. Julia Butler Hansen (D Wash.).

The Hansen plan as passed did make some jurisdictional shifts, such as giving the Public Works Committee control over most transportation matters, but mainly it kept the existing committee structure. Hansen also included procedural changes. It directed the House to organize itself in December of election years for the next Congress, and gave the Speaker wider latitude in referring bills to committees.

In January 1975, the Democratic caucus voted to abolish the House Internal Security Committee, which was known before 1969 as the House Committee on Un-American Activities. The action ended 30 years of controversy during which the committee zealously pursued subversives in every segment of American society.[85]

Conflicts With the President

The end of 1976 would mark the first time in American history that one party controlled Congress while the opposition party occupied the White House for eight years in succession. The government divided between four Democratic Congresses and Republican Presidents Nixon and Ford was replete with many confrontations on legislation, and extensive use of the presidential veto. Congress often proved unable to override bills the Presidents refused to sign.

Some of the conflicts involved institutional issues, including the impoundment of funds appropriated by Congress. When in 1972, Congress denied Nixon authority he demanded to limit federal spending to $250-billion in fiscal 1973, the President responded by impounding funds. He also vetoed a $30.5-billion funding bill for labor and health, education and welfare programs for fiscal 1973, and 15 other bills, most of them on budgetary grounds, in 1972.

Nixon provided Congress with a detailed list of impoundments in 1972, the largest single item being $2.5-billion in federal aid funds for highway construction. Nixon also refused to spend $1.9-billion on defense funds and $1.5-billion for such Agriculture Department programs as food stamps, rural water and waste disposal grants and rural electrification loans. The administration argued that the

President had "an implied constitutional right" to impound funds.

Congress asserted that impoundment was used by Nixon as an instrument for thwarting the will of Congress and threatening its constitutional control of the purse strings. The lawmakers proposed various measures aimed at releasing impounded funds, and finally wrote anti-impoundment features into the Congressional Budget Act of 1974. However, the act permitted the President to withhold funds temporarily or to cancel their spending under certain conditions, provided Congress approved the non-spending within a 45-day period. On the other side of the issues, the anti-impoundment provisions coupled with other features of the budget law were seen as having the potential to erode the President's fundamental power to direct and control federal spending.[86]

President Ford's Vetoes

The Democratic Congress, counting its biggest majority in 10 years, experienced a disappointing year in 1975. During the year, President Ford vetoed 17 major bills, and four were overridden. Seven bills involved major economic and energy legislation; none of the seven was overridden.

Bills that succumbed to the presidential veto included a measure to regulate strip mining, a bill to restrict the President's authority to impose increased import fees on foreign oil, and an emergency farm bill that would have raised price supports for certain 1975 crops.[87]

Watergate and Impeachment

Only once before in American history did the House set in motion the machinery of impeachment of a President of the United States. The impeachment power, the most crucial congressional check upon presidential abuse of power, had been used against President Andrew Johnson more than a century earlier.

When President Nixon fired Special Prosecutor Archibald Cox over access to the Watergate tapes in October 1973, several House members introduced impeachment resolutions. In November, the House voted $1-million for an investigation, and its Judiciary Committee, chaired by Rep. Peter W. Rodino Jr. (D N.J.) began assembling an investigative staff that numbered 100 persons, including 45 attorneys. On Feb. 6, 1974, the House, on a 410-4 vote, formally charged the Judiciary Committee with determining whether there were grounds to impeach Nixon, and granting the committee special subpoena power.

Throughout many weeks, the committee took testimony from witnesses and clashed with the President over access to the White House tape recordings. Nixon, who had promised to cooperate with the impeachment inquiry, in May refused to honor two Judiciary Committee subpoenas for tapes, adding he would not surrender any more Watergate evidence to the committee. That prompted Rodino to say the President's defiance could ultimately be considered grounds for impeachment.

At the end of July, before a national television audience, the Judiciary Committee voted three articles of impeachment against Nixon—obstruction of justice, abuse of presidential powers and contempt of Congress. In the case of the first article, Rodino noted it would be reported to the House, stating on television that "Richard M. Nixon has prevented, obstructed, and impeded the administration of justice...has acted in a manner contrary to his trust as President and subversive of constitutional government, to the great prejudice of the cause of law and justice, and to the manifest injury of the people of the United States...[and] warrants impeachment and trial and removal from office."

On Aug. 2, 1974, under Supreme Court order, Nixon surrendered to U.S. District Court Judge John J. Sirica three recorded conversations of June 23, 1972, six days after the burglary of Democratic National Headquarters in Watergate. On Aug. 5, Nixon released transcripts of those conversations to the press. The transcripts showed Nixon's participation in the Watergate coverup and approval of CIA involvement as a means of obstructing the FBI investigation of the Watergate break-in. What support Nixon had left in Congress evaporated; he resigned Aug. 9, 1974, nine days before the House was to begin debate on impeachment.[88]

PART III

History of the Senate

Chapter 17

Formative Years: 1789-1809

To English Prime Minister William Gladstone it was "the most remarkable of all the inventions of modern politics."[1] To Viscount James Bryce, a British ambassador to the United States, it was the "masterpiece of the constitution makers." Prominent British political analyst Walter Bagehot disagreed. "It may be necessary to have the blemish, but it is a blemish just as much," he wrote.[2] Whether effusively praised or vigorously condemned, the United States Senate clearly ranks as the most powerful upper legislative chamber in the world. *(Footnotes, p. 304)*

It is not, however, precisely what its creators had in mind. Edmund Randolph said its purpose was to provide a cure for the "turbulence and follies of democracy,"[3] and James Madison asserted that "the use of the Senate is to consist in its proceeding with more coolness, with more system, and with more wisdom, than the popular branch."[4] In the Constitutional Convention, Madison maintained that the purpose of the Senate was first "to protect the people against their rulers; secondly to protect the people against the transient impressions into which they themselves might be led.... They themselves, as well as a numerous body of Representatives, were liable to err also, from fickleness and passion. A necessary fence against this danger would be to select a portion of enlightened citizens, whose limited number, and firmness might seasonably interpose against impetuous councils...."[5] Gouverneur Morris hoped simply "that the Senate will show us the might of aristocracy."[6] Opponents feared it might become an American House of Lords.

Compromise of 1787

Under the Great Compromise of 1787, the House of Representatives was to represent the "national principle," while the Senate was to be an expression of the "federal principle." Not only would each state have two votes in the Senate, but the election of senators by the state legislatures was thought to be a means of making the states a constituent part of the national establishment. However, although the basis of representation assured each state an equal voice, senators voted as individuals, they were paid by the federal government rather than the states, and the legislatures that elected them had no power to recall them. Thus it is not surprising that most senators refused to consider themselves merely the agents of the state governments. Efforts by state legislatures to instruct their senators had only mixed success, but the practice did not die out entirely until 1913, when the adoption of the Seventeenth Amendment took the election of senators out of legislative hands.

The framers of the Constitution left unsettled many questions concerning the relationships among the branches of government, and it remained for the Senate—born of compromise and fashioned after no serviceable model—to seek its own place in the governmental structure. In the unending competition for a meaningful share of power, the Senate for nearly two centuries has been trying to define its role, and the history of the Senate is in large part the story of this quest.

Early Conceptions of Senate Role

It had been confidently predicted that the popularly elected House of Representatives would be the predominant chamber in the national legislature, with the Senate acting chiefly as a revisory body. At first the House did overshadow the Senate, both in power and prestige, but within a few decades the Senate—endowed with executive functions which the House did not share and blessed with a smaller and more stable membership—had achieved primacy over the lower chamber. Later the balance of power shifted from time to time, but the Senate never followed the British House of Lords into decline.

As the nation's population expanded, the size of the House mushroomed, while the Senate, in which the large and small states were equally represented, remained a comparatively small body. Growth compelled the House to impose stringent limitations on floor debate, to rely heavily on its committee system and to develop elaborate techniques to channel the flow of business—all steps that diminished the power of individual representatives. Such restrictions were not considered necessary in the Senate, where in any case members tended to view themselves as ambassadors of sovereign states, and the right of unlimited debate became the most cherished tradition of the upper chamber. To the House, action was the primary object; in the Senate, deliberation was paramount.

It had also been expected that the Senate would serve as an advisory council to the President, but natural friction between the two, aggravated by the rise of the party system, made such a relationship impracticable. As time passed, the Senate was far more likely to try to manage the President than to advise him. In the 19th century the Senate was often the dominant force in the government, but the rapid expansion of presidential power in the 20th century was accompanied by a corresponding decline in the power of the legislative branch, and the Senate increasingly felt that its existence as a viable legislative institution was threatened.

Insulation From Popular Pressure

The framers had expressed their distrust of democracy by providing for election of senators by the state legislatures rather than directly by the people. In "refining the popular appointment by successive filtrations," they hoped to assure excellence, guard against "mutability" and incidentally protect the interests of the propertied classes.[7] Under this system, which Madison in *The Federalist* described as "probably the most congenial with public opinion," the Senate enjoyed its periods of greatest prestige.[8] But as suffrage expanded and the democratization of government increased, pressure arose for direct election of senators. At length, the Senate was forced to participate in its own reform, and in 1912 Congress approved a proposed constitutional amendment providing for direct election. The Seventeenth Amendment, ratified in 1913, curtailed the abuses that so frequently had been associated with legislative election, but its other effects were difficult to measure. At any rate, no revolutionary change in the overall character of the institution could be discerned.

So successful were the framers in insulating the Senate from popular pressure that the body often seemed to care more for what Bryce called its "collective self-esteem" than it did for public opinion.[9] Sometimes it could be forced to act—as in the case of the Seventeenth Amendment and the adoption of the cloture rule in 1917—but its resistance to impetuous action was for the most part all its creators could have wished.

Only eight senators had reached New York City by March 4, 1789, the date fixed for the first meeting of Congress, and a quorum of the 22-member Senate—two of the 13 states had not yet ratified the Constitution—did not appear until April 6, five days after the House had organized. Crucial questions concerning the nature of the Senate and its proper role in the new government remained to be worked out.

Was the upper chamber to be principally a council to revise and review House measures, or a fully coequal legislative body? Should it also serve in a quasi-executive capacity as an advisory council to the President, particularly with respect to appointments and treaties? Was the Senate primarily the bastion of state sovereignty, the defender of propertied interests, a necessary check on the popularly elected House, or was it, as its opponents charged, a threat to republican principles and an incipient American House of Lords? Even the method of electing senators was in dispute: Were they to be chosen by joint or concurrent vote of bicameral state legislatures? This issue, which was not resolved until 1866, cost New York its Senate representation during most of the first session of Congress. The terms of individual senators were also in doubt. Under the Constitution, the first senators were to be divided into three classes—with terms of two, four and six years respectively—so that one-third of the Senate might be chosen every second year. To avoid charges of favoritism, the Senate resorted to choice by lot in making the division.

The first Senate, preoccupied with questions of form and precedence, was quick to claim for itself superiority over the House, but the lower chamber initially was the more important legislative body. James Madison stated in a letter to Virginia Governor Edmund Randolph that he would prefer serving in the House to the Senate. He wrote: "...I prefer the House of Representatives, chiefly because, if I can render any service there, it can only be to the public, and, not even in imputation, to myself."[10] (Madison was subsequently elected to the House of Representatives in the First Congress after being defeated for a Senate seat.)

In the earliest days of the first session, while the House was addressing itself to the financial problems of the infant nation, the Senate devoted three weeks to the consuming problem of an appropriate title of dignity for the President. The debate apparently was instigated by Vice President John Adams, whose penchant for ceremony earned him the mocking title of "His Rotundity."

The Senate's early insistence on form and its claim to deference from the House led to disputes over such matters as the method of transmitting communications between the two chambers, wording of the enacting clause in proposed legislation and proposals (briefly accepted) for differential pay for senators. With a mixture of resentment and amusement, the House rebuffed most Senate efforts to enhance its own prestige, the Senate soon abandoned its aristocratic claims, and relations between the two chambers became generally cordial.

Although the Senate initiated bills from the very beginning, in the earliest years most laws originated in the House (78 per cent from 1789 to 1809) with the Senate acting as a revisory body. During the first session of the First Congress only five bills were introduced in the Senate, of which four—including the important Judiciary Act, which established the framework of the judicial system—were passed. During the same period, the House originated and passed 26 bills; two of these were rejected by the Senate, one was lost in conference, and the Senate modified at least 20 of the remaining 23.[11]

Relations With the President

The concept of the Senate as an advisory council to the President never was realized. President Washington took informal advice, not from the Senate as a body, but from Alexander Hamilton, Madison (a House member) and others. The constitutional role of the Senate in the appointment process also fell short of the consultative role that some framers of the Constitution had envisioned. Washington's exercise of the appointment power carefully stressed the separate natures of the nomination and confirmation processes, a point underscored by his decision to submit nominations to the Senate in writing rather than in person. The Senate's role as an advisory council was further restricted in 1789, when the Senate narrowly accepted House-passed language vesting in the President alone the power to remove executive officers. Under Washington's successors, members of Congress had greater influence over appointments, but the principle of executive initiative remained firmly established.

In 1789 Washington attempted to put into practice his early view that "in all matters respecting treaties, oral communications [with the Senate] seem indispensably necessary."[12] On Aug. 22 and 24, he appeared in the Senate chamber to consult with the Senate concerning a treaty with southern Indians. His presence during Senate proceedings, however, created a "tense" atmosphere which was uncomfortable for the senators and the President.[13] It was an experience Washington did not wish to repeat. The result was that Senate participation in the early stages of treaty-making declined. This development made possible greater freedom of action when the time came to vote on ratification of treaties.

Indeed, in 1795 when the treaty with Great Britain negotiated in 1794 by Chief Justice John Jay was brought before the Senate for ratification, a bitter dispute occurred. The controversial treaty secured American frontier posts in the Northwest but permitted Britain to search American merchant ships and confiscate provisions destined for Britain's enemy, France. Ultimately, the treaty was ratified by a bare two-thirds majority June 24, 1795, but not before the Senate deleted a clause limiting U.S. trading rights in the British West Indies.

Relations With the States

The concept of senators as agents of state sovereignty led to repeated but largely unsuccessful efforts to make senators accountable to their state legislatures. Some members of Congress, representatives as well as senators, felt an obligation to make periodic reports on their activities to the state governments, and a continuing controversy raged over the right of state legislatures to instruct their senators. Instruction was more general in the South than in the North, but there was no unanimity of opinion on the question. However, with the emergence of political parties, party loyalty gradually took the place of the expected state allegiance.

Early Senate Procedure

Courtesy, dignity and informality marked the proceedings of the early Senate. A body that on a chill morning might leave its seats to gather around the fireplace had no need for an elaborate system of regulation. At the first session in 1789 the Senate adopted only 20 short rules, a number deemed sufficient to control the proceedings of a Senate no larger than some modern-day congressional committees. In 1806, the number of rules rose to 40; most of the new ones dealt with nominations and treaties.[14]

The rules left a wide area of decision to the Senate president, particularly Rule 16 which gave him sole authority to decide points of order. Vice President Adams presided over the Senate (1789-97) with no specific guides on procedure, but his successor, Thomas Jefferson (1797-1801), felt the need of referring "to some known system of rules, that he may neither leave himself free to indulge caprice or passion nor open to the imputation of them."[15] The result was Jefferson's *Manual of Parliamentary Procedure*, which was also adopted by the House in 1837.

Closed Sessions

Following the practice of the Congress of the Confederation, the Senate originally met behind closed doors. Total secrecy was not maintained, however, since senators often freely discussed their activities outside the chamber, and the Senate *Journal* and sketchy reports of Senate action appeared in print from time to time. The principal result of the closed-door policy was to focus public attention on the widely reported debates of the House and to encourage suspicion of the aristocratic Senate. Beginning in 1790, various state legislatures determined to press for open

179

sessions of the Senate, in part as a means of enforcing accountability from their senators.

After four defeats in four years, the Senate in 1794 finally voted to open its sessions "after the end of the present session of Congress, and, so soon as suitable galleries shall be provided for the Senate chamber."[16] Almost two years went by before the galleries were erected and the rule put into effect, but at the beginning of the first session of the Fourth Congress, in December 1795, the Senate's doors were finally opened to the public. The immediate effects of this action were not great, since the Senate sessions were too decorous to attract widespread attention, and the more spirited House remained the center of public interest. Furthermore, there were no official reporters of debates, and no accommodation for newspaper reporters was made in the Senate until 1802, after the government had moved to Washington.

Light Workload

The demands upon early senators do not appear to have been unduly burdensome. Ordinarily the Senate met at 11 a.m., except near the end of the session when the press of business was great, and 3 p.m. adjournments were common. Sen. William Maclay of Pennsylvania, whose *Journal* provides a prejudiced but invaluable record of the Senate in the First Congress, frequently noted that the Senate adjourned its own tedious debates so that members could go and listen to the livelier ones in the House. Absenteeism, a continuing problem, was only in part attributable to the difficulties of travel at this period. Accordingly, in 1798 the Senate finally added enforcement machinery to its rule prohibiting absence without leave.

Because most legislation originated in the House, the Senate had little to do early in the session; under the so-called *de novo* rule of 1790, all bills died at the end of each session of Congress, so the Senate did not have House-passed bills from a previous session on which to work. The House scornfully rejected Senate proposals that the two chambers jointly prepare a legislative program for an entire session; however, joint committees often were appointed near the end of sessions to determine what business had to be completed before adjournment. Much of the legislative output of each session was pushed through in the closing days. In the second session of the Sixth Congress, for example, the Senate passed 35 bills, one-third of them on the final day.

Presidential messages provided a partial agenda for each session. Washington and Adams delivered their messages in person annually, and each chamber prepared a reply which was delivered orally with great ceremony. Since these replies were carefully debated and amended, they provided a valuable opportunity for consideration of the overall legislative situation. Jefferson abandoned his predecessors' practice and delivered his messages in writing; such messages were not thought to require a reply.

Rules on Debate

Dilatory tactics occasionally appeared in the early Senate, but apparently they did not present a serious problem. Only three of the 1789 rules had any direct bearing on limitation of debate: Rule 4, providing that no member should speak more than twice in any one debate on the same day without permission of the Senate; Rule 6, providing that no motion should be debated until seconded; and Rule 16, providing that every question of order should be decided by the president without debate. The previous question, authorized under Rule 9, was not then used to close debate but rather to remove a question from further consideration by reverting to a previous one. The previous question was dropped when the rules were revised in 1806. At the same time, a motion to adjourn was made undebatable.

Although bills could be introduced by individual members with the permission of the majority after one day's notice, the more common practice was to move the appointment of a committee to report a bill. Thus only a limited number of bills were introduced and most of those introduced were passed.

Committee System

Standing committees as they are known today did not exist in the early Senate. Legislation was handled by ad hoc committees, which were appointed to consider a particular issue and disbanded once their work was finished, with the full Senate maintaining firm control over their activities. Membership was flexible, although the same senators were frequently assigned to committees dealing with a particular field of legislation. Following British precedent, opponents of a measure were excluded from the committee that considered it, and the Federalist majority frequently excluded Republicans from committees that were to consider bills involving party issues.

Membership and Turnover

In terms of previous experience, members of the early Senate were well qualified to serve in the national legislature. Of the 94 men in the Senate between 1789 and 1801, 18 had served in the Constitutional Convention, 42 in the Continental Congress or the Congress of the Confederation, and 84 in their state or provincial legislatures. Only one or two were without experience in some governmental capacity. A majority were men of wealth and social prominence, but they were a young "council of elders"—the average age in 1799 was only 45 years.[17]

Experience did not bear out the warnings of those who feared that senators would entrench themselves in office for life. Of the 94 senators who served between 1789 and 1801, 33 resigned within that period before completing their terms, and only six did so in order to take other federal posts. Frequent resignations continued for many years—35 in the period 1801-13—and the rate of re-election also was low.[18]

Emergence of Parties

Political parties had no place in the constitutional framework, and early Senate voting indicated chiefly sectional or economic divisions within the chamber. But upon the presentation of Alexander Hamilton's financial measures, the Senate—like the House—began to exhibit a spirit of partisanship. Supporters of a strong central government, chiefly representatives of mercantile and financial interests, banded together as Federalists under the leadership of Hamilton, while exponents of agrarian democracy, led by Madison and Jefferson, became known as Republicans. Party alignments, still quite fluid in 1791, gradually hardened in the next two years as they were inflamed by the excesses of the French Revolution and troubled relations with Great Britain. By 1794 Sen. John Taylor of Virginia wrote:

"The existence of two parties in Congress is apparent. The fact is disclosed almost upon every important question.

Whether the subject be foreign or domestic—relative to war or peace—navigation or commerce—the magnetism of opposite views draws them wide as the poles asunder."[19]

The Federalists held the Senate until 1801, but in 1794 the Republicans came close to overturning that control. The Federalists succeeded in unseating Albert Gallatin on the charge that he had not been a citizen of the United States for the number of years required to be a senator. He was deprived of his seat on a 14-12 party-line vote, but on six other occasions during the session they needed the vote of Vice President Adams to carry their program.

Approval of the Jay Treaty in 1795 united the Federalists and firmly identified the Senate in the public mind as the focus of the Federalist Party. From that time on, both Federalists and Republicans voted with a high degree of party regularity. During the Fourth, Fifth and Sixth Congresses, the Federalists enjoyed a roughly 2-1 edge over the Republicans in the Senate, while the House was closely divided between the two parties. But the rapprochement with France, engineered by President Adams, deprived the Federalists of their principal issue, and this development, combined with invasion of the chamber by members from newly admitted southern and western states, broke the power of the Federalists in the Senate. In the elections of 1800, Jefferson's Republicans won the presidency and both houses of Congress. When the Seventh Congress convened in December 1801, the Republicans held a narrow Senate majority. Federalist strength in the Senate continued to decline throughout Jefferson's term of office.

Leadership in the Senate

The Constitution solved the problem of a job for the Vice President by making him president of the Senate and it directed the Senate to choose a president pro tempore to act for him in his absence. But there were good reasons why neither of these officers could supply effective legislative leadership.

The Vice President was not chosen by the Senate but imposed upon it from outside, and there was no necessity for him to be sympathetic to its aims. Precedent was set by John Adams who, although clearly in general agreement with the majority of the Senate during his term as Vice President, perceived his role as simply that of presiding officer and made little effort to guide Senate action. His successor, Republican leader Thomas Jefferson, could not have steered the Federalist-controlled Senate even if he had wished to do so, although he did maintain a watching brief for the Republican Party in the upper chamber.

The president pro tempore was elected by the Senate from among its own members, but he could not supply legislative leadership because his term was too random and temporary. By custom a president pro tempore was elected only for the current absence of the Vice President, and his term ended with the reappearance of the Vice President. From the First through the Sixth Congresses (1789-1801), 15 senators served as president pro tempore.[20]

Thus the mantle of legislative leadership soon fell upon individual senators—Oliver Ellsworth, Rufus King and others—and more importantly upon the executive branch. Presidents Washington and Adams shared a strong belief in the separation of powers. Neither was willing to take upon himself the role of legislative leader, but Alexander Hamilton had no such qualms. As Secretary of the Treasury until 1795—and even after his retirement to private life—Hamilton not only developed a broad legislative program but functioned, in the words of one historian, "as a sort of absentee floor leader," in almost daily contact with his friends in the Senate.[21]

Under Jefferson and his Secretary of the Treasury, Albert Gallatin, legislative leadership continued to emanate from the executive branch. Jefferson, wrote Sen. Timothy Pickering of Massachusetts, tried "to screen himself from all responsibility by calling upon Congress for advice and direction.... Yet with affected modesty and deference he secretly dictates every measure which is seriously proposed."[22]

By the end of Jefferson's administration, the Senate had established internal procedures and sampled its various functions. It had both initiated and revised proposed legislation, given its advice and consent to treaties and nominations, conducted its first investigations and held two impeachment trials—the first resulting in the removal from office of a federal judge and the second in the acquittal of Supreme Court Justice Samuel Chase. But the breadth of its powers was not yet clear; relations with the House, the executive branch and the state governments were still only tentatively charted and awaited further tests.

Chapter 18

Emerging Senate: 1809-1829

Two decades of legislative supremacy began with the administration of Jefferson's successor, James Madison, for the "Father of the Constitution" proved himself incapable of presidential leadership. He soon lost control of his party to the young "war hawks" of the House, who succeeded in forcing him into the War of 1812, and thereafter he suffered repeated defeats at the hands of Congress.

James Monroe was no more fortunate in his relations with Congress than Madison had been. At the time of his second inauguration Henry Clay commented that "Mr. Monroe has just been re-elected with apparent unanimity, but he had not the slightest influence on Congress."[23]

Neither Madison nor Monroe was temperamentally fit for legislative leadership, and both were further handicapped by their obligation to the congressional caucus that had nominated them for the presidency. The situation of John Quincy Adams was even more difficult, since he owed his very election to the House of Representatives.

Rising Senate Influence

Under the speakership of Henry Clay, the House took a commanding role in government, but the influence of the Senate was on the rise. The trend toward Senate dictation of executive appointments, which had begun late in Jefferson's term of office, continued and increased under

Madison. When he sought to make Gallatin Secretary of State, the Senate blocked his choice and forced him to accept a secretary of its own choosing.

The importance of the Senate's treaty and appointment powers, in which the House had no share, was only one factor in the Senate's rise. The rapidly expanding size of the House soon suggested the advantages of serving in a smaller body; in 1820, there were still only 46 senators.[24] The Senate's longer term and more stable membership also made it seem a more desirable place in which to serve. Henry Clay moved from the Senate to the House in 1811, but by 1823 Martin Van Buren was able to claim that the Senate, more than any other branch, controlled all the efficient power of government. Clay returned to the Senate in 1831.

The Senate's legislative importance increased only gradually. In the early years, most proposed legislation originated in the House, and the great debates surrounding the War of 1812 occurred there. But the Senate took a leading role in the struggle over the Missouri Compromise of 1820 and succeeded in imposing upon the House an amendment barring slavery in any future state north of 36°30' north latitude. Since this was the part of the country in which the population was expanding most rapidly, proponents of slavery could no longer hope to uphold the cause of states' rights in the House. The Senate—where the two sides were more evenly matched—inevitably became the forum for the great anti-slavery debates of the following decades.

Change of Party Alignments

Party alignments changed during the 1809-29 period. The withering Federalist Party ceased to be a factor in national politics after the election of 1816, but Republican supremacy was marred by increasing factionalism. Suffrage expanded, and the newly enfranchised small farmers of the South and West had little in common with the landed aristocracy that was the backbone of the Republican Party. Thus the democratic masses turned from slave-holding planters to the leadership of Andrew Jackson of Tennessee, an exponent of their fiercely egalitarian philosophy. In 1825 when the House of Representatives made Adams President, although Jackson had led in popular voting, the Republican

Party split and a new Democratic Party was organized by Jackson's lieutenants. In 1826, the Democrats won control of both houses of Congress, and in 1828 they placed Jackson in the presidency of which they thought he had been defrauded four years earlier.

Growth of Standing Committees

The Senate lagged behind the House in establishing a formal committee structure. In its first quarter century it created only four standing committees, all chiefly administrative in nature: the Joint Standing Committee on Enrolled Bills, the Senate Committee on Engrossed Bills, the Joint Standing Committee for the Library, and the Senate Committee to Audit and Control the Contingent Expenses of the Senate.

During this period most of the legislative committee work fell to ad hoc select committees, usually of three members, appointed as the occasion demanded.[25] But eventually the need to appoint so many committees (between 90 and 100 in the session of 1815-16) exhausted the patience of the Senate, and in 1816 it added 11 standing committees to the existing four: Foreign Relations, Finance, Commerce and Manufactures, Military Affairs, the Militia, Naval Affairs, Public Lands, Claims, the Judiciary, the Post Office and Post Roads, and Pensions. Most of the new committees were parallel in function to previously created committees of the House. The usual membership was five; this number would rise to seven by mid-century and to nine by 1900.[26]

Senate committees were chosen by ballot until 1823, but in that year the Senate adopted an amendment to its rules giving the presiding officer authority to name committees, unless otherwise ordered by the Senate. At first this power was exercised by the president pro tempore, an officer of the Senate's own choosing, but early in the 19th Congress (1825-27) Vice President John C. Calhoun assumed the appointment power and used it to place Jackson supporters in key committee posts. In the face of this patent effort to embarrass the Adams administration, the Senate quickly returned to the rule of choice by ballot. In 1828 the rule was changed again, this time to give appointment power to the president pro tempore, but in 1833 the Senate once more reverted to choice by ballot.

A general revision of the Senate rules in 1820, bringing the total number of rules to 45, was remarkable chiefly for incorporating the provisions relating to standing committees that the Senate had adopted four years earlier. No great spirit of reform was involved; as in the case of other general revisions of Senate rules, the 1820 revision represented chiefly an attempt to codify changes that had accumulated over a number of years.

'A Senate of Equals'

Daniel Webster was to describe the upper chamber in 1830 as a "Senate of equals, of men of individual honor and personal character, and of absolute independence," who knew no master and acknowledged no dictation.[27] In such a body it is not surprising that no single leader had emerged to parallel the rise of Henry Clay in the House.

Statesmen of prominence served in the Senate during the 1809-29 period. The roster included four future Presidents—Andrew Jackson, Martin Van Buren, William Henry Harrison and John Tyler—and a number of presidential hopefuls. By the close of the period, the great figures of the ensuing "Golden Age" were beginning to gather in the chamber: Thomas Hart Benton of Missouri arrived in 1821, Robert Y. Hayne of South Carolina in 1823 and Daniel Webster of Massachusetts in 1827. Henry Clay of Kentucky, after serving briefly in the Senate in 1810-11, went to the House; he was to return to the Senate in 1831. Calhoun would resign as Vice President in 1832 to succeed Hayne as senator from South Carolina.

Until Calhoun took office in 1825, the Vice Presidents of the period did not play significant roles. Madison's first Vice President, George Clinton, was old and feeble and died in office, as did his successor, Elbridge Gerry. Monroe's Vice President, Daniel D. Tompkins, hardly ever entered the Senate chamber.

Vice President Calhoun, hostile to the Adams administration and harboring presidential ambitions of his own, had no desire to alienate the Senate by exercising undue authority, but he was a commanding figure and his influence was felt. Hayne generally served as his spokesman on the floor.

Calhoun took advantage of his position to make obviously biased committee appointments, but in other respects he assumed as little authority as possible. Although all of his predecessors in the chair had assumed direct authority to call senators to order for words used in debate, Calhoun contended that his power was appellate only and refused to act unless an offending senator was first called to order by another senator. He would not "for ten thousand worlds look like a usurper," Calhoun declared.[28] His refusal to act on his own initiative led the Senate in 1828 to amend its rules; henceforth the chair would have the power to call a senator to order, but for the first time in Senate history the rule permitted an appeal from the chair's decision on a question of order.

During the 1809-29 period, greater continuity of service developed in the office of president pro tempore. John Gaillard occupied the post for most of the period between 1814 and 1825 and presided over the Senate almost continuously during the five years when Tompkins was Vice President. Elected by the Senate and thus considering himself entitled to its support, Gaillard enforced the rules rigidly but did not exercise a true leadership role.

Chapter 19

The Golden Age: 1829-1861

In the years leading up to the Civil War, the Senate became the chief forum for the discussion of national policy. The preeminent national issue in the period between the Missouri Compromise of 1820 and the outbreak of war in 1861 was the struggle between North and South over slavery. The Senate, where the two sides were equally matched due to the system of representation, inevitably became the principal battleground.

Sectional interests were more important than party during these years preceding the Civil War, and party divisions were often blurred. The Jacksonian Democrats adopted the agrarian and states' rights philosophy of the Jeffersonian Republicans, but their concept of strong executive leadership was at odds with Jeffersonian views. Meanwhile, the Whig Party was formed of the coalition of eastern financial and business interests that had once constituted the strength of the Federalists, but the Whigs were committed to a doctrine of legislative supremacy that was alien to Federalist thought.

The Democratic Party split over the question of slavery, and many southern Democrats allied themselves with the Whigs, in the hope of finding protection for states' rights and the institution of slavery under the Whig banner of legislative supremacy. However, the Whig Party had no answer to the slavery question, and in the 1850s it gave way to the new Republican Party, an alliance of northern interests dedicated to preventing the spread of slavery into the territories. Mounting southern defiance of northern opinion led to a North-South split in the Democratic Party, and secession and war soon followed.

In this age of giants three men dominated the Senate chamber. All were former representatives, and all suffered from presidential aspirations that were to influence the shifting coalitions of a turbulent era. Daniel Webster of Massachusetts—Whig, spokesman for eastern moneyed interests, sectionalist turned nationalist, supreme orator—entered the Senate in 1827 and remained there for most of the period until 1850. Henry Clay of Kentucky—Whig, westerner, brilliant tactician and compromiser—returned to the Senate to serve between 1831 and 1842 and again in 1849-52. John C. Calhoun of South Carolina—outstanding logician, devoted son of the South and champion of the right of secession—stepped down from the vice presidency in 1832 to defend his nullification doctrine on the Senate floor and remained a senator for most of the period until his death in 1850. (Nullification was the refusal of a state to recognize or enforce a federal law it regarded as an infringement on its rights.)

French historian and politician Alexis de Tocqueville in 1834 contrasted the "vulgarity" of the House with the nobility of the Senate, where "scarcely an individual is to be found...who does not recall the idea of an active and illustrious career." The Senate, "is composed of eloquent advocates, distinguished generals, wise magistrates, and statesmen of note, whose language would, at all times, do honor to the most remarkable parliamentary debates of Europe."[29]

Senate's Preeminence Over House

De Tocqueville could think of only one explanation for the Senate's superiority: its members were elected by elected bodies, whereas representatives were elected by the people directly. Thomas Hart Benton disputed this analysis. Not only did the Senate enjoy advantages of smaller membership, longer term and greater age and experience on the part of its members, he said, but it was composed of "the pick of the House of Representatives, and thereby gains doubly—by brilliant accession to itself and abstraction from the other."[30]

Undoubtedly the Senate's greater stability of membership contributed to its preeminence over the House, where the Jacksonian concept of rotation in office led to great turnover. More significant, perhaps, was the introduction of the spoils system and the Senate's increasing domination of the appointment process. Finally, growth had strengthened the Senate by turning it from a small intimate body into one large enough for oratory and the exercise of brilliant parliamentary skills. With the addition of two senators from every new state, the Senate increased from 48 members at the beginning of Jackson's administration to 66 in Buchanan's. Its roster included such luminaries as Benton of Missouri, Lewis Cass of Michigan, Sam Houston of Texas, Jefferson Davis and Henry S. Foote of Mississippi, William H. Seward of New York, Stephen A. Douglas of Illinois and Charles Sumner of Massachusetts.

Quarrel With President Jackson

The eclipse of presidential power that had begun under Madison came to an end when Andrew Jackson became President in 1829. Backed by strong popular majorities and skilled in the use of patronage, Jackson was able to dominate the House, but in the Senate he met vigorous opposition from the new Whig Party, a combination of commercial and industrial interests dedicated to the principle of legislative supremacy. The Whigs were quick to challenge Jackson on questions of policy and executive prerogative, and his term was marked by repeated and acrimonious contests with the Senate over legislation and appointments.

These disputes reached a peak in 1834 when the Senate, outraged by Jackson's removal of deposits from the Bank of the United States and his refusal to hand over communications to his Cabinet relating to that subject, adopted a resolution censuring the President for his actions. The resolution, pushed through by Clay, charged "that the President, in the late executive proceedings in relation to the public revenue, has assumed upon himself authority and power not conferred by the Constitution and laws and in derogation of both."[31]

Jackson countered with a message, which the Senate refused to receive, declaring that so serious a charge as that contained in the censure resolution called for impeachment. Because impeachment could originate only in the House, he protested the Senate's action as a violation of the Constitution.

Benton, Jackson's leader in the Senate, promptly undertook a campaign to vindicate Jackson by expunging the censure resolution from the Senate *Journal.* Under pressure from the President, some state legislatures instructed their senators to support Benton's efforts, while others forced anti-Jackson senators into retirement. By the time Jackson's second term was drawing to a close in 1837, the Jacksonian Democrats had gained control of the Senate, and the expunging resolution finally was adopted by a 24-19 vote.

In one of the most dramatic scenes of Senate history the terms of the resolution were carried out: "[T]he Secretary of the Senate...shall bring the manuscript journal of the session of 1833-34 into the Senate, and, in the presence of the Senate, draw black lines round the said resolve, and write across the face thereof, in strong letters, the following words: 'Expunged by order of the Senate, the 16th day of January, in the year of our Lord 1837.' "³²

Whigs vs. President Tyler

Undeterred by their failure to dominate Jackson, the Whigs persisted in their efforts to establish the doctrine of legislative supremacy. With the election of Whig President William Henry Harrison, they thought their moment had come. Daniel Webster was named Secretary of State, Clay supporters were put in other Cabinet positions, and Harrison's inaugural address—revised by Webster—was a model statement of Whig doctrine. But Harrison died after only one month in office, to be succeeded by John Tyler, a states' rights Virginian who had been elected Vice President on the Whig ticket.

At first Clay, as the leading Whig member of Congress, thought he could assume effective leadership of the government, and he even introduced a set of resolutions that were designed to be the party's legislative program. But Tyler, it turned out, was determined to be President in fact as well as title, and the two men soon clashed head-on. Tyler's exercise of the veto power drove the Whigs to threats of impeachment and abortive efforts to force his resignation, but Clay was unable to push through his own legislative program. Although all Presidents had trouble with appointments during this period, Tyler, who lacked support in either party, was more unfortunate than most. Many of his nominations, including four to the Cabinet, were rejected by the Senate.

After Tyler's presidency the Whigs were never again able to muster a majority in the Senate that would permit them to put their doctrine of legislative supremacy to a test. Difficulties with nominations continued, for this was the height of the spoils system, but a succession of strong Presidents established a pattern of executive leadership that even the weakness of Pierce and Buchanan could not entirely destroy.

Great Debates Over Slavery

Oratory in the Senate reached its peak in the years leading up to the Civil War, and visitors often thronged the galleries to hear the great debates over slavery. Never had the Senate seemed so splendid as in this period when it served as the forum for the nation.

But the courtesy and decorum of the early Senate gradually began to crumble under the mounting pressures of the time. Although debates were for the most part still close and brief, passions sometimes ran high and legislative obstruction became increasingly common. Filibusters were now often threatened and occasionally undertaken, but they were not yet fully exploited as a means of paralyzing the Senate, and senators seldom admitted that they were employing dilatory tactics.

The first notable Senate filibuster occurred in 1841, when dissident senators held the floor for 10 days in opposition to a bill to remove the Senate printers. Later in the same year a Whig move to re-establish the Bank of the United States was subject to an unsuccessful two-week filibuster. Henry Clay said the tactics of the minority would "lead to the inference that embarrassment and delay were the objects aimed at," and he threatened to introduce a rule to limit debate. Unabashed, the filibusterers invited Clay to "make his arrangements at his boarding house for the winter" and warned that they would resort to "any possible extremity" to prevent restriction of debate. Unable to obtain majority support for his "gag rule," Clay never carried out his threat, and the bank bill eventually passed, only to be vetoed by President Tyler.[33]

In 1846 a bill providing for U.S.-British joint occupancy of Oregon was filibustered for two months. The measure was finally brought to a vote through use, apparently for the first time, of the unanimous consent agreement—a device still employed to speed action in the Senate. Later in 1846 the Wilmot Proviso was talked to death in the closing hours of the session. The proviso, which the House had attached as a rider to an appropriation bill in the early months of the Mexican War, stipulated that slavery be excluded from any territory that might be acquired from Mexico.

Slavery was again the issue in the extended debates over the Compromise of 1850, Clay's valiant attempt to resolve the sectional controversies that were tearing the nation apart. In a crowded chamber, the great triumvirate—Webster, Clay and Calhoun—made their last joint appearance in the Senate. The dying Calhoun dragged himself into the chamber to hear his final speech read by his colleague James Murray Mason of Virginia.

Violence in the Senate. Violence threatened when Sen. Henry S. ("Hangman") Foote of Mississippi brandished a pistol at Missouri's Benton, who was well known as a deadly duelist. Only the intervention of other senators prevented bloodshed.

Greater violence marked the 1856 debate on the Kansas statehood bill. Two South Carolina representatives attacked Charles Sumner while he sat at his desk in the Senate chamber and bludgeoned him so severely that the Massachusetts senator was unable to resume his seat until 1859.

In the next few years, as the nation drifted toward war, debates continued to reflect the rancor of the period. Oratory had little place in a chamber where all members were said to carry arms, and by the time the Senate moved into its present quarters in 1859 the great epoch of Senate debate was at an end. Oratory had flourished in the intimate grandeur of the old hall; in the new chamber—vast and acoustically poor—a new style of debate emerged.

The Committee System

The most important procedural development of the 1829-61 period occurred in 1846 when the Senate transferred responsibility for making committee assignments to the party organizations in the chamber. As long as committee assignments were determined by ballot, majority party control of the committees could not be assured, and, although by 1829 the majority usually controlled the working committees, the opposition party still held important chairmanships.

When the second session of the 29th Congress met in December 1846, the Senate first rejected a proposal to let the Vice President name the committees and then, in accordance with the regular rule, began balloting for chairmen. Midway through this process the balloting rule was suspended, and the Senate proceeded to elect on one ballot a list of candidates for all of the remaining committee vacancies that had been agreed upon by the majority and minority. From that time on, the choice of committees has usually amounted to a routine acceptance by the Senate of lists agreed upon by representatives of the caucus or conference of the two major parties.

The fact that the party organizations did not become the standard instrument of committee selection until 1846 gives some indication of the limited use of party discipline in the early years of the Senate. During this period, party authority was confined to organizational questions; when it came to substantive issues, senators voted as individuals rather than as Democrats or Whigs.

Party influence in the Senate was enhanced by the new method of committee selection, but rank within committees was thereafter increasingly determined by seniority, thus making chairmanships less subject to party control. Experience had always played a major role in making committee assignments, but as long as committees were elected by ballot, rigid adherence to seniority was impossible. However, with the introduction of party lists in 1846 strict compliance with seniority began to be enforced. The bitter sectional disputes leading up to the Civil War may well have encouraged the use of seniority to avoid fierce inter-party struggles for committee control.

The system was not, of course, impartial in distributing its favors. In 1859 a northern Democrat called the seniority usage "intolerably bad" and complained that it had "operated to give to senators from slave-holding states the chairmanship of every single committee that controls the public business of this government. There is not one exception."[34]

There had been one exception earlier in the same year; Stephen A. Douglas of Illinois was chairman of the Committee on Territories. But the Democratic Caucus had removed him from the chairmanship, in spite of his seniority, because he refused to go along with President James Buchanan and the southern wing of the party on the question of slavery in the territories.

By the time of the Civil War the committee structure of the Senate had changed from a loose aggregation of ad hoc committees appointed for the occasion to a formal system of standing committees, whose members owed their appointments to the party organization and their advancement within committees to the seniority system.

Chapter 20

Party Government: 1861-1901

During the Civil War and Reconstruction periods, the Republicans controlled the presidency, the Senate and the House throughout seven consecutive Congresses, ending in 1875. Not only did the Democrats lose the southern seats in Congress, most of which were vacant from 1861 to 1869, but many northern Democrats defected to the Republicans rather than remain in a party so closely tied to the southern cause.

This period of Republican hegemony was marked by a power struggle between Congress and the White House. During the war Congress sought to assert its authority through such mechanisms as the Joint Committee on the Conduct of the War, consisting of three senators and four representatives, which exercised a wide range of authority. Yet President Lincoln managed not only to retain his independence of Congress, but also to increase the armed forces, call for volunteers, spend money on defense, issue a code of regulations for the armed forces, suspend the writ of habeas corpus, and even emancipate the slaves in the states in rebellion without waiting for authority from Congress.

When the President issued a proclamation of Reconstruction in December 1863, Congress passed the Wade-Davis bill transferring Reconstruction powers to itself. In response to the President's pocket veto of this measure, the Radical Republicans in Congress issued the

Wade-Davis Manifesto, which declared: "[T]he authority of Congress is paramount and must be respected; that the body of Union men in Congress will not submit to be impeached by him [the President] of rash and unconstitutional legislation; and if he wishes our support he must confine himself to his executive duties—to obey and execute, not to make the laws—to suppress by arms and armed rebellion, and leave political reorganization to Congress."[35]

Era of Radical Republicans

The Republican Congress achieved its aims after Lincoln was assassinated. It passed its own Reconstruction Act, overrode President Andrew Johnson's veto of a civil rights bill and set up Gen. Ulysses S. Grant as General of the Army in Washington, requiring all Army orders to be issued through him (thus bypassing the President as commander in chief) and forbidding the President to remove or transfer the general without prior consent of the Senate. Over Johnson's veto, Congress passed the Tenure of Office Act which required approval by the Senate of the removal of officials appointed with its advice and consent. When Johnson dismissed his Secretary of War to test in the courts the constitutionality of the act, the House impeached him, and the Senate came within one vote of removing him from office. Congress had broken the authority of the executive. Under a compliant President Grant, the Republican Congress governed.

In this period of one-party government, the House, led by Radical Republican Thaddeus Stevens of Pennsylvania, overshadowed the Senate. But following the failure of the effort to impeach Johnson and the death of Stevens, House prestige declined, and the Senate rapidly became the dominant arm of the national legislature. During the remainder of the 19th century, while control of the House shifted back and forth between the two parties, the Republicans managed to maintain control of the Senate in all except two Congresses, and during this period modern party government developed in the upper chamber.

Meanwhile, later Presidents were able to recoup some of the power lost under Grant. With public support, Rutherford B. Hayes refused to let the Republican Senate dictate his Cabinet and customs appointments, and Grover

Cleveland's defense of the presidential appointment power led to repeal of the Tenure of Office Act, but on the whole the Senate remained the most powerful force in the government. When William McKinley became President in 1897, Congress and the White House entered a period of almost unprecedented harmony. "We never had a President who had more influence with Congress than McKinley," said Sen. Shelby M. Cullom (R Ill.). "I have never heard of even the slightest friction between him and the party leaders in Senate and House."[36]

Power of Party Bosses in Senate

The character of the Senate underwent a marked change in the post-Civil-War era. Its membership grew from 74 in 1871 to 90 in 1901, and, as state politics became more centralized, a new breed of senator entered the chamber. The great constitutional orators of the pre-war period were succeeded by "party bosses"—professional politicans who had risen through the ranks of their state party organizations and who came to Washington only after they had consolidated their power over the state party structure. As long as they maintained state control, they were immune from external political reprisal, but their dedication to party and their acceptance of the need for discipline made them good "party senators," willing to compromise their differences in order to maintain harmony within the party. To these men the Senate was a career, and a striking increase in average length of Senate service occurred during this period.

The public viewed the Senate's changing character with grave suspicion, and the growing power of party organizations was widely attributed to the "trusts." Political analyst Moisei Ostrogorski charged in 1902 that the economic interests "equipped and kept up political organizations for their own use, and ran them as they pleased, like their trains."[37] Other observers held that political centralization and business concentration were parallel developments, not directly related, but they agreed that the corporations contributed to the power of the party chiefs.

Loss of Public Esteem

Lobbying by business groups became a vital element in government during the last part of the 19th century, but business itself was not unified and its efforts were too haphazard for it to attain great political control. Still, some of the lobbying practices of the period—ranging from wholesale distribution of railroad passes to loans and sales of stock at attractive prices to members of Congress—fostered the impression of Senate corruption.

The Senate's "usurpation" of executive power, its failure to impose limitations on debate and the undoubted existence of corruption all contributed to the chamber's loss of public esteem. By the close of the 19th century, the Senate was described in derogatory—and somewhat un-fair—fashion as a "Millionaires' Club," and it was without question the most unpopular branch of the national government. Dissatisfaction with the Senate led to the movement for direct election of senators, through which reformers hoped to curtail both the power of political parties and the political influence of the corporations. By 1900, it had become clear that a constitutional amendment providing for direct election would eventually be enacted.

Development of Party Leadership

Political parties assumed responsibility for organizational matters in the pre-Civil-War Senate, and party authority was extended during the war to substantive questions as well. However, the Senate had no strong tradi-tion of leadership and party discipline was expected to lapse after the war ended. Indeed, the Republican and Democratic Parties themselves were expected to dis-integrate, as other parties had done before them, once the issues that had brought them together were resolved.

Although the parties failed to dissolve, party influence in the upper chamber did decline for a time; when Grant's administration began in 1869, political parties compelled unity only on organizational questions. Disputes over com-mittee assignments were settled in the caucus, and pressing issues were discussed there, but caucus decisions could hardly be considered binding as long as there was no leader to enforce discipline or exact reprisals. The Republican caucus did remove Charles Sumner of Massachusetts from the chairmanship of the Foreign Relations Committee in 1871 when his differences with President Grant had become so extreme that he would communicate neither with the President nor the Secretary of State.

Conkling's Influence. The possibilities of party leadership first became apparent in the Senate career of Roscoe Conkling of New York in the 1870s. Conkling gathered around him a loyal following, and after 1873 his faction usually controlled the Committee on Committees and thus was able to reward his supporters with valuable committee posts. But the Conkling forces stood together only on organizational questions; their influence on substantive legislation was not great. When Conkling resigned his Senate seat in 1881, following an altercation with President Garfield over appointments, the Senate reverted to its old independent ways. "No one," wrote Woodrow Wilson in 1885, "is *the* Senator. No one may speak for his party as well as for himself; no one exercises the special trust of acknowledged leadership. The Senate is merely a body of individual critics...."[38]

Modern Party Discipline

Republican Leadership. Modern party discipline made its appearance in the Senate in the 1890s under the leadership of William B. Allison of Iowa, Nelson W. Aldrich of Rhode Island and their fellow members of the School of Philosophy Club, an informal group that met regularly for poker at the home of Joseph McMillan of Michigan. When Allison, because he had served in the Senate longer than any other member of his party, was elected chairman of the Republican Caucus in March 1897, this group assumed control of the Senate. Previous caucus chairmen had not viewed the office as a vehicle for concentrating party authority, but Allison was quick to see the possibilities of his new position. Holding that "both in the committees and in the offices, we should use the machinery for our own benefit and not let other men have it," Allison took advantage of his appointment powers to monopolize party offices.[39]

Since the mid-1880s, a Republican Steering Committee had been appointed biennially to help schedule legislative business. Unlike previous caucus leaders, Allison determined to chair this committee himself, and he filled the committee with other members of his group. Under Allison, the Steering Committee arranged the order of business in minute detail and also managed proceedings on the floor.

Allison likewise dominated the Committee on Committees, which had responsibility for assignments to the working committees. The caucus chairman had great leeway in making appointments to this group, and Allison was able to staff it with a majority that would be receptive to his wishes; its chairman was always a member of the ruling faction. Committee chairmanships were by this time invariably filled through seniority, and Allison and Aldrich made no attempt to overturn the seniority rule, to which they owed their own committee chairmanships (Allison on Appropriations and Aldrich on Finance). But seniority did not apply to the filling of committee vacancies, and here the party leaders found an opportunity to reward their supporters and punish dissidents. Access to positions of influence soon depended on the favor and support of the party leaders. When Albert J. Beveridge of Indiana entered the Senate in 1899, he directed his appeal for committee preferment to Allison, in shrewd recognition of the existing order. "I feel that the greatest single point is gained in the possession of your friendship," Beveridge said. "I will labor very hard, strive very earnestly to deserve your consideration."[40]

Caucus approval of the committee slates and order of business became a mere formality, but the caucus still met to consider important issues. Through the caucus mechanism divisive questions were compromised in privacy, and the party was enabled to speak with a united voice on the floor. Caucus decisions were not formally binding ("We can get along without that," Allison remarked), but once the party leadership was capable of enforcing discipline on those who broke ranks, party solidarity became the norm. "Senators willing to abandon the opportunity to increase their authority could act freely, following their own inclinations," historian David Rothman noted. "The country might honor their names but the Senate barely felt their presence."[41]

Democratic Leadership. Under the leadership of Arthur P. Gorman of Maryland, Senate Democrats developed a power structure similar to that devised by the Republicans. As chairman of the Democratic Caucus in the 1890s, Gorman chaired not only the Steering Committee but the Committee on Committees as well, and in some ways his control over his party was greater than that of Allison and Aldrich over the Republicans. But the Democrats were in the minority most of the time, they often split on substantive issues, and Gorman never attained the power that his

Republican counterpart achieved. The lack of harmony within Democratic ranks led, in 1903, to the adoption of a rule making the decisions of the Democratic Caucus binding upon a two-thirds vote. Allison had considered such a rule unnecessary for the Republicans, but Gorman enthusiastically supported it.

Attitude Toward Party Control

The growth of party government was viewed with grave misgivings by the country at large and was by no means always popular in the Senate itself. As early as 1872 the Liberal Republicans (dissident Republicans opposed to the Grant administration) were protesting efforts by "a few Members of the Senate" to use the party organization to "seek to control first a majority of the members belonging to that organization and then of the Senate."[42] Similar complaints came from the Mugwumps (Republicans opposed to the party leadership) in the 1880s and from the Populist Party in the 1890s. The Senate in 1899 took one step toward dispersing authority within the chamber when it transferred responsibility for major appropriations bills from the Appropriations Committee to various legislative committees. The change was pressed, not in caucus, but on the floor where dissidents within both parties were able to carry it over the combined opposition of the Republican and Democratic leaders.

By the end of the 19th century, political parties had assumed a decisive role in the legislative process. The parties named the committees which made the first tentative decisions on proposed legislation, and they also determined what bills would be considered on the floor. When divisive legislative questions arose, party members resolved their differences within the caucus and went forth in disciplined ranks to ratify caucus decisions on the floor, often acting without debate or the formality of a roll-call vote.

The Republicans had a plurality, but not a majority, of the Senate when a bill proposed by representative Nelson Dingley raising tariffs to a new high came from the House in April 1897. Allison, with only the help of the Republican members of the Finance Committee, framed the schedules, which all but three of the Republicans agreed in advance to support. After limited debate in the caucus, the bill went to the Senate floor where united Republican support passed it over solid Democratic opposition. The Republicans, said Benjamin R. Tillman of South Carolina, "under the stress of party orders, I suppose, given by the caucus, sit by quietly and vote. They say nothing...and every schedule prepared by the party caucus is voted by them unanimously."[43] Tillman was wrong in only one particular; he credited the caucus with more influence than it actually had.

Election Law of 1866

For more than 75 years after the adoption of the Constitution, Congress took no advantage of its constitutional power to regulate congressional elections, and the method of electing senators was left to the states. At first, senators generally were chosen by concurrent vote of the two houses of the state legislature, each sitting separately. Later, in about half the states it became common for the two houses to elect senators by per capita voting in joint session.

The election system had serious flaws. Insistence on a majority vote in each house caused frequent deadlocks, which not only kept the legislature from handling other business but also caused the state to lose its representation in the Senate. Irregular practices abounded, and the Senate itself was forced to decide many election contests resulting from the lack of a uniform election law.

Accordingly, Congress in 1866 enacted legislation designed to correct these problems. The 1866 law provided that on the second Tuesday after the organization of a legislature when a senator was to be elected, the two houses should meet separately and by voice vote name a person for senator. On the following day the results of the voting were to be canvassed at a joint session of the two houses. If one candidate had won a majority of both houses, he was to be declared elected, but if this was not the case, "the joint assembly shall meet at twelve o'clock, meridian, of each succeeding day during the session of the legislature, and take at least one vote until a senator shall be elected."[44]

Senatorial elections were regulated by this law for almost half a century, until the adoption of the Seventeenth Amendment in 1913, but the measure was not a success. Deadlocks continued to occur, and irregularities increased. George H. Haynes summarized the problems of legislative election that led to the direct election movement: "...not a few, but nearly half the states of the Union suffered from serious deadlocks. These contests, the outcome of which was often as much a matter of chance as would be the throw of dice, aroused men's worst passions and gave rise now to insistent charges of bribery, now to riot, to assault and to threats of bloodshed, such that legislative sessions had to be held under protection of martial law. Fourteen contests lasted throughout an entire session of the legislature without effecting an election. Four states submitted to the heavy cost and inconvenience of special sessions to elect senators. Six states preferred to accept vacancies, thus losing their 'equal suffrage in the Senate,' while the country was deprived of a Senate constituted as the fathers had intended. At times legislative election led to positive and flagrant misrepresentation of the state in the Senate. To the individual state it brought a domination of state and local politics by the fierce fight for a single federal office, and interference with the work of lawmaking, ranging all the way from the exaction of a few hours of the legislators' time to the virtual annihilation of the legislature, which had been constituted to care for the interests of the state."[45]

Rise of the Filibuster

The oratorical splendor that had brought renown to the Senate in the years preceding the Civil War disappeared with the settlement of the slavery question, and for the remainder of the 19th century Senate debate was not noted for its brilliance. As crucial legislative decisions came to be made in party councils, few floor speeches were delivered for the purpose of swaying votes, and attendance at formal sessions of the Senate became a tedious duty. "It would be a capital thing," wrote George F. Hoar in 1897, "to attend Unitarian conventions if there were not Unitarians there, so too it would be a delightful thing to be a United States Senator if you did not have to attend the sessions of the Senate."[46]

Filibusters, increasingly common as the century advanced, became virtually an epidemic in the 1880s and 1890s. As a result, the Senate suffered a marked loss of public esteem for its failure to impose stringent curbs on debate. Cloture proposals were introduced from time to time, but the Senate held fast to its cherished tradition of unlimited speech.

Wartime pressures had produced two notable filibusters during the 1860s. In 1863 the conference report on a bill to secure the President against loss in any action brought against him for having suspended the writ of habeus corpus sparked an intense filibuster in the closing hours of the session. But the filibuster failed when the presiding officer, in the face of obvious obstruction, called for a vote and refused to entertain an appeal. The tactics of the filibusters were described by Sen. Lyman Trumbull (R Ill.): "Motion after motion was made here last night to lay on the table, to postpone indefinitely, to adjourn, to adjourn, to adjourn and to adjourn again, and the yeas and nays called on each occasion."[47] Similar tactics were employed by Charles Sumner in 1865 to postpone the readmission of Louisiana. He felt so strong on the issue that he declared himself "justified in employing all the instruments that I find in the arsenal of parliamentary warfare."[48]

Democratic proposals to suspend or repeal statutes allowing the use of federal troops in state elections were the subject of the next great filibusters, in 1876 and 1879. In the 1879 filibuster Republicans relied on dilatory motions, roll-call votes and refusal to answer quorum calls, whereupon the president pro tempore ruled that he could determine whether enough senators were present to constitute a quorum.

Famous Filibusters

In a famous filibuster of 1881, the Democratic minority prevented the Republicans from organizing the Senate until the resignations of two senators (Roscoe Conkling and Thomas C. Platt of New York) had given the Democrats numerical control. The filibuster made it impossible for the upper chamber to take action on any legislation from March 24 to May 16 of that year.

In 1890 a bill to provide federal aid to education sponsored by Henry W. Blair (R N.H.) was filibustered from Feb. 26 to March 20 by Blair himself in an effort to get sufficient support for passage. Believing he had won the requisite strength, Blair permitted the bill to come to a vote, but two senators at the last minute decided to vote against it. The bill was defeated, 31-37, with Blair himself voting nay in order to be eligible to move reconsideration. The measure was never revived.

A filibuster against the "Force Bill," sponsored by Rep. Henry Cabot Lodge (R Mass.), lasted from Dec. 2, 1890, to

Jan. 26, 1891. The measure would have established federal supervision over polling places at national elections in order to prevent exclusion of black voters in southern states. After seven weeks of debate, the bill's supporters tried to put through a rule for majority cloture. When this failed, the Senate was held in continuous session for four days and nights in an effort to exhaust filibusters. Eventually, after 33 days of actual obstruction, the bill was dropped to permit the enactment of vital appropriation bills before the 51st Congress expired in March 1891. During the debate, West Virginia Democrat C. J. Faulkner nominally held the floor for 11½ hours, although for nearly eight hours of that time he was relieved of the necessity of speaking through the absence of a quorum.

In 1893, a filibuster against repeal of the 1890 Silver Purchase Act lasted from Aug. 29 to Oct. 24. After 46 days of actual filibuster and 13 continuous day-and-night sittings, the repeal was passed Oct. 30 and sent to the President. The minority made use of every weapon in the filibuster arsenal—dilatory motions, roll-call votes and quorum calls, in addition to talk. A new record was set by Nebraska Populist William V. Allen who held the floor, with interruptions, for 14 hours.

This filibuster aroused widespread public concern over the conduct and future of the Senate. "To vote without debating is perilous, but to debate and never vote is imbecile," wrote Sen. Henry Cabot Lodge (R Mass.) shortly after the struggle ended. "As it is, there must be a change, for the delays which now take place are discrediting the Senate.... A body which cannot govern itself will not long hold the respect of the people who have chosen it to govern the country...."[49]

In 1897, during a mild filibuster on a naval appropriation bill, the chair ruled that a quorum call could not be ordered unless business had intervened since the last quorum call. However, since there was as yet no suggestion that debate was not business, this ruling had only limited value in curbing the excesses of the filibuster.

In 1901, Montana Republican Thomas H. Carter, who was retiring from the Senate in a few hours, filibustered against a "pork-barrel" rivers and harbors bill from the night of March 3 until the Senate adjourned *sine die* at noon March 4 (legislative day of March 3). The bill was a raid on the Treasury, Carter said, and he was performing a "public service" in preventing it from becoming law. He readily yielded for other business but resumed his item-by-item denunciation of the bill whenever necessary. No determined attempt was made to stop him, and the bill died.[50]

Early filibusters had not been notably successful, but as obstructionists gradually shifted to bolder techniques the Senate was unable to restrain them, and by the beginning of the 20th century the filibuster had assumed scandalous proportions. This was, says Franklin Burdette, "the heyday of brazen and unblushing aggressors. The power of the Senate lay not in votes but in sturdy tongues and iron wills. The premium rested not upon ability and statesmanship but upon effrontery and audacity."[51]

Senate Rules on Debate

The House of Representatives, whose entire membership is elected anew every two years, must adopt its rules at the beginning of each new Congress. But the Senate, as a continuing body, faces no such task; its rules remain in force from Congress to Congress unless the Senate decides to change them. Several revisions of the Senate rules have occurred since the first rules were adopted in 1789, but these revisions have been chiefly codifications of changes that had accumulated over a number of years.

Two such codifications occurred in the 1861-1901 period. The first, in 1868, increased the number of rules to an all-time maximum of 53, and it reflected some wartime strains. Another codification, in 1884, brought the number of rules down to 40. Although many changes in Senate rules have been adopted since that time, no further codification has taken place.

"Rules are never observed in this body; they are only made to be broken. We are a law unto ourselves," said John J. Ingalls (R Kan.) in 1876.[52] His comment may explain why rules reform has not played as significant a role in the history of the Senate as it has in the House.

Efforts to limit Senate debate provide a notable exception. In the last half of the 19th century, many proposals were offered to curtail debate either through the use of the previous question or some other means. Most of the proposals were simply ignored, but a few minor changes affecting debate were agreed to.

In 1862, the Senate adopted a resolution stating that "in consideration in secret session of subjects relating to the rebellion, debate should be confined to the subject matter and limited to five minutes, except that five minutes be allowed any Member to explain or oppose a pertinent amendment."[53] Adoption of this resolution was attributable to the exigencies of wartime. In later years it also became customary for the Senate, in the closing days of a session when the need for haste was great, to apply a five-minute limit on debate on appropriations bills.

Anthony Rule. In 1870, the Senate first adopted the Anthony Rule named after its originator Sen. Henry B. Anthony (R R.I.). The rule was the most important limitation of debate it had yet agreed to as a means of expediting its business. The rule was so successful in speeding action on noncontroversial bills that in 1880 it became part of the Standing Rules, where it now appears as Rule VIII:

"At the conclusion of the morning business for each day, unless upon motion the Senate shall at any time otherwise order, the Senate will proceed to the consideration of the Calendar of Bills and Resolutions, and continue such consideration until 2 o'clock; and bills and resolutions that are not objected to shall be taken up in their order, and each senator shall be entitled to speak once and for five minutes only upon any question; and the objection may be interposed at any stage of the proceedings, but upon motion the Senate may continue such consideration; and this order shall commence immediately after the call for 'concurrent and other resolutions,' and shall take precedence of the unfinished business and other special orders. But if the Senate shall proceed with the consideration of any matter notwithstanding an objection, the foregoing provisions touching debate shall not apply."[54]

The Anthony Rule greatly speeded the handling of routine measures without prejudice to the right of senators to demand longer debate on controversial bills. Another change that helped to facilitate the business of the Senate was the decision in 1875 that action on an amendment to an appropriation bill could be postponed without prejudice to the bill itself. This rule was so successful that its application was later extended to amendments to any bill.

Chapter 21

Era of Reform: 1901-1921

The "Progressive Era," which had begun with movements for economic reform in the 1880s and 1890s, gathered momentum and a radical democratic character after the turn of the century and gradually faded into the background during World War I. The progressive program was foreshadowed in the platform of the Populist Party, which in 1892 polled over a million votes for its presidential candidate, James B. Weaver. Though the party, centered in the agrarian Midwest and West, soon declined, many of its programs were gradually adopted by the two major parties.

Early Progressive Legislation. Under popular pressure, Congress had enacted such early "progressive" legislation as civil service reform (1883), the Interstate Commerce Act (1887), the Sherman Antitrust Act (1890), conservation legislation (1891) and an income tax law (1894). But the income tax was invalidated by the Supreme Court, and the other measures were rendered ineffective by their vagueness and their loopholes, by court rulings and by unenthusiastic administration.

Finding themselves thus frustrated, and laying the blame on the supposed sinister influence of vested interests, reformers concluded that more democratic control of the government was necessary to secure the laws they sought. Accordingly, the reform movement turned increasingly toward such measures as direct election of senators, direct primaries, women's suffrage and laws against corrupt election practices. In the House, the reformers were determined to break the power of the Speaker.

The power of the Senate declined after Theodore Roosevelt became President in 1901. Roosevelt was an aggressive leader who took an active role in promoting legislation. Concentration of authority in the House Speaker had brought cohesion to the lower chamber, which was now prepared to challenge senatorial leadership, and Roosevelt worked mainly through informal contacts with the Speaker of the House to advance his legislative program.

Insurgent Movement in Congress

Congress went along, somewhat reluctantly, with Roosevelt's progressive program, passing such measures as the Hepburn Act, which strengthened the Interstate Commerce Commission, pure food and drug laws and a workmen's compensation act. But William Howard Taft, who was elected in 1908, failed to press Roosevelt's policies in the face of Old Guard opposition, and the defeat of legislation sought by progressives in both parties led to the development of an insurgent movement among western Republicans in Congress.

In the House, Republican insurgents led the revolt against Speaker Joseph G. Cannon, while in the Senate the "Band of Six"—Robert M. La Follette of Wisconsin, Albert J. Beveridge of Indiana, Jonathan P. Dolliver and Albert B. Cummins of Iowa, Francis Bristow of Kansas and Edwin Clapp of Minnesota—unsuccessfully challenged the Nelson W. Aldrich machine on a tariff bill sponsored by Aldrich. Enactment of this distinctly protectionist measure led to resounding Republican defeats in the congressional elections of 1910 and the formation of the Progressive ("Bull Moose") Party which nominated Roosevelt for President in 1912. The split between the Roosevelt and Taft wings of the Republican Party gave an easy victory to the Democrats, and under President Woodrow Wilson the government entered a period of progressive rule that lasted through most of Wilson's first term.

Wilson Reforms. The President's early relations with Congress were easy. He returned to the pre-Jeffersonian practice of addressing the Congress in person and frequently went to the President's room in the Capitol to confer with committees or individual members. Under his leadership a caucus of Democratic senators was proposed in 1913, to marshal party support for a tariff-cutting bill sponsored by Oscar W. Underwood. Other legislative victories included the income tax (made valid by a constitutional amendment submitted to the states in 1909 and belatedly ratified on the eve of Wilson's inauguration), direct election of senators, the Clayton Antitrust Act and the Federal Reserve and Federal Trade Commission Acts.

This flow of progressive legislation ended when the United States entered World War I in 1917. During the war, Wilson assumed almost dictatorial powers, and criticism of his policies was silenced, but with the President's ill-timed appeal for election of a Democratic Congress in the fall of 1918, the opposition surfàced. In the ensuing election, Republicans captured control of both houses of Congress, and the President went off to the Paris Peace Conference a rejected hero. Wilson's health broke in his futile efforts to enlist support for the League of Nations, and the Republican Senate first emasculated, then rejected the Treaty of Versailles in which the League Covenant was embedded. With the election of a Republican Congress in 1918, a new period of congressional hegemony was at hand.

The Seventeenth Amendment, providing for direct election of senators, was undoubtedly the most important development in the evolution of the Senate during the Progressive Era, but other significant changes also occurred. Political parties were beginning to assume their modern place in the legislative structure, and as party leadership roles became institutionalized during the early years of the century, formally identifiable majority and minority leaders emerged. With the admission of Arizona to statehood in 1912, the membership of the Senate increased to 96; no further changes in size would occur for nearly half a century. Finally, in 1917 the Senate was driven by the excesses of filibustering to adopt its first cloture rule, permitting two-thirds of those present and voting to bring debate to a close.

Direct Election of Senators

The Constitution provided for the election of senators by the state legislatures. But the Seventeenth Amendment, ratified in 1913, changed the Constitution to provide for direct election of senators. The change was part of the

Progressive Era's movement toward more democratic control of government. Being less immediately dependent on popular sentiment than the House, the Senate did not seek to reform itself. Only strong pressure from the public, expressed through the House of Representatives, the state governments, pressure groups, petitions, referenda and other means, convinced the Senate that it must reform.

It was common in the Progressive Era to attribute legislative disappointments to the dealings of vested interests operating behind the scenes. A Senate chosen by state legislatures, whose decisions were often made in closed-door party caucuses, could not easily escape suspicion. Moreover, the high-tariff views of the Senate served to link this body in the public mind with the great corporations that were widely accused of improper influence on politics. The popular image of the Senate in the Progressive Era was a far cry from the picture presented by de Tocqueville in an earlier age.

Pressures on the Senate. Andrew Johnson, who as President subsequently came within one vote of removal from office at the hands of the Senate, was an early advocate of Senate reform. Twice as representative, once as a senator, and again as President in 1868, Johnson presented resolutions calling for direct election of senators. But in the first 80 years of Congress, a total of only nine resolutions proposing a constitutional amendment to that effect were introduced in Congress. In the 1870s and 1880s the number increased, and by 1912 a total of not less than 287 such joint resolutions had been introduced. Not until 1892 was a resolution reported favorably from committee in the House. In the next decade such a resolution was carried five times in the House with only a handful in opposition. But the proposed amendment to the Constitution was not allowed to reach a vote in the Senate until 1911.

Petitions from farmers' associations and other organizations, particularly in the West, and party platforms in state elections pressed the issue until the national parties took it up. Direct election of senators was a plank in the Populist program at every election, beginning in 1892, and in the Democratic platform in each presidential election year from 1900 to 1912. Starting in California and Iowa in 1894, state legislatures addressed Congress in favor of a direct election amendment, until by 1905 the legislatures in

31 of the 45 states had taken this step, many of them repeatedly. Referenda held in three states showed approval of the amendment by votes of 14 to 1 in California, 8 to 1 in Nevada, and 6 to 1 in Illinois. Support was strongest in the West and North Central states, where every legislature petitioned Congress at least once, and weakest in the Northeast, where only Pennsylvania's legislature voted to address Congress in support of direct election.

In 1900, when the House voted 240-15 in favor of submitting an amendment for direct election of senators, it was favored by a majority of the representatives from every state except Maine and Connecticut.[55]

Other Tactics. Still the Senate did not act. Since the senators would not even consider a change in the method of electing them, other tactics were adopted. Between 1902 and 1911 even the House did not vote on any resolution for direct election of senators. But the states were finding ways to achieve the same results without a constitutional amendment.

The spread of direct primaries in the 1890s led in many states to expressions of popular choice of senator on the primary ballot. Though not legally binding on the legislatures, this choice was likely to be ratified. In the South, the primary winners were soon being "elected" by the one-party legislatures almost as a matter of course. But in states that did not have a one-party system, especially those lacking clear party lines, primaries were less effective in guaranteeing that the popular choice would be ratified by the legislature.

Oregon led the way in devising a system to guarantee popular choice of senators in spite of the Constitution's assignment of this task to the legislatures. In 1901 an Oregon law was enacted enabling voters to express their choice for senator in the same manner as they voted for governor, except that the vote for senator had no legal force. But the law specified that when the legislature assembled to elect a senator, "it shall be the duty of each house to count the votes and announce the candidate having the highest number, and thereupon the houses shall proceed to the election of a senator." In the first test of this system, the man who led the field with 37 per cent of the popular vote for senator secured scant support from the legislators, who scattered their votes among 14 candidates. After a five-week deadlock, the legislature chose a man who had not received a single vote in the popular election.

Far from being discouraged at this mockery of "the people's choice," the people of Oregon in 1904 used their new initiative and referendum powers to petition for and approve a new law. Henceforth each candidate for senator was to be nominated by petition, and allowed to include on the petition a 100-word statement of principles, and on the ballot a 12-word statement to be printed after his name. The legislators, who could not be denied their constitutional power to name senators, were permitted to include in their nomination petitions their signatures to either "Statement No. 1" or "Statement No. 2." The former pledged the signer always to vote "for that candidate for United States Senator in Congress who has received the highest number of the people's votes...without regard to my individual preference." The second statement was a pledge to regard the popular vote "as nothing more than a recommendation, which I shall be at liberty to wholly disregard...." Meanwhile, citizen groups circulated pledges, which were widely subscribed to, that the signer would not support or vote for any candidate to the legislature who did not endorse "Statement No. 1."

The first legislature elected after enactment of this law promptly ratified the "people's choice" for senator. And two years later, when 83 of the 90 members of the legislature were Republicans, the Democratic popular choice was elected. He received 53 votes, including all 52 who had endorsed "Statement No. 1."

The "Oregon System" was adopted in other states in modified forms. By December 1910 it was estimated that 14 of the 30 senators about to be named by state legislatures had already been designated by popular vote.[56]

The Issue in the Senate. Gradually the mounting external pressures began to be felt within the Senate. Some of the senators were themselves products of the new systems of popular election. In fact, the leader within the Senate in the fight for the Seventeenth Amendment, Sen. William E. Borah (R Idaho), had entered the Senate through a popular mandate after an earlier defeat at the hands of the Idaho legislature.

Beginning in 1901, some of the legislatures were no longer content to request Congress to submit a con-

stitutional amendment to the states. They called for a convention to amend the Constitution, a method as yet untried
but obligatory once two-thirds of the states so petition
Congress. Some senators, though they opposed popular election, feared that such a convention, like the original Constitutional Convention, might exceed its original mandate
and preferred to submit to the states a specific amendment
for direct election of senators.

When a resolution for the constitutional amendment
was referred to the Senate Judiciary Committee, rather
than to the more hostile Committee on Privileges and Elections that had considered it on previous occasions, a
favorable report was at last obtained on Jan. 1, 1911.
However, a committee amendment, supported by southern
senators, which would have modified Congress' power under
Article I, Section 4 of the Constitution to control state
regulation of Senate and House elections, provoked such a
storm of controversy that at times it overshadowed the popular election itself. The amendment would have transferred
to the states exclusive power to regulate the election of
senators; it would have left unchanged Congress' power to
regulate House elections. Once on the floor, the northern opposition prevailed and the committee amendment was
removed by a vote of 50-37. But on Feb. 28, 1911, the resolution itself failed, 54-33, to secure the necessary two-thirds
majority.[57]

In a special session later that year, the House passed
296-16 the direct election resolution. But the House version
was the same as that reported by the Senate committee, giving the states exclusive power to regulate Senate elections.
The Senate, on a 45-44 roll call decided by Vice President
James S. Sherman's tie-breaking vote, again rejected the
committee amendment, and adopted the original
resolution, 64-24. A deadlock between the two houses was
broken in the next session when on May 13, 1912, the House,
238-39, finally concurred in the Senate version. By May 31,
1913, three-fourths of the states had ratified.[58]

The immediate effects of the Seventeenth Amendment
were difficult to assess. Even before its adoption, the direct
primary movement had diminished the power of the
legislatures, and by 1913 three-fourths of the candidates for
the Senate were being nominated in direct primaries. The
terms of the senators in office at the time the amendment

was ratified ended variously in 1915, 1917 and 1919, so the 66th Congress (1919-21) was the first in which all members of the Senate were the products of direct election. "By that time," George B. Galloway pointed out, "56 of the senators who owed their togas originally to state legislatures had been re-elected by the people, three had died, and 37 had disappeared from the scene either voluntarily or by popular verdict. In other words, more than half of those last chosen by legislative caucus were subsequently approved by the people."[59]

Restraining the Filibuster

In the early years of the 20th century, filibusters continued to be undertaken with frequency and a high degree of success. But mounting opposition to the practice led, in 1908, to efforts to curb obstruction through interpretation of existing rules and, in 1917, to the Senate's first cloture rule.

Meanwhile, 1903 proved to be a vintage year for the filibuster. Democratic Sen. Benjamin R. ("Pitchfork Ben") Tillman of South Carolina filibustered against an appropriation bill until an item for payment of war claims to his state was restored. The item was put back in the bill after Tillman threatened to read Byron's "Childe Harold" and other poems into the record until his colleagues surrendered from boredom.

While Tillman resorted to "legislative blackmail," in the words of House Speaker Joseph G. Cannon (R Ill.), Republican Sen. Albert J. Beveridge of Indiana chose a different method. Beveridge, chairman of the Territories Committee and an opponent of statehood for Arizona and New Mexico, led a filibuster against an omnibus statehood bill. Taking advantage of a custom that no vote should be taken on a measure in the absence of the chairman of the committee that had handled it, Beveridge hid for days in Washington and finally slipped away to Atlantic City. The bill ultimately was dropped.

In 1908, a bitter two-day filibuster against the conference report on an emergency currency measure sponsored by Aldrich and Rep. Edward B. Vreeland (R N.Y.) brought the first significant steps to curb obstruction. Republican Sen. Robert M. La Follette Sr. of Wisconsin held the floor for 18 hours and 23 minutes, a record that stood until 1938, but he was interrupted by 29 quorum calls and three roll calls on questions of order. La Follette fortified himself periodically with eggnogs from the Senate restaurant. According to one account, he rejected one of these eggnogs as doped, and it later was found to contain a fatal dose of ptomaine. No charge of a deliberate poisoning attempt was made.

The filibusterers' cause finally was lost when blind Sen. Thomas P. Gore (D Okla.) yielded the floor after learning that Sen. William J. Stone (D Mo.), who was scheduled to relieve him, was in the chamber. But Stone had been called to the cloakroom, and the blind Gore surrendered the floor. The conference report was approved on a hastily demanded roll call.

First Curbs on Obstruction

Three important curbs on obstruction resulted from the 1908 filibuster. They were rulings that: (1) the chair could count a quorum if enough senators were present, even on a vote, whether or not they answered to their names; (2) debate did not count as intervening business for the purpose of deciding if a quorum call was in order; and (3) senators could by enforcement of existing rules be prevented from speaking more than twice on the same subject in one day.

During a 1914 Republican filibuster against a rivers and harbors bill, the chair ruled that senators could not yield for any purpose, even for a question, without unanimous consent. The Senate tabled an appeal from this ruling, 28-24, but reversed itself the next day and the rules remained unchanged.

In 1915, a successful filibuster was organized against President Wilson's Ship Purchase bill. Republican Sen. Reed Smoot of Utah spoke for 11 hours and 35 minutes without relief and without deviating from the subject. After almost a month of obstruction, seven Democrats who thought the filibuster should give way to other important legislation joined the Republicans to move that the bill be recommitted. Other Democrats supporting the bill then staged a five-day reverse filibuster until they regained control of the chamber. The Republican filibuster then was renewed. A Democratic motion to close the debate was blocked, and the bill finally was dropped, but as a result of the filibuster three important appropriation bills failed.

Eleven Willful Men

The public was disgusted by this episode, but it took one more great filibuster to force the Senate into action. The occasion came in 1917 when the administration's Armed Neutrality bill was talked to death by an 11-man bloc in the closing days of the 64th Congress. Seventy-five senators who signed a statement in support of the measure asked that it be entered in the record "to establish that the Senate favors the legislation and would pass it, if a vote could be had."[60] Not all of the obstruction came from the Republican side of the aisle. On the last day of the session, when it was clear that the bill was doomed, the Democrats staged their own filibuster to keep an outraged La Follette from being able to speak against the measure before crowded Senate galleries.

No sooner had the session ended than President Wilson issued an angry statement: "The Senate of the United States is the only legislative body in the world which cannot act when its majority is ready for action. A little group of willful men, representing no opinion but their own, have rendered the great government of the United States helpless and contemptible...." Wilson immediately called the Senate into special session and demanded that it amend its rules so that it could act and "save the country from disaster."[61]

The Senate yielded, and a conference of Republican and Democratic leaders hastily drew up the Senate's first cloture rule. After only six hours of debate, Rule 22 was adopted by the chamber March 8, 1917, by a vote of 76-3.

Rule 22's Limits on Debate

The new rule provided for limitation of debate upon any pending measure by vote of two-thirds of the senators present and voting, two days after a cloture motion had been submitted by 16 senators. Thereafter, debate was limited to one hour for each senator on the bill itself and all amendments and motions affecting it. No new amendments could be offered except by unanimous consent. Amendments that were not germane to the pending business, and amendments and motions clearly designed to delay action, were out of order.

An amendment was offered to authorize cloture by majority instead of two-thirds vote. The amendment was attacked as a breach of faith and was withdrawn before a vote could be taken. And in 1918 the Senate rejected, 34-41, a proposal to allow use of the previous question to limit debate during the war period.

For a time it looked as if the Senate would never make use of its new tool against obstruction, but the interminable debates on the Treaty of Versailles in 1919 finally provided an occasion. The Senate adopted its first cloture motion Nov. 15, 1919, on a 78-16 roll call, and four days later the treaty itself was brought to a vote, after 55 days of debate.

Party Leadership

The system of party leadership that had evolved in the Senate in the closing years of the 19th century became institutionalized in the early years of the 20th with the creation of formally designated majority and minority leadership positions.

Both Republicans and Democrats for many years had elected chairmen of the party caucuses, but the caucus chairman was not necessarily the effective leader of his party in the Senate. William B. Allison (R Iowa) and Arthur P. Gorman (D Md.) served as chairmen of their respective caucuses, but the position was not essential to their control; Nelson W. Aldrich (R R.I.), the most powerful member of the Senate until his retirement in 1911, never held any official position other than the chairmanship of the Finance Committee.

With the departure of these dynamic leaders from the chamber, power was fragmented within the parties. It became common for both Republicans and Democrats to elect a different floor leader in each session, and the floor leadership did not necessarily correspond with the caucus chairmanship. Under these conditions party unity was hard to maintain.

In 1911, the Democrats—already in control of the House and looking forward to the election of a Democratic Senate two years later—instituted the practice of electing a single, readily identifiable leader, who held the dual posts of floor leader and chairman of the party caucus. The Republicans, threatened by insurgents within their ranks, took a similar course in 1913. Subsequently party whips (assistant floor leaders) were added to the leadership structure—in 1913 by the Democrats and in 1915 by the

221

Republicans. Since this period, the majority and minority leaders have usually been the acknowledged spokesmen for their parties in the Senate.

The importance of the leadership role was underscored in 1913, when progressive Senate Democrats deposed conservative leader Thomas S. Martin (Va.) and engineered the election as majority leader of John W. Kern (Ind.), who had served in the Senate only two years. The Steering Committee, appointed by Kern and dominated by progressives, made committee assignments in such a way as to assure administration control of major committees; seniority was ignored when necessary. The Steering Committee also recommended rules, later adopted by the caucus, that permitted a majority of committee members to call meetings, elect subcommittees and appoint conferees. Thus party authority was augmented and the power of committee chairmen curbed in a movement that somewhat paralleled the revolt against Cannonism in the House.

Early in the 20th century, both parties replaced the title "caucus" with "conference," in formal recognition of the non-binding nature of thse party meetings. The Democratic Caucus in 1903 adopted a binding caucus rule, but there is no evidence that it was ever used, and when Kern in 1913 proposed holding a binding caucus on the tariff bill, opposition was so vigorous that the idea had to be dropped. The compromise finally achieved preserved the appearance of a non-binding "conference," though Democratic senators were under such strong pressure to support caucus decisions that the effect of a binding caucus was maintained.

Chapter 22

Republican Stalemate: 1921-1933

After its victory over Woodrow Wilson on the League of Nations, the Senate was in no mood to submit to presidential leadership. It expected to assume control of the government in the Republican administrations that followed Wilson, but after the House revamped its appropriations procedures in 1920 the lower chamber increasingly challenged Senate primacy.

Wilson's three Republican successors, faithful to the GOP doctrine of legislative independence, made little effort to direct Congress in legislative matters. Wilson's immediate successor, Warren G. Harding, promised prior to his election that he would take a hands-off approach with respect to legislation and that the Senate would "have something to say about the foreign relations as the Constitution contemplates." Harding added, "I had rather have the counsel of the Senate than all the political bosses in any party."[62] Harding, who was an ex-senator, appeared before his former colleagues on several occasions. In an unprecedented move in 1921, he personally delivered his nominations for Cabinet positions to the Senate. But he came to regret his promise not to intervene in legislative matters. When he appeared before the Senate in 1921 to urge a balanced budget, the Senate berated him for interfering in its business and the House was offended that the issue had not been raised in the chamber where money bills must originate. Harding's subsequent feeble efforts to exert leadership were rebuffed by Congress, and his administration tarnished by scandals that were exposed by Senate investigators after his death in 1923.

Harding's successor, Calvin Coolidge, was even less inclined to leadership than Harding had been. "I have never felt that it was my duty to attempt to coerce senators or representatives, or to make reprisals," Coolidge wrote. "The people sent them to Washington. I felt I had discharged my duty when I had done the best I could with them."[63] The Senate rejected Coolidge's nomination of Charles Beecher Warren as Attorney General, the first rejection of a Cabinet nomination since 1868, but in other respects it largely ignored the passive President.

More aggressive leadership was expected of Herbert Hoover, but he lacked political experience and, as a recent convert to Republicanism, was distrusted by many members of his own party. Friction with the legislative branch thwarted his efforts to deal with the economic depression that engulfed the nation early in his single term of office.

If the Presidents of the 1920s were unable to lead the government, Congress itself was not much more successful. Although Republicans controlled the White House from 1921 to 1933, the House from 1919 to 1931 and the Senate from 1919 to 1933, the party solidarity that had characterized the McKinley era no longer existed. Throughout the 1920s a "progressive" farm bloc dominated by western Republicans held the balance of power in Congress, and the decade was marked by persistent deadlocks on major issues.

Meanwhile, significant internal developments took place in the chamber. A major consolidation of the committee system occurred in 1921, and exclusive authority over spending was restored to the Appropriations Committee in 1922 after introduction of the new budget system. In 1932, the Senate finally succeeded in winning House concurrence to the Lame-Duck Amendment, which altered the terms and sessions of Congress. But experience did not bear out the hope of Sen. George W. Norris (R Neb.), sponsor of the amendment, that it would end the filibusters that continued to plague the Senate in the 1920s. Of the nine cloture votes taken during that decade, only three succeeded, and opponents of the filibuster continued to seek new ways to halt obstruction.

Republican Insurgency

Agriculture did not share in the prosperity of the 1920s, and efforts to relieve the farmers' plight led to a breakdown of party government and the development of legislative blocs representing sectional and economic interests. Efforts to enact agricultural relief legislation brought a split between eastern and western Republicans and the establishment of a powerful bipartisan farm bloc within Congress. Insurgent Republicans, mostly from the Great Plains and Rocky Mountain areas, usually kept their formal ties to the Republican Party but cooperated with the Democrats on sectional economic legislation. In the House, Republican regulars for the most part kept the upper hand. In the Senate, Republican control was often only nominal. Insurgents frequently succeeded in blocking administration legislation although they lacked the strength to carry their own legislative program. The divisions of the period extended to organizational matters within the chamber.

The congressional elections of 1922 were a disaster for the regular Republicans. Not only did the Republican majority decline from 167 to 15 in the House and from 22 to 6 in the Senate, but throughout the farm states progressive Republicans won over regulars. When the 68th Congress met in December 1923, the insurgents challenged the regulars' control.

The insurgent Republicans and the two Farmer-Labor senators from Minnesota accepted committee assignments from the Republicans but did not attend the Republican conference. When the committee lists came to the floor, Robert M. La Follette (R Wis.) led an effort to remove Albert B. Cummins of Iowa from the chairmanship of the Interstate Commerce Committee. A month-long deadlock ensued. La Follette was the second-ranking Republican on the committee, and the regular Republicans, unable to elect Cummins, had no intention of letting La Follette succeed to the chairmanship. Finally, on the 32nd ballot, the regulars threw their support to the committee's ranking Democrat, Ellison D. Smith of South Carolina, and Smith was elected chairman although he was of the minority party. Cummins continued as a member of the committee and also retained his office as president pro tempore.

In 1924, La Follette ran for President under the Progressive banner, polling 16 per cent of the vote but carrying only his own state of Wisconsin. The Republicans gained five seats in the Senate, and party leaders felt strong enough to retaliate against the irregulars who had supported the Progressive ticket. Thus the Republican Conference adopted a resolution that the disloyal senators "be not invited to future Republican conferences and be not named to fill any Republican vacancies on Senate committees."[64] The irregulars were permitted to keep the committee assignments they then held, but in many instances they were placed at the bottom of the list. In the Senate reorganization two years later, however, they were welcomed back into the Republican fold.

The Progressives continued to be a thorn in the side of the regular Republicans. In his last two years in office, Hoover had to contend with a Democratic House in which the Republican Progressives regularly sided with the opposition. The situation in the Senate was not much better. The Senate of the 72nd Congress consisted of 48 Republicans, 47 Democrats and one Farmer-Labor. Since some Progressive Republicans continually voted with the Democrats, President Hoover advised James Watson, the Republican leader, to let the Democrats organize the Senate "to convert their sabotage into responsibility." Hoover said he "could deal more constructively with the Democratic leaders if they held full responsibility in both houses, than with an opposition in the Senate conspiring in the cloakrooms to use every proposal of his for demagoguery."[65] Watson, who wanted to be majority leader, and his Republican colleagues, who wanted to be committee chairmen, rejected Hoover's proposal.

Cloture in Practice

Early experience with the Senate cloture rule bore out the predictions of those who expected it to be used only sparingly. Between 1917, when the rule was adopted, and the end of the Hoover administration in 1933, the Senate took only 11 cloture votes, of which five occurred in one two-week period in 1927.

Four of the 11 votes were successful. In addition to the 1919 vote on the Treaty of Versailles, the Senate in 1926 ended a 10-day filibuster against the World Court Protocol by adopting cloture on a 68-26 vote, and in 1927 it voted cloture twice—on a branch banking bill, 65-18, and on a prohibition reorganization measure, 55-27. The seven measures on which cloture failed included two tariff bills, a bill for development of the Lower Colorado River Basin and a banking bill against which Huey Long (D La.) staged his first filibuster early in 1933. On this occasion cloture failed by a single vote.

Some issues were too touchy for cloture even to be attempted. During the third session of the 67th Congress in 1922, a group of southern senators mounted a filibuster against an anti-lynching bill. On behalf of the obstructionists, Oscar W. Underwood (D Ala.) said: "It is perfectly apparent that you are not going to get an agreement to vote on this bill.... I want to say right now to the Senate that if the majority party insist on this procedure, they are not going to pass the bill and they are not going to do any other business.... We are going to transact no other business until we have an understanding about this bill.... We are willing to take the responsibility, and we are going to do it."[66] The obstructionists were as good as their word: the Senate was unable to transact any legislative business until the anti-lynching bill was formally put aside on the last day of the session, but no cloture vote was ever taken.

Similarly, in 1927 no attempt was made to invoke cloture on a filibuster against extending the life of a special campaign-investigating committee headed by James A. Reed (D Mo.). A small group of senators succeeded in killing the committee, which had exposed corruption in the 1926 election victories of Frank L. Smith (R Ill.) and William S. Vare (R Pa.), although a majority of the Senate clearly favored its extension.

As it became apparent that Rule 22 was not an effective weapon against the filibuster, new curbs on obstruction were proposed. During the 1922 filibuster on an anti-lynching bill, Republican Whip Charles Curtis (R Kan.) asked the chair to follow the precedent of Speaker Reed that, notwithstanding the absence of a specific rule on the question, dilatory motions could be ruled out of order under general parliamentary law. Such a precedent would have established a significant tool against obstruction, but Vice President Coolidge declined to rule.

The next Vice President, however, was made of sterner stuff. When Charles G. Dawes made his inaugural address to the Senate in 1925, he coupled a scathing denunciation of the existing Senate rules with a call for new curbs on debate. Not content with attacking the Senate on its own turf, Dawes took his campaign to the country, where he encountered the rather surprising opposition of the American Federation of Labor. The Dawes scheme, said the AFL ominously, "emanates from the secret chambers of the predatory interests."[67] Although Dawes aroused widespread public interest in the problem, the Senate took no action on rules reform proposals.

The Lame-Duck Amendment

One member of the Senate thought he saw a way to end the filibuster. George W. Norris (R Neb.), a progressive who earlier had participated in the House revolt against Speaker Cannon, proposed a constitutional amendment that would eliminate the short, post-election sessions of Congress in which so many filibusters occurred.

Under the Constitution and existing law, a Congress that was elected in November of an even-numbered year did not take office until March 4 of the following odd-numbered year and did not meet in its first regular session until December of that year, 13 months after its election. Meanwhile, the old Congress regularly met in December following the election of its successor and remained in session until the term of the new Congress began in March. This was known as the short session, in which "lame-duck" members who had been repudiated at the polls often determined the course of legislation. The fixed adjournment date was an invitation to filibusters, because merely by talking long enough members could block action until the old Congress expired; it was hardly surprising that the short sessions were seldom productive.

Accordingly, Norris proposed an amendment to the Constitution to abolish the short session by starting the terms of Congress and the President in January instead of March and providing that Congress should meet annually in January rather than December. The Senate approved the change six times before the House agreed to it in 1932. The Twentieth Amendment became part of the Constitution in 1933.

The first Senate vote on the Norris amendment came early in 1923, during the short session of the 67th Congress. Reported from the Senate Agriculture Committee, of which Norris was chairman, the resolution proposing the amendment was adopted by the Senate Feb. 13 on a 63-6 vote. In the House the amendment was reported by the Election Committee and approved by a majority of the Rules Committee, but Rules Chairman Philip P. Campbell (R Kan.), himself a lame duck, managed to keep it from the floor.

In 1924, the Norris amendment was again approved by the Senate, 63-7, and again reported by the House Election Committee, but this time it was blocked in the Rules Committee. The same thing happened in 1926, when the Senate approved the amendment by a vote of 73-2.

The Norris amendment finally reached the House floor in 1928, after the Senate had approved it for a fourth time, 65-6. However, the House vote of 209-157 fell 35 short of the two-thirds required for approval under the Constitution.

In the next Congress, the 71st, the Senate approved the Norris resolution for a fifth time, 64-9. The House adopted a different version, 290-93, and the measure died in conference.

Final action came in the following Congress, when the Democrats had won control of the House. Early in 1932, the Senate adopted the Norris resolution for a sixth time, 63-7, and the House quickly cleared it, 335-56. It became the Twentieth Amendment upon ratification by the 36th state early in 1933.

The amendment established Jan. 3 of the year following election as the day on which the terms of senators and representatives would begin and end, and Jan. 20 as the day on which the President and Vice President would take office. It provided also that Congress should meet annually on Jan. 3 "unless they shall by law appoint a different day."

The second session of the 73rd Congress was the first to convene on the new date, Jan. 3, 1934. And the first President to take office on Jan. 20 was Franklin D. Roosevelt at the beginning of his second term in 1937. It quickly became clear, however, that the amendment would not eliminate the filibuster, as Norris had hoped. The final sessions of the

73rd and 74th Congresses, the first to function under it, both ended in filibusters.

Committee Reorganization

The Senate's standing committee system had expanded fantastically since the middle of the 19th century, and by 1921 it was ripe for pruning. The 25 standing committees of 1853 increased to 42 by 1889, and in the next quarter-century this number almost doubled. Five select committees graduated to standing-committee status in 1884, three more did so in 1896, and all of the remaining select committees were made standing committees in 1909. At the same time, nine new standing committees were created, followed by three more in 1913, bringing the total number to an all-time high of 74.

The expansion of the committee system was only in part a reflection of the increasing · complexity of Senate business; committees also provided welcome clerical service and office space for their chairmen in the days before such assistance was available to all members. Thus "sinecure committees" had a way of surviving long after any need for them was gone. (Benefits did not go only to the party in power; in 1907, the Republicans took 61 chairmanships but assigned 10 others to the minority, and several committees were established solely for the purpose of creating chairmanships.)

When the 67th Congress convened in April 1921, the Senate effected a major consolidation of its committee system by reducing the number of committees from 74 to 34 and abolishing a number of long-defunct bodies such as the Committee on Revolutionary Claims.

The revision of the committee system was initiated by the Republican Committee on Committees, which at the same time proposed to increase the Republican margin on each of the major committees to reflect Republican gains in the Senate. To Democratic protests against "steam roller" tactics, Sen. Frank B. Brandegee (R Conn.), the committee chairman, replied: "Criticisms are purely professional. The Republicans are responsible to the country for legislation and must have control of committees. That's not tyranny; that's representative government—the rule of the majority."[68] The Republican proposal was adopted, 45-25, without substantial change.

A further modification of the committee system occurred in 1922 when the Senate, following the lead of the House, restored exclusive spending powers to the Appropriations Committee (from which they had been taken in 1899). When the eight appropriation bills previously considered by other Senate committees were taken up, three ad hoc members (one in the case of a conference) from the committee which previously had considered the bill were to serve with the Appropriations Committee. At the same time, Appropriations was deprived of its power to report amendments proposing new or general legislation.

The change in appropriations procedure was part of a larger effort to develop a more systematic approach to federal expenditures in both the executive and legislative branches. The Budget and Accounting Act of 1921 set up a Bureau of the Budget to assist the President in preparing an annual budget that reconciled federal revenues and expenditures; it also created a General Accounting Office to strengthen congressional surveillance over government spending.

Chapter 23

Democratic Leadership: 1933-1945

The United States was in the depths of a great economic depression when Franklin D. Roosevelt entered the White House in 1933 with overwhelming popular support and commanding majorities in both houses of Congress. Asked prior to his election what authority he would seek from Congress, Roosevelt had answered, "Plenty," and he was as good as his word.

Called into special session March 9, 1933, Congress in the next "hundred days" embarked on a whirlwind legislative course dictated by the President. The House on March 9 passed an emergency banking bill, which had not then even been printed, in 38 minutes; the Senate took a little longer, two hours and 15 minutes, but the measure was ready for the President's signature before the day ended.

With time the pace slackened somewhat, but the pattern of action remained the same. The President would send a brief message to Congress, accompanied by a detailed draft of the legislation he proposed. Congress had been outraged when President Lincoln dared to submit his own draft bills, but it readily accepted such action from Roosevelt and the practice became routine. Given the President's popularity and the prevailing economic conditions, opposition was futile and often nonexistent, and the President's proposals were promptly enacted. Congress did not long continue to be a rubber stamp, but throughout his first term

(1933-37) Roosevelt was able—through negotiation, compromise and the exercise of his patronage powers—to obtain the enactment of a broad range of New Deal social and economic programs.

In his second term (1937-41), a conservative coalition of Republicans and southern Democrats frequently opposed Roosevelt on domestic issues. The coalition thwarted his plan to enlarge the Supreme Court and successfully opposed him on other measures. During the President's unprecedented third term (1941-45), wartime issues were paramount. As in previous wars, the executive branch assumed extraordinary powers, and Congress became increasingly restive under executive domination. As the war drew to a close, opposition to Roosevelt's domestic policies mounted, and by the time the President died shortly after the start of his fourth term in 1945, Congress was in open revolt. His successor, Harry S Truman, won broad congressional support for his foreign policy measures, but his domestic programs were largely ignored.

Even before the war ended, Congress began to consider ways of modernizing its machinery so that it would be able to handle its mounting volume of business and regain some of the initiative it had lost to the executive branch. The resulting Legislative Reorganization Act of 1946 was only partially successful in meeting these goals. In the Senate no action was taken to strengthen the cloture rule, although filibusters were used repeatedly to defeat civil rights legislation.

President and Senate

President Roosevelt, at times assisted by Vice President Garner, was his own legislative leader in the Senate during his first term, and Senate Democratic leaders viewed themselves as the loyal lieutenants of the President. Senate rules and procedures precluded the close control exercised by party leaders in the House, but the Senate leaders were more experienced than their House counterparts and they were often more successful in advancing administration programs.

Roosevelt in Control. When Sen. Joseph T. Robinson (D Ark.) became majority leader in 1933, he revived the Democratic Caucus and won from Democratic senators an agreement, adopted by a vote of 50-3, to make caucus decisions on administration bills binding by majority vote. The rule read:

"Resolved, That until further order the chairman [Robinson] is authorized to convene Democratic senators in caucus for the purpose of considering any measure recommended by the President; and that all Democratic senators shall be bound by the vote of the majority of the conference; provided, that any senator may be excused from voting for any such measure upon his expressed statement to the caucus that said measure is contrary to his conscientious judgment or that said measure is in violation of pledges made to his constituents as a candidate."[69]

Although there is no evidence that Robinson ever made use of the binding caucus rule, non-binding caucuses frequently were held to mobilize party support. In the House the majority leadership worked through the Steering Committee and the whip organization, but in the Senate the Steering Committee served only as a committee on committees, while it is doubtful if the Policy Committee ever even met.

The Senate had more potential dissidents than the House, among them many southern Democrats who had risen to key committee chairmanships through the seniority system, but Roosevelt was remarkably successful at keeping them in line. Agriculture Chairman Ellison D. Smith (S.C.) was not sympathetic to the proposed Agricultural Adjustment Act of 1933, but after a conference at the White House his committee reported the measure with this comment: "This bill...was drafted by the Department of Agriculture and is practically unchanged from the bill as presented to Congress. Considerable hearings were had by the Senate committee, but on account of the desire of the administration that no change be made the bill is presented to the Senate in practically an unchanged form...."[70]

As long as the Democrats maintained their tremendous margins in Congress and were able to curb the dissidents within their own party, the leadership could afford to ignore the minority—especially since many Republicans supported early New Deal proposals. But by the beginning of Roosevelt's second term in 1937, these conditions no longer prevailed, and a conservative coalition of Republicans and southern Democrats emerged opposed to the New Deal.

Failure of Court Packing

Stung by the Supreme Court's invalidation of major administration acts, Roosevelt sent to the Senate, Feb. 5, 1937, a proposal to enlarge the court by providing for the appointment of additional justices, up to a total of six, to assist those who did not retire within six months after reaching the age of 70. For once, public opinion was not with the President, and Senate Republicans sat on their hands while conservative and New Deal Democrats contested the issue. A series of court decisions favorable to New Deal programs weakened support, as did the sudden death of Sen. Robinson, the administration floor leader, on July 13.

In the leadership contest that followed, Alben W. Barkley (D Ky.), with Roosevelt's implied support, defeated Pat Harrison (D Miss.) for the majority leadership in a fight that brought to the surface the deep split in Democratic ranks. It also cost Roosevelt his court plan, which was rejected shortly thereafter.

Struggling to reassert his party leadership, Roosevelt decided to intervene in Democratic primaries in 1938 in an effort to block the renomination of conservative Democrats in Congress. The "purge" was notably unsuccessful; senators on the purge list were triumphantly returned to office, and the President's only victory was in unseating Rep. John J. O'Connor (D N.Y.), chairman of the House Rules Committee. As a further embarrassment, Republicans gained eight seats in the November election.

Growing Opposition to Roosevelt

With the onset of World War II, opposition to Roosevelt was muted. Wartime supplies were freely voted, and in the Senate the Special Committee to Investigate the National Defense Program, set up in 1941 under the chairmanship of Harry S Truman (D Mo.), earned the President's gratitude for serving as a "friendly watchdog" over defense spending without embarrassing the administration. However, as the war went on, it became apparent that opposition to the President on domestic issues was rising.

The antagonism between Roosevelt and Congress came to the surface in February 1944, when the President against the advice of party leaders vetoed a revenue bill, the first veto of such a measure by any President. The action was denounced by Barkley on the floor of the Senate, Feb. 23, as "a calculated and deliberate assault upon the legislative integrity of every member of Congress." Barkley said: "Other members of Congress may do as they please, but as for me I do not propose to take this unjustifiable assault lying down.... I dare say that, during the last seven years of tenure of majority leader, I have carried the flag over rougher territory than ever traversed by any previous majority leader. Sometimes I have carried it with little help from the other end of Pennsylvania Avenue."[71] The following day Barkley's resignation as floor leader was accepted, but he was at once re-elected by unanimous vote of the Democratic Caucus.

Roosevelt's problems with Congress increased after his election to a fourth term in 1944. His proposals for postwar economic and social legislation were ignored, and his nomination of Henry A. Wallace as Secretary of Commerce was confirmed only after the Reconstruction Finance Corporation had been removed from Commerce Department control. By the time of his death in April 1945, Congress was in open revolt.

When Truman succeeded Roosevelt, many observers predicted a renewal of the happy relationship between Congress and the Executive that had prevailed in the McKinley administration. Like McKinley, Truman was a former member of Congress who enjoyed the goodwill of his colleagues, but his honeymoon with Congress did not last long. Although he was markedly successful in pushing his foreign policy programs, the old conservative coalition stood ready to oppose him on domestic issues. With the election of a Republican House and Senate in 1946, the Democrats' 14-year leadership of Congress came to an end.

Reorganization Act of 1946

Even before World War II ended, the tremendous expansion of the size and the authority of the government, especially the executive branch, led to a debate on reform of Congress. Proposals ranged from granting the President constitutional power to dissolve Congress to limiting selection of page boys to residents of the District of Columbia.

But two themes dominated the debate—the relationship between the organization of Congress and its increased workload, and the relations between Congress and the executive branch.

The feeling of many members of Congress was expressed by Rep. Jerry Voorhis (D Calif.) when he urged approval of a concurrent resolution to set up the Joint Committee on the Organization of Congress. Voorhis on Jan. 18, 1945, said, "[I]n the midst of this war we have to grant executive power...of the most sweeping nature." But he wanted the groundwork laid "in order that this Congress may perform its functions efficiently, effectively, and in accord with the needs of the people of this nation and so that it will become not merely an agency that says yes or no to executive proposals, but an agency capable of, and actually performing the function of bringing forth its own constructive program for the needs of the people of this nation. Thus it will take its place and keep its place as an altogether coequal branch of our government."[72]

In February 1945, Congress set up a Joint Committee on the Organization of Congress, with Sen. Robert M. La Follette Jr. (Prog. Wis.) as chairman, and Rep. A. S. Mike Monroney (D Okla.) as vice chairman. After extensive hearings the committee submitted a detailed report that formed the basis of the Legislative Reorganization Act of 1946 (PL 79-601). Passed with bipartisan support in both houses, the most important provisions of the act concerned congressional salaries, the number of standing committees, committee staffs and the legislative budget.

Filibusters and Civil Rights

Obstruction continued to plague the Senate throughout the New Deal era, but no significant new curbs on the filibuster were imposed. The Senate took no cloture votes in the 73rd and 74th Congresses, but in the years 1938-46 it took eight such votes—four in 1946 alone. None of the eight votes came within striking distance of the required two-thirds majority.

The most notorious filibusterer of the early New Deal period was Huey P. Long (D La.), who was at odds with the Roosevelt administration over patronage in Louisiana and other matters. Long staged his most famous filibuster in 1935, during debate on a proposed extension of the National Industrial Recovery Act. The "Kingfish" spoke for 15½ hours, a record for the time, filling 85 pages of the *Congressional Record* with remarks that ranged from commentaries on the Constitution to recipes for southern "potlikker," turnip greens and corn bread. His avowed intent was "to save to the sovereign states their rights and prerogatives" and "to preserve the right and prerogative of the Senate as to the qualifications of important officers."[73] Long conducted his last filibuster, against a deficiency appropriation bill, less than two weeks before his assassination in the summer of 1935.

As time went by, the filibuster increasingly came to be associated with civil rights legislation. Southern senators might lack the votes to defeat civil rights measures outright, but they found they could accomplish the same objective through obstruction. Proponents of civil rights legislation could not muster the requisite two-thirds majority to invoke cloture on a southern filibuster even if they had the simple majority needed for action on substantive issues. Accordingly, the southerners used the filibuster to keep civil rights bills from coming to a vote.

Most of the great filibusters of the period involved civil rights. Anti-lynching bills were filibustered in 1935 and 1938, and anti-poll-tax measures were filibustered in 1942, 1944 and 1946. Fair employment practices legislation was filibustered in 1946.

It was hard to keep senators in the chamber during these exhibitions. At one point during the 1942 debate when a quorum could not be mustered and the business of the Senate halted, the sergeant at arms was directed to "request the attendance" of absent senators, and at length 44 senators—five short of a quorum—appeared. He was then directed to "compel the attendance" of absent members. After some delay, he reported that 43 senators were out of town and eight others were in Washington but could not be located. The exasperated Senate finally ordered him to "execute warrants of arrest" upon absent senators. He was saved from this embarrassing duty by the timely appearance of five senators to complete the quorum. (The sergeant at arms had not always been so fortunate; during debate on the Lower Colorado River project in 1927, several infuriated senators actually were brought into the chamber under arrest.)

Rule 22 proved totally ineffectual against these sustained and organized southern filibusters. Six of the eight unsuccessful cloture votes in the years 1938-46 dealt with civil rights issues; on four of the six votes, cloture did not win even a simply majority.

Two minor curbs on obstruction were imposed during the period. The first dealt with the quorum call, a favorite obstructionist tool. During a 1935 filibuster by Long, the chair ruled that a quorum call constitutes business and that senators who yield for a quorum call lose the floor. Under this ruling a senator who yields twice for a quorum call while the same question is before the Senate may be denied the right to speak again on that question during the same legislative day. The second curb, contained in the Reorganization Acts of 1939 and 1945, limited debate on presidential reorganization plans.

The Legislative Reorganization Act of 1946 contained no provisions on debate limitation, since that subject was outside the purview of the Joint Committee on the Organization of Congress, but by 1946 many senators were convinced that further debate curbs were needed if the Senate was to meet its postwar responsibilities.

Chapter 24

Postwar Developments: 1945-1969

The election of a Republican Congress in 1946 marked the beginning of a period of divided government in which the White House and Congress were often in the hands of opposing political parties. From 1947 through 1976, Congress was controlled for 16 of the 30 years by the party in opposition to the President.

Democratic President Harry S Truman (1945-53) faced a Republican House and Senate in the 80th Congress (1947-49). His successor, Republican Dwight D. Eisenhower (1953-61) had a Republican Congress only in his first two years in office (1953-55). The Democrats controlled Congress throughout the terms of Democratic Presidents John F. Kennedy (1961-63) and Lyndon B. Johnson (1963-69), but when Republican Richard M. Nixon was elected in 1968, he became the first President since Zachary Taylor to fail to win control of at least one house of the new Congress in his initial election. The House and Senate remained in Democratic hands for the duration of the Nixon presidency and the term completed by Gerald R. Ford after Nixon resigned.

In only two Congresses did Republicans organize the Senate. In the 80th Congress (1947-49) they enjoyed a 51-45 margin, but in the 83rd (1953-55) their margin was so narrow that the death of Majority Leader Robert A. Taft (R Ohio) gave temporary numerical superiority to the

Democrats. In the 82nd, 84th and 85th Congresses, the Democratic margin of control was also razor-thin, but after the Democratic sweep in the 1958 elections the Democrats had comfortable majorities.

Need of Presidents for Bipartisan Support

Throughout the postwar period the parties themselves were often badly split, and both Republican and Democratic Presidents were forced to seek bipartisan support to get their programs enacted. Although Truman and the Republicans were often at loggerheads on domestic issues, Sen. Arthur H. Vandenberg (R Mich.) led his once-isolationist party colleagues into a new bipartisan foreign policy in cooperation with the Democratic administration. President Eisenhower often received more support from Democrats than he did from members of his own party, particularly on foreign policy questions in the early years of his administration, but partisanship increased as the 1960 elections approached, and many domestic bills were not enacted.

President Kennedy's relations with Congress were far from ideal, although the Senate was generally more responsive to his proposals than the House, but much of Kennedy's program was enacted after Johnson succeeded him in November 1963. Early in his administration, Johnson won spectacular legislative victories, but with the escalation of the war in Vietnam and the rise of disorder at home he lost his influence over Congress and was forced into retirement in 1968. During the Nixon administration, as well as the term completed by Ford, Congress and the White House were repeatedly in conflict.

Congress and the Public

Throughout the postwar period, the Senate—like Congress as a whole—was preoccupied with the problem of preserving for itself a viable role in the governmental process. The rapid expansion of the power of the executive branch in the 20th century had seriously weakened legislative authority, but at the same time the volume and complexity of legislative business continued to mount. Meanwhile, Congress as an institution suffered increasing public disfavor.

241

In an effort to reassert its eroded prerogatives and improve its legislative machinery, Congress in 1946 and 1970 enacted major legislative reorganization bills. In an effort to improve its public image, both chambers in 1968 adopted codes of ethics and rules requiring limited financial disclosure. But sensitive internal matters, such as the seniority system and limitation of Senate debate, remained vexing problems.

Party Leadership

Senate leadership in both parties was fairly stable during the years following World War II.

Barkley. On the Democratic side, Alben W. Barkley (Ky.) retained the floor leadership until his resignation in 1949 to become Vice President. The Democrats then had two majority leaders in as many Congresses—Scott W. Lucas (Ill.) in the 81st and Ernest W. McFarland (Ariz.) in the 82nd, both of whom lost their Senate seats after two years in the leadership post.

Johnson. When the 83rd Congress met in January 1953, with the Republicans in control, the Democrats chose as their minority leader Lyndon B. Johnson (Texas), a former House member who had served only four years in the Senate. Johnson was close to House Speaker Sam Rayburn (D Texas) and had the backing of powerful Senate conservatives, notably Robert S. Kerr (D Okla.) and Richard B. Russell (D Ga.), but he promptly built bridges to the liberal Democratic faction in the Senate in an effort to heal the deep liberal-conservative split within the party. Johnson soon became one of the most powerful leaders in Senate history, serving as minority leader in 1953-54 and as majority leader from 1955 until his resignation to become Vice President in 1961.

As a leader, Johnson was celebrated for his powers of persuasion and his manipulative skills. He revitalized the Democratic Policy Committee, saw to it that liberals won seats both on it and on the Steering Committee (committee on committees) and modified the seniority system to assure freshman senators at least one major committee assignment (a practice later adopted by the Republicans as well). On the floor, efficiency was promoted through the use of such devices as unanimous consent agreements, aborted quorum calls and night sessions. Through an active intelligence operation headed by Robert G. (Bobby) Baker, secretary to the senate majority, Johnson kept himself informed about what the Senate was really thinking, and he was adept at rounding up votes for acceptable compromises. A system of rewards and punishments supplemented the famous Johnson "treatment." An apostle of "moderation" and "consensus government," Johnson supported the Eisenhower administration on many major questions and frequently solicited Republican support in the Senate. Such was his skill that in 1957 he was able to bring about passage of the first civil rights bill since Reconstruction without a filibuster and without splitting the Democratic Party.

Mansfield. Johnson's successor as majority leader was Mike Mansfield (D Mont.). Mansfield had served as party whip under Johnson, but his permissive style of leadership was in sharp contrast to the Johnson methods. Mansfield held the respect of his colleagues, but he was not an aggressive leader, and under him the Johnson system gave way to a collegial leadership pattern in which the Policy Committee and the legislative committees played important roles.

Republican Leaders

On the Republican side, party authority was less concentrated than under the Democrats. Robert A. Taft Sr. (Ohio) had been the de facto Republican power in the Senate since the early 1940s and chairman of the Policy Committee from the time it was created in 1947, but he did not feel it necessary to assume the floor leadership of his party until the Eisenhower administration took office in 1953.

After Taft's death in July 1953, the floor leadership went to William F. Knowland (Calif.), a conservative who frequently split with the Eisenhower administration on major issues, but H. Styles Bridges (N.H.) often spoke for the Republicans as chairman of the Policy Committee. Knowland was succeeded as minority leader in 1959 by Everett McKinley Dirksen (Ill.), one of the most colorful party leaders in recent history. His style, noted one observer, was "one of remaining vague on an issue, or taking an initial position from which he could negotiate: bargaining with the majority party, the President and his own colleagues, and eventually accepting a compromise."[74] When Dirksen died in 1969, he was succeeded as minority leader by Hugh Scott (Pa.), a liberal Republican who sometimes found it difficult to serve as spokesman for the Nixon and Ford administrations in the Senate.

Use of Cloture to Pass Civil Rights Acts

As filibusters continued to block civil rights legislation in the years following World War II, liberal senators made persistent efforts to revise the Senate cloture rule to make it easier to cut off debate. Amendments to Rule 22 in 1949 and 1959 did not bring an end to obstruction in the Senate, and during the 1960s cloture votes were taken with increasing frequency.

Four such votes were successful. In 1962 the Senate voted 63-27 for a Mansfield-Dirksen motion to invoke cloture on a liberal filibuster against the administration's communications satellite bill. This was the first successful cloture vote since 1927 and only the fifth since the adoption of Rule 22 in 1917. In 1964, the Senate for the first time in its history invoked cloture, by a 71-29 vote, on a southern filibuster against civil rights legislation. This action was followed by successful cloture votes on two other civil rights measures—the voting rights bill of 1965 and, on the fourth try, the open housing bill of 1968.

The discovery that it was possible to impose cloture on civil rights bills under the existing rule took some of the steam out of liberal efforts to reform Rule 22. But in the closing days of the 91st Congress in 1970, the Senate became embroiled in a confusion of filibusters on a variety of major questions. Although this spectacle led to soul-searching within the Senate and to calls from President Nixon for procedural reform, when the 92nd Congress met a few weeks later the Senate once again declined to strengthen its curbs on the filibuster.

Revision of Cloture Rule in 1949

In its original form, Rule 22 required the votes of two-thirds of the Senators present and voting to invoke cloture. Over the years, however, a series of rulings and precedents rendered Rule 22 virtually inoperative by holding that it could not be applied to debate on procedural questions. By

1948 such were the precedents that President Pro Tempore Arthur H. Vandenberg (R Mich.) ruled, during a filibuster against an attempt to bring up an anti-poll-tax bill, that cloture could not be used on a motion to proceed to consideration of a bill. In making his ruling, Vandenberg conceded that "in the final analysis, the Senate has no effective cloture rule at all."[75]

In 1949, the Truman administration, desiring to clear the way for a broad civil rights program, backed a change in the cloture rule. After a long and bitter floor fight, the Senate adopted a proposal, backed by conservative Republicans and southern Democrats, that was actually more restrictive than the rule it replaced. The new rule required the votes of two-thirds of the entire Senate membership (instead of two-thirds of those present and voting) to invoke cloture, but allowed cloture to operate on any pending business or motion with the exception of debate on motions to change the Senate rules themselves (on which cloture previously had operated).

Because under this rule cloture could not be used to cut off a filibuster against a change in the rules, and because any attempt to change Rule 22 while operating under this rule appeared hopeless, Senate liberals devised a new approach. Senate rules had always continued from one Congress to the next in accordance with the theory that the Senate was a continuing body, but the liberals now challenged this conception, arguing that the Senate had a right to adopt new rules by general parliamentary procedure—majority vote—at the beginning of a new Congress.

Accordingly, in 1953 and 1957, at the opening of the 83rd and 85th Congresses, respectively, Sen. Clinton P. Anderson (D N.M.) moved that the Senate consider the adoption of new rules. On both occasions his motion was tabled, but during the 1957 debate Vice President Richard M. Nixon offered a significant "advisory opinion" on how the Senate could proceed to change its rules. Citing the section of the Constitution which provides that "each house may determine the rules of its proceedings," Nixon said he believed the Senate could adopt new rules "under whatever procedures the majority of the Senate approves."[76]

Although each incoming Senate had traditionally operated under existing rules, Nixon said that in his opinion the Senate could not be bound by any previous rule "which denies the membership of the Senate the power to exercise its constitutional right to make its own rules."[77] In this light he said he regarded as unconstitutional the section of Rule 22 banning any limitation of debate on proposals to change the rules. The Vice President explained that he was stating his personal opinion and that the question of constitutionality of the rule could be decided only by the Senate itself. The Senate did not take a vote on the question.

Change in Cloture in 1959

A modest revision of Rule 22 was accomplished in 1959. Senate liberals hoped to make it possible to invoke cloture by a simple majority or by a three-fifths vote, but they were defeated in their efforts to bring about such a substantial change. Instead, a bipartisan leadership group engineered a slight revision of the rule which the southern bloc opposed but did not really fight. The changes were basically designed and put through by Johnson, who seized the initiative from the liberals, and were adopted on a 72-22 roll call.

The 1959 revision permitted cloture to be invoked by two-thirds of those present and voting (rather than two-thirds of the full membership as the 1949 rule had required) and also applied the cloture rule to debate on motions to change the Senate rules. At the same time the Senate added a new provision to Rule 32, the rule concerning the continuation of Senate business from the first session of a Congress to the second session. The new language stated: "The rules of the Senate shall continue from one Congress to the next unless they are changes as provided in these rules."[78] This language buttressed the position of those who maintained that the Senate was a continuing body, but liberal opponents of the filibuster never conceded the point.

Later Efforts at Revision

In 1969, liberal strategy focused on obtaining a ruling from Vice President Hubert H. Humphrey, who was about to retire as presiding officer of the Senate, that a simple majority could invoke cloture on rules debates at the start of a new Congress. After a cloture motion was filed on a liberal proposal to reduce the requirement for cloture from two-thirds to three-fifths of those present and voting, Humphrey announced, in answer to a parliamentary inquiry, that if a majority, but less than two-thirds, of those present and voting voted for cloture he would rule that the majority prevailed. He said that such a ruling, because it could be appealed by the Senate, would enable the Senate to decide the constitutional issue by a simple majority vote, without debate. Humphrey added that if he held that the cloture motion had failed because of the lack of a two-thirds vote, he would be inhibiting the Senate from deciding the constitutional question.

In explaining the ruling he proposed to make, Humphrey said: "On a par with the right of the Senate to determine its rules, though perhaps not set forth so specifically in the Constitution, is the right of the Senate, a simple majority of the Senate, to decide constitutional questions."[79]

When the cloture motion came to a vote Jan. 16, 1969, a slim majority (51-47) voted for cloture, and Humphrey ruled that debate would proceed under the limitations of Rule 22. Opponents of the rules change immediately appealed his decision, and Humphrey's ruling was reversed, 45-53. The vote on the appeal meant that cloture was not invoked and left the Senate to continue the debate on the motion to consider the rules change proposal. Proponents of the change did not have enough support to limit debate under the two-thirds rule, and so ended another round in the rules reform fight.

The real breakthrough for senators seeking changes in the filibuster rule came in 1975.

Other Rules Changes

Two minor changes in Senate rules were adopted in 1964. The first amended Rule 8 to provide for a three-hour period after the morning hour when debate on a pending measure, or amendments to that measure, must be germane. The period could be waived by unanimous consent or motion without debate. The intent of the proposal was to speed passage of pending bills by preventing speeches on irrelevant matters until late in each day's session, and it was adopted over proposals for more stringent germaneness rules. Senators immediately found one loophole: a nongermane amendment could be offered (and later withdrawn), and debate on that amendment would be in order. The rule was seldom applied in practice.

In the second change, the Senate amended Rule 25 to permit Senate standing committees to meet until completion of the morning hour—a period of up to two hours at the beginning of each legislative day when routine business is conducted. Previously unanimous consent had been required for committees to meet at any time when the Senate was in session.

Integrity of the Senate

To much of the American public the Senate did not present a favorable image in the years following World War II. Not only did it often seem unable, by virtue of its antiquated procedures, to do the work the public expected it to do, but the integrity of its personnel was frequently under attack. The Senate is not a body to be stampeded by public opinion, and it approached this problem in its own way.

McCarthy. From 1950 until 1954, Sen. Joseph R. McCarthy (R Wis.) was by all odds the most controversial member of the Senate. McCarthy's career as a Communist-hunter began with a speech in Wheeling, W.Va., in February 1950 in which he charged that 205 Communists were working in the State Department with the knowledge of the Secretary of State. From that time until his formal censure by the Senate in 1954, McCarthy and his freewheeling accusations of Communist sympathies among high and low-placed government officials absorbed much of the public's attention. The phenomenon of "McCarthyism" had a major impact on the psychological climate of the early 1950s. Taking over the chairmanship of the Senate Government Operations Committee in 1953, McCarthy investigated the State Department, the Voice of America, the Department of the Army and other agencies. An opinion-stifling climate of fear was said to be one of the results of his probes.

For several years McCarthy's colleagues showed no disposition to tangle with him, but the Army-McCarthy hearings, televised in the spring of 1954, led finally to his censure by the Senate in a special session following the mid-term election of 1954. In the end McCarthy was censured, by a vote of 67-22, not for his "habitual contempt of people" as Sen. Ralph E. Flanders (R Vt.) had originally proposed, but for contemptuous treatment of the Senate itself—for his failure to cooperate with the Subcommittee on Privileges and Elections in 1952 and for his abuse of the select committee that had considered the censure charges against him. The censure resolution asserted that McCarthy had "acted contrary to senatorial ethics and tended to bring the Senate into dishonor and disrepute, to obstruct the constitutional processes of the Senate, and to impair its dignity. And such conduct is hereby condemned."[80]

McCarthy remained in the Senate until his death in 1957, but he lost his committee and subcommittee chairmanships in the next, Democratic-controlled Congress, and his activities no longer attracted much attention in the Senate, the press or elsewhere.

Meanwhile, alleged excesses in treatment of witnesses by congressional committees led in 1954 to an extensive search for a "fair-play" code to govern congressional investigations. Most criticism was directed at the Senate Permanent Investigations Subcommittee, headed by McCarthy, and at the House Un-American Activities Committee. In 1955, the House amended its rules to provide a minimum standard of conduct for House committees. The Senate adopted no general rules on the subject, but the Permanent Investigations Subcommittee under the chairmanship of John L. McClellan (D Ark.) adopted new safeguards for the protection of witnesses.

Bobby Baker. In 1963, the Senate was shaken by charges that Robert G. (Bobby) Baker had used his position as secretary to the Senate majority to promote outside business interests. Baker, who served as secretary from 1955 until his resignation under fire in August 1963, was no ordinary Senate functionary. Exposure of his numerous "improprieties" led to criticism of the Senate as a whole and prompted a review of congressional ethics.

A protégé of Lyndon B. Johnson, to whom the case was particularly embarrassing, Baker had access to leadership councils and was known as the Senate's "most powerful employee." He headed Johnson's intelligence network in the Senate and was celebrated for his ability to forecast the outcome of close votes. Johnson once hailed "his tremendous fund of knowledge about the Senate, which is almost appalling in one so young."[81]

In the wake of disclosures about Baker's wide-ranging business ventures, the Senate instructed its Rules and Administration Committee to investigate his activities from the standpoint of congressional ethics. The committee's Democratic majority, in reports issued in 1964 and 1965, accused Baker of "many gross improprieties" but cited no actual violations of law. Committee Republicans charged that the investigation was incomplete and a "whitewash." Both Republicans and Democrats called for rules requiring financial-disclosure statements by members of Congress and their employees.

Baker ultimately was convicted in court and imprisoned for income tax evasion, theft and conspiracy to defraud the government. Meanwhile, largely because of embarrassments caused by the Baker scandal, the Senate in 1964 created a Select Committee on Standards and Conduct to investigate allegations of improper conduct by senators and Senate employees, to recommend disciplinary action and to draw up a code of ethical conduct. The House established a similar committee in 1967.

Dodd. The Select Committee's first investigation began in 1966. It involved charges by syndicated columnists Drew Pearson and Jack Anderson that Sen. Thomas J. Dodd (D Conn.) had misused political campaign funds contributed to him and had committed other offenses. The Committee in April 1967 recommended that the Senate censure Dodd for misuse of political funds and for double-billing for official and private travel. The Senate on June 23 censured Dodd on the first charge by a 92-5 roll-call vote but refused, on a 51-45 vote, to censure him on the second charge. The action marked the seventh time in its history that the Senate had censured one of its members. After the vote was taken, the issue was closed, and Dodd continued to serve in the Senate until he was defeated for re-election in 1970.

Adoption of Ethics Codes

Concern over conflicts of interest at all levels of government had been rising since World War II, but Congress showed no inclination to adopt self-policing measures.

Pressures generated by the Baker and Dodd cases in the Senate and by investigation of the activities of Rep. Adam C. Powell (D N.Y.) in the House were largely responsible for the adoption of limited financial-disclosure rules in both chambers in 1968.

In the Senate, a code of conduct proposed by the Select Committee on Standards and Conduct was adopted without substantial change on March 22, 1968, by a 67-1 vote. Included were provisions to regulate the outside employment of Senate employees, to require a full accounting of campaign contributions and limit the uses to which they could be put, and to require senators and top employees to file detailed financial reports each year. However, these reports were to be available only to the Select Committee, and the only public accounting required was of gifts of $50 or more and honoraria of $300 or more. The Senate rejected, 40-44, a proposal for full public disclosure of members' finances. The proposal had been pressed by Sen. Joseph S. Clark (D Pa.), who was a persistent advocate of congressional reform.

The code of conduct was embodied in four additions to the Senate Rules:

Rule 41. Stipulated that no officer or employee of the Senate might engage in any other employment or paid activity unless it was not inconsistent with his duties in the Senate. Directed employees to report their outside employment to specified supervisors, including senators, who were to take such action as they considered necessary to avoid a conflict of interest by the employee.

Rule 42. Directed that a senator or a declared candidate for the Senate might accept a contribution from a fund-raising event for his benefit only if he had given express approval before funds were raised and if he received a full accounting of the sources and amounts of each contribution. Official events of his party were exempted from these restrictions.

Permitted a senator or candidate to accept contributions from an individual or an organization provided that a complete accounting of the sources and amounts were made by the recipient.

Specified that a senator or candidate might use such contributions for the expenses of his nomination and election and for the following purposes: travel expenses to and from the senator's home state; printing and other expenses of sending speeches, newsletters and reports to his constituents; expenses of radio, television and other media reports to constituents; telephone, postage and stationery expenses not covered by Senate allowances; and subscriptions to home-state newspapers.

Required disclosure of gifts, from a single, non-family source, of $50 or more under the provisions of Rule 44.

Rule 43. Prohibited employees of the Senate from receiving, soliciting or distributing funds collected in connection with a campaign for the Senate or any other federal office. Exempted from the rule senators' assistants who were designated to engage in such activity and who earned more than $10,000 a year. Required that the senator file the names of such designated aides with the secretary of the Senate, as public information.

Rule 44. Required each senator, declared candidate and Senate employee earning more than $15,000 a year to file with the U.S. Comptroller General, by May 15 each year, a sealed envelope containing the following reports:

● A copy of his U.S. income tax returns and declarations, including joint statements.

● The amount and source of each fee of $1,000 or more received from a client.

● The name and address of each corporation, business or professional enterprise in which he was an officer, director, manager, partner or employee, and the amount of compensation received.

● The identity of real or personal property worth $10,000 or more that he owned.

● The identity of each trust or fiduciary relation in which he held a beneficial interest worth $10,000 or more and the identity, if known, of any interest the trust held in real or personal property over $10,000.

● The identity of each liability of $5,000 or more owed by him or his spouse jointly.

● The source and value of all gifts worth $50 or more received from a single source.

Specified that the information filed with the Comptroller General would be kept confidential for seven years and then returned to the filer or his legal representative. If the filer died or left the Senate, his reports would be returned within a year.

Provided that the Select Committee on Standards and Conduct might, by a majority vote, examine the contents of a confidential filing and make the file available for investigation to the committee staff. Required that due notice be given to an individual under investigation and an opportunity provided for him to be heard by the committee in closed session.

Required each senator, candidate and employee earning more than $15,000 a year to file with the secretary of the Senate by May 15 each year the following information, which was to be kept for three years and made available for public inspection:

● The accounting required under Rule 42 of all contributions received in the previous year (amounts under $50 might be totaled and not itemized).

● The amount, value and source of any honorarium of $300 or more.

Senate-Executive Contests for Power

One of the principal purposes of the Legislative Reorganization Act of 1946 was to help Congress hold its own against the rapidly expanding power of the executive branch. In this it was only partly successful. By the end of World War II it seemed clear that legislative initiative had shifted, apparently irretrievably, from Congress to the President, and during the postwar era Congress was for the most part concerned with preserving its powers to approve, revise or reject presidential programs.

In these years the Senate's sense of itself was frequently offended by what it viewed as presidential encroachments on its constitutional functions. In 1954 the Senate came within one vote of approving a proposed constitutional amendment—the so-called Bricker Amendment—to restrict the President's power to negotiate treaties and other international agreements. Other conflicts arose over the spending power, the war power and to a lesser extent, the appointment power. Frequently the Senate was in contention with the House as well as the executive branch.

Disputes Over Spending Power

In the 1946 act Congress tried to assert new and meaningful control over the budget process through the creation of a legislative budget. After three unsuccessful attempts to use this device, it was abandoned as an unqualified failure.

In 1947, the Joint Committee on the Legislative Budget, composed of members of the House Ways and Means and Appropriations Committees and the Senate Finance and Appropriations Committees, agreed to ceilings on appropriations and expenditures that were substantially lower than the amounts projected in President Truman's budget. The House approved the ceilings, but the Senate increased them and insisted that an expected budget surplus be applied to debt retirement rather than to reduction of taxes as House leaders proposed. As a result, the budget resolution died in conference.

In 1948, both houses adopted the same legislative budget, but Congress appropriated $6 billion more than the agreed-upon ceiling. In 1949, the process broke down entirely when the deadline for a budget was moved from Feb. 15 to May 1. By that date 11 appropriation bills had passed the House and nine had passed the Senate; the legislative budget was never produced.

Failure of the legislative budget prompted a serious effort in Congress in 1950 to combine the numerous separate appropriation bills into one omnibus measure. The omnibus measure was approved by Congress about two months earlier than the last of the separate measures in 1949. In addition, the appropriations total was about $2.3 billion less than the President's combined budget requests. Chairman Clarence Cannon (D Mo.) of the House Appropriations Committee hailed the omnibus approach as "the most practical and efficient method of handling the annual budget."[82] In spite of his support the House Appropriations Committee in 1951 voted 31-18 to return to the traditional method of separate handling of appropriation bills; the omnibus approach had undercut the authority of subcommittees and their chairmen. Following the vote, Cannon charged that "every predatory lobbyist, every pressure group seeking to get its hands into the U.S. Treasury, every bureaucrat seeking to extend his empire downtown is opposed to the consolidated bill."[83]

The Senate in 1953 voted to make another attempt at an omnibus bill and to place limitations on various forms of spending, but the proposal was not acted on in the House.

Another Senate proposal, for the creation of a Joint Budget Committee to provide Congress with meaningful fiscal information, was approved by the Senate eight times between 1952 and 1967 but was never accepted by the House.

As years went by, Congress discovered that the "power of the purse," long considered one of its principal sources of power over the executive branch, was not the bulwark of legislative authority it had thought. Congress generally managed to authorize less spending than was proposed by postwar Presidents, but it proved unable to consider the budget as a whole and it lacked effective control over actual expenditures. This point was underscored by repeated conflicts with the White House over "backdoor spending" and the impounding by executive agencies of funds appropriated by Congress. Congressional frustration found expression in the frequent enactment of spending ceilings not to be exceeded by the executive branch.

Meanwhile, long-standing disagreement between the Senate and House over their respective roles in the appropriations process caused a rift between the two chambers. In 1962 this issue produced a Senate-House feud that delayed final action on appropriation bills and kept Congress in turmoil through much of the session. The feud started as a spat over the physical location of conference committee meetings and quickly moved on to the larger issues of whether the Senate could (1) initiate its own appropriation bills and (2) add to House-passed appropriation bills funds for items either not previously considered by the House or considered and rejected.

When the Senate passed a continuing resolution to provide temporary financing for federal agencies pending final congressional action on their regular appropriations, the House called the action an infringement on its "immemorial" right to initiate appropriation bills. In retaliation, the Senate adopted a resolution stating that "the acquiescence of the Senate in permitting the House to first consider appropriation bills cannot change the clear language of the Constitution nor affect the Senate's coequal power to originate any bill not expressly 'raising revenue.' "[84] Although the two chambers eventually reached a truce, the basic issues were not resolved. It was not until a decade later that the House and Senate agreed on a new congressional budget control system.

Exercise of the War Power

Events of the post-World-War-II era frequently reminded Congress that its constitutional power to declare war counted for little in the modern world. But in the late 1960s the Senate began to mount a substantial challenge to the President's authority over military involvement.

Truman. Congress did not seriously challenge President Truman's war powers until 1951. At issue then was the President's authority to dispatch troops to Korea and to Western Europe. Sen. Robert A. Taft Sr. (R Ohio) opened a three-month-long debate on Jan. 5, 1951, by asserting that Truman had "no authority whatever to commit American troops to Korea without consulting Congress and without Congressional approval." Moreover, he said, the President had "no power to agree to send American troops to fight in Europe in a war between members of the Atlantic Pact and Soviet Russia."[85]

The debate revolved principally around the troops-to-Europe issue. It came to an end April 4, when the Senate adopted two resolutions approving the dispatch of four divisions to Europe. One of the resolutions stated that it was the sense of the Senate that "no ground troops in addition to such four divisions should be sent to Western Europe...without further Congressional approval."[86] But neither resolution gained the force of law because the House took no action.

Truman never asked Congress for a declaration of war in Korea, and he waited until Dec. 16, 1950—six months after the outbreak of hostilities—to proclaim the existence of a national emergency. In defense of this course, it was argued that the Russians or Chinese or both had violated post-World-War-II agreements on Korea and that emergency powers authorized during World War II could still be applied.

The Korean conflict provided two further tests of presidential powers. In 1951, the nation was split when Truman dismissed Gen. Douglas A. MacArthur from his command of United Nations and U.S. forces in the Far East because of a dispute over policy. The Senate Foreign Relations and Armed Services Committees reviewed the ouster, and their joint hearings were credited with cooling the atmosphere throughout the country. So bitter was the controversy that the committees refrained from making any formal report, but the President's right to remove MacArthur was conceded and the principle of civilian control over the military upheld. In 1952, Congress ignored Truman's request for approval of his seizure of the nation's steel mills, an action taken under his war powers, and the Supreme Court later ruled that the seizure was without statutory authority and constituted a usurpation of the powers of Congress.

Eisenhower. Presidents who followed Truman made frequent use of their war powers, sometimes in cooperation with Congress. For example, President Eisenhower asked Congress in 1955 for advance approval of the use of American armed force in the event of a Communist attack on Formosa or the Pescadores Islands. A resolution to that effect was adopted within a week. However, Eisenhower landed toops in Lebanon in July 1958 strictly on his own authority. In a special message to Congress, July 15, he said the action was designed to protect American lives and "to assist the Government of Lebanon in the preservation of Lebanon's territorial integrity and independence, which have been deemed vital to U.S. national interests and world peace."[87]

Kennedy. President Kennedy, responding to Soviet threats to Allied rights in West Berlin, asked Congress on July 16, 1961, for authority to call up ready reservists and to extend the enlistments of men already on active duty. Such authority was granted in a joint resolution signed by the President Aug. 1. Kennedy did not wait for congressional approval of his actions in the Cuban missile crisis of October 1962. Confronted with a buildup of Soviet missile bases in Cuba. he ordered an immediate "naval quarantine" of Cuba to prevent delivery of additional Russian missiles. More than any other crisis of the post-war period, the Cuban episode illustrated the vast sweep of presidential power in times of great emergency.[88]

Johnson. Congress virtually abdicated its power to declare war in Vietnam when it adopted, in August 1964, the Gulf of Tonkin resolution authorizing the President to "take all necessary measures" to stop aggression in Southeast Asia.[89] The resolution was requested by President Johnson and adopted by a vote of 88-2 in the Senate and 414-0 in the House. The President considered the resolution adequate authority for expanding U.S. involvement in the Vietnam War, but in following years, as public support for the war deteriorated, Congress was to have second thoughts about its 1964 action; the Tonkin Gulf resolution was repealed in January 1971.

Chapter 25

Liberal Advances: 1970-1976

While the House was initiating many procedural reforms in the first half of the 1970s, the Senate was making a parallel effort on its side of the Capitol.

Senate reforms were not as broad as those in the House mainly because the 100-member Senate was already a more open body than the 435-member House. The Senate—unlike the House—did not use a closed rule. This difference meant any senator could propose floor amendments. Similarly, the Senate did not have a system of unrecorded teller votes; thus each senator could be held more closely accountable for his actions. And the Senate had admitted television and radio coverage of Senate committees, sanctioned in the Legislative Reorganization Act of 1946, long before the House generally ended its broadcast bans on committee hearings through enactment of the Legislative Reorganization Act of 1970.

The principal obstacle to a more democratic Senate, in the view of reformers, was unlimited debate, the minority's use of the filibuster to obstruct the majority. After years of trying, the reformers succeeded in 1975 in reducing the number of votes needed to invoke cloture. The modification did not destroy the power of a minority from talking legislation to death; it merely modified that power by lowering the vote needed to end debate from two-thirds of those present and voting to three-fifths of the 100-member Senate.

In an attempt to place Congress on a par with the presidency in the control of foreign policy, certain senators focused their attention on the Vietnam war. One of the leaders was Chairman J. William Fulbright (D Ark.) of the Foreign Relations Committee. The committee held nationally televised hearings on the Vietman war in 1966. Secretary of State Dean Rusk testified on Jan. 28 that the United States had obligations to South Vietnam under the Southeast Asia Collective Defense Treaty (SEATO) of 1954 and the Gulf of Tonkin resolution of 1964. In addition, Rusk stated, "We have bilateral assistance agreements with South Vietnam."

On the Senate floor July 31, 1967, Fulbright called Rusk's statement of agreements beyond SEATO and the Tonkin resolution "casual reference to other acts." The senator added, "Thus, so far as I know, none of the bilateral assistance agreements referred to has ever been submitted to the Congress." He described them as informal executive agreements presumably signed by Rusk or the American ambassador in Saigon and a representative of South Vietnam. Fulbright maintained that Congress had abandoned its constitutional role to several Presidents bent upon acting in foreign affairs without consulting Congress. He said the Foreign Relations Committee by functioning "as a forum of free and wide-ranging discussion can serve valuable democratic purposes...."

But by 1973, Congress was able to muster its strength to win enactment of the historic Senate-inspired War Powers Act despite intensive White House lobbying against it and a presidential veto. Principal sponsors of the war powers movement, which sought to codify presidential war powers left vague by the Constitution, were Sens. Jacob K. Javits (R N.Y.), John C. Stennis (D Miss.) and Thomas F. Eagleton (D Mo.). And in 1975, Congress defeated President Ford's proposals for supplementary military aid funds to South Vietnam and Cambodia as they were collapsing before a communist military offensive; put restrictions on his request for similar funds to Turkey; and legislated against his proposals to provide military aid funds to anticommunist factions in Angola.[90]

The Senate also played an important role in reforming the federal campaign laws, instituting a congressional budgetary control system and exposing the crimes of

Watergate. Congress had long been faulted for ignoring its oversight function, unless embarked upon a publicity-laden probe. The Watergate investigation, however, rated as a high point of publicly-aired investigations. It was the Senate Watergate Committee which discovered the existence of the tape recordings that ultimately brought about President Nixon's resignation.

Party Leaders

Majority Leader Mike Mansfield (D Mont.) and Minority Leader Hugh Scott (R Pa.), leaders respectively since 1961 and 1971, remained in their positions through early 1976 after they had announced their retirements from Congress effective at the conclusion of the 94th Congress. Mansfield was called "the gentle persuader" because he held that each senator should conduct his affairs with minimal pressure from the leadership. Despite his reticence on the national stage, Mansfield was a strong defender of Senate prerogatives during the Johnson and Nixon administrations, and differed openly with Democrat Johnson on the Vietnam war. His 16-year tenure (1961-1976) as leader was the longest in Senate history.

Scott defended U.S. actions in Indochina long after much of his Pennsylvania constituency had turned against them. He promised that White House tapes would exonerate President Nixon and suffered embarrassment when the Watergate evidence indicated Nixon's guilt.[91]

Legislative Reorganization

The Legislative Reorganization Act of 1970 was designed to improve the floor and committee operations of Congress, by providing better means to evaluate the federal budget and by increasing congressional resources for research and information. Rules changes, applying to the Senate only and aiming at accountability, openness and efficiency, focused primarily on the operations of committees.

Changes affecting committee operations included allowing a committee majority to call a meeting when the chairman does not do so on request, requiring committees to adopt and publish rules of procedure, and guaranteeing that a majority of minority members of a committee be allowed to call witnesses during hearings.

Rules governing committee assignments and seniority were changed so that senators could be members of only two major committees and one minor, select or joint committee; so that no senator could serve on more than one of the Armed Services, Appropriations, Finance or Foreign Relations Committees; and so that no senator could hold the chairmanship of more than one full committee and one subcommittee of a major committee.

In a move to give senators more information on committee actions, the new rules prohibited Senate consideration of any bill (exceptions included declarations of war and emergency) unless the committee report was available three days prior to floor action, and required conference committees to explain conference action.[92]

Filibuster Reform

Rule 22, which prescribed the way to terminate filibusters, was modified in 1975 after years of battle. The existing rule required two-thirds of senators present and voting to invoke cloture and bring a proposal to a vote. The 1975 change set the number of votes required at three-fifths of the full Senate, or 60 if there were no vacancies. Advocates believed the change would ease the task of ending filibusters.

The old rule had required a two-thirds vote of those senators present and voting to shut off debate. The change was accomplished after a three-week struggle in the Senate and after an almost ritualistic attempt by liberals at filibuster modification every two years since 1959, with the exception of 1973.

The 1975 reformers wanted a simple majority or a three-fifths majority of senators present and voting to cut off debate, but had to settle for the compromise that set the necessary figure at three-fifths of all 100 members, called "a constitutional majority." The new rule to invoke cloture would apply to any matter except a proposed change in the Standing Rules of the Senate, for which the old two-thirds rule to end a talkathon would still hold.

The limited nature of the filibuster change left it unclear as to how major a victory had been won. Another consideration in evaluating the change was the place of the filibuster as a tool to kill legislation in the mid-1970s.

In practical terms, the two-thirds majority rule general-ly meant that between 61 and 67 senators had to support cloture. This was because most issues that were controver-sial enough to draw a filibuster also were important enough to prompt many of the 100 senators to vote on a cloture motion.

For example, between 1960, when frequent use of the filibuster and cloture began, and 1975 there were 79 cloture votes. Only a handful of the 79 cloture votes—18—succeeded during this 15-year period under the two-thirds requirement.

The record of cloture votes left some doubt about whether the reform bloc had won all that it claimed from the 1975 change. Of the 79 cloture votes between 1960 and 1975, only 22—or 28 per cent—recorded at least 60 senators sup-porting an end to debate.

Moreover, the record showed that the three-fifths "con-stitutional" majority rule would have made almost no difference in the actual outcome of legislation on which filibusters and cloture votes occurred. During the entire history of the two-thirds cloture rule from 1917 to 1975, only one additional cloture vote would have been successful had the three-fifths rule been in effect. This is because 60 votes or more, but not a two-thirds majority, were obtained on several bills, but in each case cloture was reached on sub-sequent votes under the two-thirds rule.

However, reformers saw the new rule speeding up the Senate's work as well as enhancing the chance of success for senators seeking cloture. In addition, the importance of the filibuster appeared diminished in view of the fact that talkathons were basically a weapon of southern senators to block civil rights legislation in the 1960s and that by 1975 civil rights legislative issues—except for busing—were largely settled.

In April 1976, Senate liberals and conservatives joined forces to persuade the Senate to amend the cloture rule by allowing the introduction of amendments to pending legisla-tion up until the announcement of the outcome of a cloture vote.

Under the existing rule for ending a filibuster, no amendment could be considered after cloture was invoked, unless it had been formally read or considered read before the cloture vote was taken. In practice, the Senate routinely granted unanimous consent to consider read all amendments at the Senate desk at the time of the vote so that they could be eligible for consideration in compliance with Rule 22. The rules change had no effect on the three-fifths voting requirement for ending filibusters. But it could delay bringing an amendment or bill to a final vote after cloture had been invoked.[93]

Seniority System

In 1971, Sens. Fred R. Harris (D Okla.) and Charles McC. Mathias Jr. (R Md.) led an unsuccessful move to scrap the seniority system, a custom, in the selection of committee chairmen in favor of what they called "a standard of merit" in making the top choices. Their plan would have amended Rule 24 to require that committee chairmen and ranking minority members be nominated individually by a majority vote of the party caucuses and elected individually by majority vote of the full Senate at the beginning of each new Congress. The proposal failed when it was adversely reported by the Senate Rules and Administration Committee. (Rule 24 merely stated that the Senate "shall proceed by ballot to appoint severally the chairmen of each committee, and then, by one ballot, the other members necessary to complete the same.")

Democratic reformers were more successful in January 1975 when they revised party rules to establish a method by which committee chairmen would have to face an election every two years, but the vote was not mandatory as it was in the House. The Democratic caucus voted to require selection of chairmen by secret ballot whenever one-fifth of the caucus requested it. The modification did not affect chairmen in the 94th Congress.

The rule change was intended to make it easier for senators to depose a chairman without fear of retribution. Under the procedure, a list of senators nominated by the Democratic Steering Committee to be committee chairmen would be distributed to all Democrats. The Democrats would check off the names of the nominees they wished to subject to a secret ballot and would submit the list without signing it. If at least 20 per cent of the caucus members wanted a secret vote on a nominee it would be held automatically two days later.

Open Committees

Almost three years after the House in March 1973 voted to open up its committee bill-drafting sessions to the public and press, the Senate in November 1975 adopted a similar rule that would require most of its committees to work in public. At the same time, the Senate approved open conference committee sessions as the House had done in January, thereby opening up one of the last bastions of congressional committee secrecy. The new rules included these features:

● All meetings were to be public unless a majority of a committee voted in open session to close a meeting or series of meetings on the same subject for not to exceed 14 days.

● A meeting could be closed only for action on the following matters: 1) national security; 2) committee staff personnel or internal staff management or procedures; 3) criminal or other charges against a person that might harm him or her professionally or otherwise or represent an invasion of privacy; 4) disclosure of the identity of an informer or law enforcement agent or a criminal investigation that should be kept secret to assist the investigation; 5) disclosure of trade secrets or financial or commercial information required by law to be kept secret or obtained by the government on a confidential basis; 6) disclosure of "matters required to be kept confidential under other provisions of law or government regulation."

● A committee on the motion of one member and a second could go into secret session to discuss whether a meeting should be closed under these standards, but required the vote to close be taken in public session.

● Every committee was required to prepare a transcript or electronic record of each meeting, including conference committees, unless a majority of the committee voted to forgo it.

● A chairman was allowed to clear a committee meeting of spectators when there was disorder or a demonstration by the audience, and to continue the meeting in secret.

In another 1975 reform, junior senators obtained committee staff assistance to aid them on legislative issues. In the past, committee staff members were controlled by chairmen and other senior members. Few junior members had regular and dependable access to staff personnel.[04]

265

Budget Control

The Senate worked closely with the House on the Congressional Budget Act of 1974, setting the foundation for reasserting congressional control over government spending. If faithfully implemented when all of its provisions were to take effect for fiscal year 1977, beginning Oct. 1, 1976, the reform bill would force Congress into more measured and timely action on budgetary legislation, tying its separate spending decisions together with fiscal policy objectives in a congressionally determined budget package. *(For provisions of the budget act, see p. 162)*

Among other items, the budget measure moved back the beginning of the federal fiscal year from July 1 to Oct. 1 and mandated a series of deadlines imposing changes in Congress' appropriations schedule. This was to allow Congress time to complete the entire budget process before the fiscal year began. It had been decades since Congress enacted its appropriations by July 1. Also, the act contained provisions seeking to curb presidential impoundment of funds as a means of cutting government spending.[95]

Campaign Finance

Long criticized for doing little to control the use of money in federal election campaigns, Congress responded by passing the Federal Election Campaign Acts of 1971 and 1974.

Until passage of the 1971 act, the entire history of campaign finance laws was one of non-enforcement. No candidate for Congress was ever prosecuted under the 1925 Corrupt Practices Act, which the 1971 Act repealed.

The new law, actually enacted in 1972, strengthened the requirements for reporting to the public how much a candidate spent on his campaign and his sources of contributions and other income. Also, all candidates and political committees were required to report names and addresses of all persons who made contributions and loans in excess of $100 and to all persons to whom expenditures of $100 were made. Disclosure was viewed by many as the most useful feature of the 1971 Act since it enabled scholars, journalists and investigators to obtain a better picture of patterns of spending and to uncover formerly concealed contributions.

The 1971 Act placed spending limits on communications media campaign spending in an effort to curb the most rapidly escalating cost of political campaigns. Also, the law defined more strictly the roles unions and corporations could play in political campaigns, but was criticized by some reformers for permitting unions and corporations having government contracts to participate in the same political activities as those not doing business with the government.

The 1974 Act provided for public financing of presidential campaigns, including provisions for primary campaigns as well as general elections. Originally, the Senate version of the bill included public financing of congressional campaign costs, but the provision was dropped in conference committee where House members strongly opposed it. Senate reformers had held that public financing would remove the influence of big money in congressional elections as well as presidential races.

The 1974 Act established the first spending limits ever for candidates in presidential primary and general elections and in primary campaigns for the House and Senate. It also set up new expenditure ceilings for general election campaigns for Congress.[96]

CIA, FBI Probe

Legislative review or congressional oversight of federal agencies and legislation was another area in which Congress drew heavy criticism. Reformers regularly charged that Congress was reluctant to pursue that function unless there was beneficial publicity attached to an investigation or some other political advantage.

Until 1975, the Central Intelligence Agency and the Federal Bureau of Investigation were almost privileged from any congressional probing. After a series of hearings, the Senate Select Intelligence Committee, in several reports issued in the spring of 1976, aired abuses committed by the two agencies. One stated that since World War II Republican and Democratic administrations alike had yielded to the temptation to use the FBI for secret surveillance with alarming consistency. The report prompted FBI Director Clarence M. Kelley, in a May 1976 speech, to place the blame for FBI wrongdoing on his predecessor, J. Edgar Hoover.[97]

Watergate

The Senate launched its inquiry into Watergate Feb. 7, 1973, when it approved by a 77-0 vote a resolution creating a Select Committee on Presidential Campaign Activities (known as the Senate Watergate Committee), to investigate and study "the extent...to which illegal, improper, or unethical activities" occurred in the 1972 presidential campaign and election. The nationally-televised committee hearings were the major focus of Watergate developments during the summer of 1973.

Several former Committee to Re-Elect the President (which directed Nixon's 1972 campaign) witnesses and former White House aides appeared, some to admit perjury during earlier investigations. They drew a picture of political sabotage that went far beyond Watergate, motivated by extreme loyalty to Nixon and by a belief that any tactics against people who had supported anti-Vietnam war demonstrations were acceptable.

The hearings brought forth details of a special White House investigative unit known as the "plumbers" which had been responsible for acts such as harassment of Daniel Ellsberg, who had released the classified Pentagon Papers on the Vietnam war to the press. Among the other highlights was the four-day appearance of former White House counsel John Dean in June. Dean turned over about 50 documents to the Senate committee. Included were a memorandum written by Dean on "dealing with our political enemies" (White House lists named about 200 important "enemies") and a memorandum commenting on 20 persons, including members of Congress, lobbyists, reporters and motion picture personalities, who were to be given priority in that White House "dealing." Dean was the only witness to implicate the President directly in the Watergate cover-up.

The most important revelation of the committee hearings came as a result of closed-door questioning of Federal Aviation Administration chief Alexander P. Butterfield, a former White House aide. He testified publicly July 16 that the President's offices were equipped with a special voice-activated system which recorded all conversations. The existence of the tapes entirely changed the Watergate case, for the evidence existed to prove or disprove Dean's allegations.

President Nixon had fought to retain possession of the tapes while the federal trial courts, Congress and Nixon's own special prosecutors sought to obtain them as evidence. The Supreme Court ruled that Nixon on the grounds of executive privilege could not keep the recordings from the trial courts, and on Aug. 2, 1974, he surrendered three critical recordings to Judge Sirica. The recordings were made June 23, 1972, six days after the Watergate burglary, and proved Nixon's early participation in the Watergate coverup. Meanwhile, the House Judiciary Committee had voted three articles of impeachment against Nixon. He resigned Aug. 9, 1974.[98]

Foreign Policy

Concerted Senate efforts to reassert its voice in the conduct of foreign affairs and decisions to go to war dated back to the late 1960s, spurred by growing congressional and popular opposition to a widening Indochina conflict. Those efforts led to the first law ever passed by Congress defining and limiting presidential war powers. President Nixon suffered a major setback on Nov. 7, 1973, when both houses voted to override his veto. Congressional determination on having a foreign policy role perhaps was reflected in the fact that the War Powers Act of 1973 was the first successful veto override in the 93rd Congress. Previously, eight other vetoes had been sustained in 1973:—five in the House and three in the Senate.

Although the final version of the act was closer to the House-passed bill, the real victory belonged to the Senate. The conference agreement culminated several years of Senate attempts to place substantive limits on executive war powers.

As enacted into law, the act:

● Stated that the President could commit U.S. armed forces to hostilities or situations where hostilities might be imminent, only pursuant to a declaration of war, specific statutory authorization or a national emergency created by an attack upon the United States, its territories or possessions, or its armed forces.

● Urged the President "in every possible instance" to consult with Congress before committing U.S. forces to hostilities or to situations where hostilities might be im-

269

minent, and to consult Congress regularly after such a commitment.

● Required the President to report in writing within 48 hours to the Speaker of the House and president pro tempore of the Senate on any commitment or substantial enlargement of U.S. combat forces abroad, except for deployments related solely to supply, replacement, repair or training; required supplementary reports at least every six months while such forces were being engaged.

● Authorized the Speaker of the House and the president pro tempore of the Senate to reconvene Congress if it was not in session to consider the President's report.

● Required the termination of a troop commitment within 60 days after the President's initial report was submitted, unless Congress declared war, specifically authorized continuation of the commitment, or was physically unable to convene as a result of an armed attack upon the United States; allowed the 60-day period to be extended for up to 30 days if the President determined and certified to Congress that unavoidable military necessity respecting the safety of U.S. forces required their continued use in bringing about a prompt disengagement.

● Allowed Congress, at any time U.S. forces were engaged in hostilities without a declaration of war or specific congressional authorization, by concurrent resolution to direct the President to disengage such troops.

● Set up congressional priority procedures for consideration of any resolution or bill introduced pursuant to the provisions of the resolution.

In 1975, Congress demonstrated to President Ford that it was opposed to further military aid to Indochina. As communist forces were overrunning South Vietnam and Cambodia, the Senate Armed Services Committee, in a series of votes, refused to approve $722-million, in whole or in part, in extra aid that Ford wanted for South Vietnam.

Within weeks after total communist conquest of the Indochina peninsula, an incident in nearby waters marked usage of the War Powers Act. On May 12, Cambodian communist forces captured the American merchant ship Mayaguez and its crew of 39. President Ford ordered combined Navy, Air Force and Marine units to retake the ship and crew. Ford's action in using force was questioned in Congress, but there was general agreement that he had authority to commit U.S. troops without regard to the War Powers Act even though the President complied with the law by issuing a report to Congress May 15 on his actions.

During 1975, Congress consistently clashed with Ford, questioning and resisting further U.S. involvements in other trouble spots around the world. They took the following forms:

● A congressionally imposed ban on arms shipments to Turkey took effect in February despite White House efforts to persuade Congress to reverse it. After intensive and lengthy lobbying, it was only partially lifted in October.

● Secretary of State Henry A. Kissinger's inability to negotiate an interim peace accord between Israel and Egypt early in the year led to the Ford administration's "total reassessment" of its Middle East policy. Many on Capitol Hill viewed it as a thinly disguised attempt to pressure Israel into making concessions for a new settlement, and Congress in turn pressured the White House to continue its traditional support for Israel. One response was a letter to Ford signed by 76 senators urging sufficient financial support for Israel to enable the country to defend itself against any aggression. After Kissinger succeeded in formulating a pact acceptable to Israel and Egypt in August, Congress ultimately gave its approval to a controversial provision calling for the stationing of American technicians in the Sinai to monitor the truce. The acceptance came only after lengthy deliberations that revealed deep suspicion of Kissinger's role.

● As the session came to a close in December 1975, the Senate voted to block the channeling of U.S. funds to two of three factions engaged in a civil war in Angola despite the objections of Ford and Kissinger. The disclosures of the secret U.S. support had aroused fears in Congress of another Vietnam-type involvement and raised anew doubts about the success of the policy of detente with the Soviet Union, which was supporting the third faction. The Angola ban was written into the defense spending bill by the Senate. The House followed the Senate lead by accepting the Senate amendment Jan. 27, 1976.[99]

Constitution
of the United States

We the People of the United States, in Order to form a more perfect Union, establish Justice, insure domestic Tranquility, provide for the common defence, promote the general Welfare, and secure the Blessings of Liberty to ourselves and our Posterity, do ordain and establish this Constitution for the United States of America.

Article I

Section. 1. All legislative Powers herein granted shall be vested in a Congress of the United States, which shall consist of a Senate and House of Representatives.

Section. 2. The House of Representatives shall be composed of Members chosen every second Year by the People of the several States, and the Electors in each State shall have the Qualifications requisite for Electors of the most numerous Branch of the State Legislature.

No Person shall be a Representative who shall not have attained to the age of twenty five Years, and been seven Years a Citizen of the United States, and who shall not, when elected, be an Inhabitant of that State in which he shall be chosen.

Representatives and direct Taxes shall be apportioned among the several States which may be included within this Union, according to their respective Numbers, which shall be determined by adding to the whole Number of free Persons, including those bound to Service for a Term of Years, and excluding Indians not taxed, three fifths of all other Persons. The actual Enumeration shall be made within three Years after the first Meeting of the Congress of the United States, and within every subsequent Term of ten Years, in such Manner as they shall by Law direct. The Number of Representatives shall not exceed one for every thirty Thousand, but each State shall have at Least one Representative; and until such enumeration shall be made, the State of New Hampshire shall be entitled to chuse three, Massachusetts eight, Rhode-Island and Providence Plantations one, Connecticut five, New-York six, New Jersey four, Pennsylvania eight, Delaware one, Maryland six, Virginia ten, North Carolina five, South Carolina five, and Georgia three.

When vacancies happen in the Representation from any State, the Executive Authority thereof shall issue Writs of Election to fill such Vacancies.

The House of Representatives shall chuse their Speaker and other Officers; and shall have the sole Power of Impeachment.

Section. 3. The Senate of the United States shall be composed of two Senators from each State, chosen by the Legislature thereof, for six Years; and each Senator shall have one Vote.

Immediately after they shall be assembled in Consequence of the first Election, they shall be divided as equally as may be into three Classes. The Seats of the Senators of the first Class shall be vacated at the Expiration of the second Year, of the second Class at the Expiration of the fourth Year, and of the third Class at the Expiration of the sixth Year, so that one third may be chosen every second Year; and if Vacancies happen by Resignation, or otherwise, during the Recess of the Legislature of any State, the Executive thereof may make temporary Appointments until the next Meeting of the Legislature, which shall then fill such Vacancies.

No Person shall be a Senator who shall not have attained to the Age of thirty Years, and been nine Years a Citizen of the United States, and who shall not, when elected, be an Inhabitant of that State for which he shall be chosen.

The Vice President of the United States shall be President of the Senate, but shall have no Vote, unless they be equally divided.

The Senate shall chuse their other Officers, and also a President pro tempore, in the Absence of the Vice President, or when he shall exercise the Office of President of the United States.

The Senate shall have the sole Power to try all Impeachments. When sitting for that Purpose, they shall be on Oath or Affirmation. When the President of the United States is tried the Chief Justice shall preside: And no Person shall be convicted without the Concurrence of two thirds of the Members present.

Judgment in Cases of Impeachment shall not extend further than to removal from Office, and disqualification to hold and enjoy any Office of honor, Trust or Profit under the United States: but the Party convicted shall nevertheless be liable and subject to Indictment, Trial, Judgment and Punishment, according to Law.

Section. 4. The Times, Places and Manner of holding Elections for Senators and Representatives, shall be prescribed in each State by the Legislature thereof; but the Congress may at any time by Law make or alter such Regulations, except as to the Places of chusing Senators.

The Congress shall assemble at least once in every Year, and such Meeting shall be on the first Monday in December, unless they shall by Law appoint a different Day.

Section. 5. Each House shall be the Judge of the Elections, Returns and Qualifications of its own Members, and a Majority of each shall constitute a Quorum to do Business; but a smaller Number may adjourn from day to day, and may be authorized to compel the Attendance of absent Members, in such Manner, and under such Penalties as each House may provide.

Each House may determine the Rules of its Proceedings, punish its Members for disorderly Behaviour, and, with the Concurrence of two thirds, expel a Member.

Each House shall keep a Journal of its Proceedings, and from time to time publish the same, excepting such Parts as may in their Judgment require Secrecy; and the Yeas and

Nays of the Members of either House on any question shall, at the Desire of one fifth of those Present, be entered on the Journal.

Neither House, during the Session of Congress, shall, without the Consent of the other, adjourn for more than three days, nor to any other Place than that in which the two Houses shall be sitting.

Section. 6. The Senators and Representatives shall receive a Compensation for their Services, to be ascertained by Law, and paid out of the Treasury of the United States. They shall in all Cases, except Treason, Felony and Breach of the Peace, be privileged from Arrest during their Attendance at the Session of their respective Houses, and in going to and returning from the same; and for any Speech or Debate in either House, they shall not be questioned in any other Place.

No Senator or Representative shall, during the Time for which he was elected, be appointed to any civil Office under the Authority of the United States, which shall have been created, or the Emoluments whereof shall have been encreased during such time; and no Person holding any Office under the United States, shall be a Member of either House during his Continuance in Office.

Section. 7. All Bills for raising Revenue shall originate in the House of Representatives; but the Senate may propose or concur with amendments as on other Bills.

Every Bill which shall have passed the House of Representatives and the Senate, shall, before it become a Law, be presented to the President of the United States; If he approve he shall sign it, but if not he shall return it, with his Objections to that House in which it shall have originated, who shall enter the Objections at large on their Journal, and proceed to reconsider it. If after such Reconsideration two thirds of that House shall agree to pass the Bill, it shall be sent, together with the Objections, to the other House, by which it shall likewise be reconsidered, and if approved by two thirds of that House, it shall become a Law. But in all such Cases the Votes of both Houses shall be determined by yeas and Nays, and the Names of the Persons voting for and against the Bill shall be entered on the Journal of each House respectively. If any Bill shall not be returned by the President within ten Days (Sunday excepted) after it shall have been presented to him, the Same shall be a Law, in like Manner as if he had signed it, unless the Congress by their Adjournment prevent its Return, in which Case it shall not be a Law.

Every Order, Resolution, or Vote to which the Concurrence of the Senate and House of Representatives may be necessary (except on a question of Adjournment) shall be presented to the President of the United States; and before the Same shall take Effect, shall be approved by him, or being disapproved by him, shall be repassed by two thirds of the Senate and House of Representatives, according to the Rules and Limitations prescribed in the Case of a Bill.

Section. 8. The Congress shall have Power To lay and collect Taxes, Duties, Imposts and Excises, to pay the Debts and provide for the common Defence and general Welfare of the United States; but all Duties, Imposts and Excises shall be uniform throughout the United States;

To borrow Money on the credit of the United States;

To regulate Commerce with foreign Nations, and among the several States, and with the Indian Tribes;

To establish an uniform Rule of Naturalization, and uniform Laws on the subject of Bankruptcies throughout the United States;

To coin Money, regulate the Value thereof, and of foreign Coin, and fix the Standard of Weights and Measures;

To provide for the Punishment of counterfeiting the Securities and current Coin of the United States;

To establish Post Offices and post Roads;

To promote the Progress of Science and useful Arts, by securing for limited Times to Authors and Inventors the exclusive Right to their respective Writings and Discoveries;

To constitute Tribunals inferior to the supreme Court;

To define and punish Piracies and Felonies commited on the high Seas, and Offences against the Law of Nations;

To declare War, grant Letters of Marque and Reprisal, and make Rules concerning Captures on Land and Water;

To raise and support Armies, but no Appropriation of Money to that Use shall be for a longer Term than two Years;

To provide and maintain a Navy;

To make Rules for the Government and Regulation of the land and naval Forces;

To provide for calling forth the Militia to execute the Laws of the Union, suppress Insurrections and repel Invasions;

To provide for organizing, arming, and disciplining, the Militia, and for governing such Part of them as may be employed in the Service of the United States, reserving to the States respectively, the Appointment of the Officers, and the Authority of training the Militia according to the discipline prescribed by Congress;

To exercise exclusive Legislation in all Cases whatsoever, over such District (not exceeding ten Miles square) as may, by Cession of Particular States, and the Acceptance of Congress, become the Seat of the Government of the United States, and to exercise like Authority over all Places purchased by the Consent of the Legislature of the State in which the Same shall be, for the Erection of Forts, Magazines, Arsenals, dock-Yards, and other needful Buildings;—And

To make all Laws which shall be necessary and proper for carrying into Execution the foregoing Powers, and all other Powers vested by this Constitution in the Government of the United States, or in any Department or Officer thereof.

Section. 9. The Migration or Importation of such Persons as any of the States now existing shall think proper to admit, shall not be prohibited by the Congress prior to the Year one thousand eight hundred and eight, but a Tax or duty may be imposed on such Importation, not exceeding ten dollars for each Person.

The Privilege of the Writ of Habeas Corpus shall not be suspended, unless when in Cases of Rebellion or Invasion the public Safety may require it.

No Bill of Attainder or ex post facto Law shall be passed.

No Capitation, or other direct, Tax shall be laid, unless in Proportion to the Census of Enumeration herein before directed to be taken.

No Tax or Duty shall be laid on Articles exported from any State.

No Preference shall be given by any Regulation of Commerce or Revenue to the Ports of one State over those of another; nor shall Vessels bound to, or from, one State, be obliged to enter, clear or pay Duties in another.

No Money shall be drawn from the Treasury, but in Consequence of Appropriations made by Law; and a regular Statement and Account of the Receipts and Expenditures of all public Money shall be published from time to time.

No Title of Nobility shall be granted by the United States: And no Person holding any Office of Profit or Trust under them, shall, without the Consent of the Congress, accept of any present, Emolument, Office, or Title, of any kind whatever, from any King, Prince or foreign State.

Section. 10. No State shall enter into any Treaty, Alliance, or Confederation; grant Letters of Marque and Reprisal; coin Money; emit Bills of Credit; make any Thing but gold and silver Coin a Tender in Payment of Debts; pass any Bill of Attainder, ex post facto Law, or Law impairing the Obligation of Contracts, or grant any Title of Nobility.

No State shall, without the Consent of the Congress, lay any Imposts or Duties on Imports or Exports, except what may be absolutely necessary for executing it's inspection Laws: and the net Produce of all Duties and Imposts, laid by any State on Imports or Exports, shall be for the Use of the Treasury of the United States; and all such Laws shall be subject to the Revision and Controul of the Congress.

No State shall, without the Consent of Congress, lay any Duty of Tonnage, keep Troops, or Ships of War in time of Peace, enter into any Agreement or Compact with another State, or with a foreign Power, or engage in War, unless actually invaded, or in such imminent Danger as will not admit of delay.

Article II

Section. 1. The executive Power shall be vested in a President of the United States of America. He shall hold his Office during the Term of four Years, and, together with the Vice President, chosen for the same Term, be elected, as follows

Constitution

Each State shall appoint, in such Manner as the Legislature thereof may direct, a Number of Electors, equal to the whole Number of Senators and Representatives to which the State may be entitled in the Congress: but no Senator or Representative, or Person holding an Office of Trust or Profit under the United States, shall be appointed an Elector.

The Electors shall meet in their respective States, and vote by Ballot for two Persons, of whom one at least shall not be an Inhabitant of the same State with themselves. And they shall make a List of all the Persons voted for, and of the Number of Votes for each; which List they shall sign and certify, and transmit sealed to the Seat of the Government of the United States, directed to the President of the Senate. The President of the Senate shall, in the Presence of the Senate and House of Representatives, open all the Certificates, and the Votes shall then be counted. The Person having the greatest Number of Votes shall be the President, if such Number be a Majority of the whole Number of Electors appointed; and if there be more than one who have such Majority, and have an equal Number of Votes, then the House of Representatives shall immediately chuse by Ballot one of them for President; and if no Person have a Majority, then from the five highest on the list the said House shall in like Manner chuse the President. But in chusing the President, the Votes shall be taken by States, the Representation from each State having one Vote; a quorum for this Purpose shall consist of a Member or Members from two thirds of the States, and a Majority of all the States shall be necessary to a Choice. In every Case, after the Choice of the President, the Person having the greatest Number of Votes of the Electors shall be the Vice President. But if there should remain two or more who have equal Votes, the Senate shall chuse from them by Ballot the Vice President.

The Congress may determine the Time of chusing the Electors, and the Day on which they shall give their Votes; which Day shall be the same throughout the United States.

No Person except a natural born Citizen, or a Citizen of the United States, at the time of the Adoption of this Constitution, shall be eligible to the Office of President; neither shall any Person be eligible to that Office who shall not have attained to the Age of thirty five Years, and been fourteen Years a Resident within the United States.

In Case of the Removal of the President from Office, or of his Death, Resignation, or Inability to discharge the Powers and Duties of the said Office, the Same shall devolve on the Vice President, and the Congress may by Law provide for the Case of Removal, Death, Resignation or Inability, both of the President and Vice President, declaring what Officer shall then act as President, and such Officer shall act accordingly, until the Disability be removed, or a President shall be elected.

The President shall, at stated Times, receive for his Services, a Compensation, which shall neither be encreased nor dimished during the Period for which he shall have been elected, and he shall not receive within that Period any other Emolument from the United States, or any of them.

Before he enter on the Execution of his Office, he shall take the following Oath or Affirmation: —"I do solemnly swear (or affirm) that I will faithfully execute the Office of President of the United States, and will to the best of my Ability, preserve, protect and defend the Constitution of the United States."

Section. 2. The President shall be Commander in Chief of the Army and Navy of the United States, and of the Militia of the several States, when called into the actual Service of the United States; he may require the Opinion, in writing, of the principal Officer in each of the executive Departments, upon any Subject relating to the Duties of their respective Offices, and he shall have Power to grant Reprieves and Pardons for Offenses against the United States, except in Cases of Impeachment.

He shall have Power, by and with the Advice and Consent of the Senate, to make Treaties, provided two thirds of the Senators present concur; and he shall nominate, and by and with the Advice and Consent of the Senate, shall appoint Ambassadors, other public Ministers and Consuls, Judges of the supreme Court, and all other Officers of the United States, whose Appointments are not herein otherwise provided for, and which shall be established by Law: but the Congress may by Law vest the Appointment of such inferior Officers, as they think proper, in the President alone, in the Courts of Law, or in the Heads of Departments.

The President shall have Power to fill up all Vacancies that may happen during the Recess of the Senate, by granting Commissions which shall expire at the End of their next Session.

Section. 3. He shall from time to time give to the Congress Information of the State of the Union, and recommend to their Consideration such Measures as he shall judge necessary and expedient; he may, on extraordinary Occasions, convene both Houses, or either of them, and in Case of Disagreement between them, with Respect to the Time of Adjournment, he may adjourn them to such Time as he shall think proper; he shall receive Ambassadors and other public Ministers; he shall take Care that the Laws be faithfully executed, and shall Commission all the Officers of the United States.

Section. 4. The President, Vice President and all Civil Officers of the United States, shall be removed from office on Impeachment for, and Conviction of, Treason, Bribery, or other high Crimes and Misdemeanors.

Article III

Section. 1. The judicial Power of the United States, shall be vested in one supreme Court, and in such inferior Courts as the Congress may from time to time ordain and establish. The Judges, both of the supreme and inferior Courts, shall hold their Offices during good Behaviour, and shall, at stated Times, receive for their Services, a Compensation, which shall not be diminished during their Continuance in Office.

Section. 2. The judicial Power shall extend to all Cases, in Law and Equity, arising under this Constitution, the Laws of the United States, and Treaties made, or which shall be made, under their Authority;—to all Cases affecting Ambassadors, other public Ministers and Consuls;—to all Cases of admiralty and maritime Jurisdiction;—to Controversies to which the United States shall be a Party;—to Controversies between two or more States;—between a State and Citizens of another State;—between Citizens of different States;—between Citizens of the same State claiming Lands under Grants of different States, and between a State, or the Citizens thereof, and foreign States, Citizens or Subjects.

In all Cases affecting Ambassadors, other public Ministers and Consuls, and those in which a State shall be Party, the supreme Court shall have original Jurisdiction. In all the other Cases before mentioned, the supreme Court shall have appellate Jurisdiction, both as to Law and Fact, with such Exceptions, and under such Regulations as the Congress shall make.

The Trial of all Crimes, except in cases of Impeachment, shall be by Jury; and such Trial shall be held in the State where the said Crimes shall have been committed; but when not committed within any State, the Trial shall be at such Place or Places as the Congress may by Law have directed.

Section. 3. Treason against the United States, shall consist only in levying War against them, or in adhering to their Enemies, giving them Aid and Comfort. No Person shall be convicted of Treason unless on the Testimony of two Witnesses to the same overt Act, or on Confession in open Court.

The Congress shall have Power to declare the Punishment of Treason, but no Attainder of Treason shall work Corruption of Blood, or Forfeiture except during the Life of the Person attainted.

Article IV

Section. 1. Full Faith and Credit shall be given in each State to the public Acts, Records, and judicial Proceedings of every other State. And the Congress may by general Laws prescribe the Manner in which such Acts, Records and Proceedings shall be proved, and the Effect thereof.

Section. 2. The Citizens of each State shall be entitled to all Privileges and Immunities of Citizens in the several States.

A Person charged in any State with Treason, Felony, or other Crime, who shall flee from Justice, and be found in another State, shall on Demand of the executive Authority of the State from which he fled, be delivered up, to be removed to the State having Jurisdiction of the Crime.

No Person held to Service or Labour in one State, under the Laws thereof, escaping into another, shall, in Consequence of any Law or Regulation therein, be discharged from such Service or Labour, but shall be delivered up on Claim of the Party to whom such Service or Labour may be due.

Section. 3. New States may be admitted by the Congress into this Union; but no new State shall be formed or erected within the Jurisdiction of any other State; nor any State be formed by the Junction of two or more States, or Parts of States, without the Consent of the Legislatures of the States concerned as well as of the Congress.

The Congress shall have Power to dispose of and make all needful Rules and Regulations respecting the Territory or other Property belonging to the United States; and nothing in this Constitution shall be so construed as to Prejudice any Claims of the United States, or of any particular State.

Section. 4. The United States shall guarantee to every State in this Union a Republican Form of Government, and shall protect each of them against Invasion; and on Application of the Legislature, or of the Executive (when the Legislature cannot be convened) against domestic Violence.

Article V

The Congress, whenever two thirds of both Houses shall deem it necessary, shall propose Amendments to this Constitution, or, on the Application of the Legislatures of two thirds of the several States, shall call a Convention for proposing Amendments, which, in either Case, shall be valid to all Intents and Purposes, as Part of this Constitution, when ratified by the Legislatures of three fourths of the several States, or by Conventions in three fourths thereof, as the one or the other Mode of Ratification may be proposed by the Congress; Provided that no Amendment which may be made prior to the Year One thousand eight hundred and eight shall in any Manner affect the first and fourth Clauses in the Ninth Section of the first Article; and that no State, without its Consent, shall be deprived of its equal Suffrage in the Senate.

Article VI

All Debts contracted and Engagements entered into, before the Adoption of this Constitution, shall be as valid against the United States under this Constitution, as under the Confederation.

This Constitution, and the Laws of the United States which shall be made in Pursuance thereof; and all Treaties made, or which shall be made, under the Authority of the United States, shall be the supreme Law of the Land; and the Judges in every State shall be bound thereby, any Thing in the Constitution or Laws of any State to the Contrary notwithstanding.

The Senators and Representatives before mentioned, and the Members of the several State Legislatures, and all executive and judicial Officers, both of the United States and of the several States, shall be bound by Oath or Affirmation, to support this Constitution; but no religious Test shall ever be required as a Qualification to any Office or public Trust under the United States.

Article VII

The Ratification of the Conventions of nine States, shall be sufficient for the Establishment of this Constitution between the States so ratifying the Same. Done in Convention by the Unanimous Consent of the States present the Seventeenth Day of September in the Year of our Lord one thousand seven hundred and Eighty seven and of the Independence of the United States of America the Twelfth In witness whereof We have hereunto subscribed our Names, George Washington, President and deputy from Virginia.

New Hampshire: John Langdon,
Nicholas Gilman.

Constitution

Massachusetts: Nathaniel Gorham,
Rufus King.

Connecticut: William Samuel Johnson,
Roger Sherman.

New York: Alexander Hamilton.

New Jersey: William Livingston,
David Brearley,
William Paterson,
Jonathan Dayton.

Pennsylvania: Benjamin Franklin,
Thomas Mifflin,
Robert Morris,
George Clymer,
Thomas FitzSimons,
Jared Ingersoll,
James Wilson,
Gouverneur Morris.

Delaware: George Read,
Gunning Bedford Jr.,
John Dickinson,
Richard Bassett,
Jacob Broom.

Maryland: James McHenry,
Daniel of St. Thomas Jenifer,
Daniel Carroll.

Virginia: John Blair,
James Madison Jr.

North Carolina: William Blount,
Richard Dobbs Spaight,
Hugh Williamson.

South Carolina: John Rutledge,
Charles Cotesworth Pinckney,
Charles Pinckney,
Pierce Butler.

Georgia: William Few,
                                Abraham Baldwin.

Amendments

Amendment I
(First ten amendments ratified Dec. 15, 1791.)

Congress shall make no law respecting an establishment of religion, or prohibiting the free exercise thereof; or
abridging the freedom of speech, or of the press; or the right
of the people peaceably to assemble, and to petition the
Government for a redress of grievances.

Amendment II
A well regulated Militia, being necessary to the security
of a free State, the right of the people to keep and bear
Arms, shall not be infringed.

Amendment III
No Soldier shall, in time of peace be quartered in any
house, without the consent of the Owner, nor in time of war,
but in a manner to be prescribed by law.

Amendment IV
The right of the people to be secure in their persons,
houses, papers, and effects, against unreasonable searches
and seizures, shall not be violated, and no Warrants shall
issue, but upon probable cause, supported by Oath or affirmation, and particularly describing the place to be
searched, and the persons or things to be seized.

Amendment V
No person shall be held to answer for a capital, or
otherwise infamous crime, unless on a presentment or indictment of a Grand Jury, except in cases arising in the land
or naval forces, or in the Militia, when in actual service in
time of War or public danger; nor shall any person be subject for the same offence to be twice put in jeopardy of life or
limb; nor shall be compelled in any criminal case to be a

witness against himself, nor be deprived of life, liberty, or property, without due process of law; nor shall private property be taken for public use, without just compensation.

Amendment VI

In all criminal prosecutions, the accused shall enjoy the right to a speedy and public trial, by an impartial jury of the State and district wherein the crime shall have been committed, which district shall have been previously ascertained by law, and to be informed of the nature and cause of the accusation; to be confronted with the witnesses against him; to have compulsory process for obtaining witnesses in his favor, and to have the Assistance of Counsel for his defence.

Amendment VII

In Suits at common law, where the value in controversy shall exceed twenty dollars, the right of trial by jury shall be preserved, and no fact tried by a jury, shall be otherwise re-examined in any Court of the United States, than according to the rules of the common law.

Amendment VIII

Excessive bail shall not be required, nor excessive fines imposed, nor cruel and unusual punishments inflicted.

Amendment IX

The enumeration in the Constitution, of certain rights, shall not be construed to deny or disparage others retained by the people.

Amendment X

The powers not delegated to the United States by the Constitution, nor prohibited by it to the States, are reserved to the States respectively, or to the people.

Amendment XI *(Ratified Feb. 7, 1795)*

The Judicial power of the United States shall not be construed to extend to any suit in law or equity, commenced or prosecuted against one of the United States by Citizens of another State, or by Citizens or Subjects of any Foreign State.

Amendment XII *(Ratified June 15, 1804)*

The Electors shall meet in their respective states and vote by ballot for President and Vice-President, one of whom, at least, shall not be an inhabitant of the same state with themselves; they shall name in their ballots the person voted for as President, and in distinct ballots the person voted for as Vice-President, and they shall make distinct lists of all persons voted for as President, and of all persons voted for as Vice-President, and of the number of votes for each, which lists they shall sign and certify, and transmit sealed to the seat of the government of the United States, directed to the President of the Senate;—The President of the Senate shall, in the presence of the Senate and House of Representatives, open all the certificates and the votes shall then be counted;—The person having the greatest number of votes for President, shall be the President, if such number be a majority of the whole number of Electors appointed; and if no person have such majority, then from the persons having the highest numbers not exceeding three on the list of those voted for as President, the House of Representatives shall choose immediately, by ballot, the President. But in choosing the President, the votes shall be taken by states, the representation from each state having one vote; a quorum for this purpose shall consist of a member or members from two-thirds of the states, and a majority of all the states shall be necessary to a choice. And if the House of Representatives shall not choose a President whenever the right of choice shall devolve upon them, before the fourth day of March next following, then the Vice-President shall act as President, as in the case of the death or other constitutional disability of the President—The person having the greatest number of votes as Vice-President, shall be the Vice-President, if such number be a majority of the whole number of Electors appointed, and if no person have a majority, then from the two highest numbers on the list, the Senate shall choose the Vice-President; a quorum for the purpose shall consist of two-thirds of the whole number of Senators, and a majority of the whole number shall be necessary to a choice. But no person constitutionally ineligible to the office of President shall be eligible to that of Vice-President of the United States.

Amendment XIII *(Ratified Dec. 6, 1865)*

Section 1. Neither slavery nor involuntary servitude, except as a punishment for crime whereof the party shall have been duly convicted, shall exist within the United States, or any place subject to their jurisdiction.

Section 2. Congress shall have power to enforce this article by appropriate legislation.

Amendment XIV *(Ratified July 9, 1868)*

Section 1. All persons born or naturalized in the United States and subject to the jurisdiction thereof, are citizens of the United States and of the State wherein they reside. No State shall make or enforce any law which shall abridge the privileges or immunities of citizens of the United States; nor shall any State deprive any person of life, liberty, or property, without due process of law; nor deny to any person within its jurisdiction the equal protection of the laws.

Section 2. Representatives shall be apportioned among the several States according to their respective numbers, counting the whole number of persons in each State, excluding Indians not taxed. But when the right to vote at any election for the choice of electors for President and Vice President of the United States, Representatives in Congress, the Executive and Judicial officers of a State, or the members of the Legislature thereof, is denied to any of the male inhabitants of such State, being twenty-one years of age, and citizens of the United States, or in any way abridged, except for participation in rebellion, or other crime, the basis of representation therein shall be reduced in the proportion which the number of such male citizens shall bear to the whole number of male citizens twenty-one years of age in such State.

Section 3. No person shall be a Senator or Representative in Congress, or elector of President and Vice President, or hold any office, civil or military, under the United States, or under any State, who, having previously taken an oath, as a member of Congress, or as an officer of the United States, or as a member of any State legislature, or as an executive or judicial officer of any State, to support the Constitution of the United States, shall have engaged in insurrection or rebellion against the same, or given aid or comfort to the enemies thereof. But Congress may by a vote of two-thirds of each House, remove such disability.

Section 4. The validity of the public debt of the United States, authorized by law, including debts incurred for payment of pensions and bounties for services in suppressing insurrection or rebellion, shall not be questioned. But neither the United States nor any State shall assume or pay any debt or obligation incurred in aid of insurrection or rebellion against the United States, or any claim for the loss or emancipation of any slave; but all such debts, obligations and claims shall be held illegal and void.

Section 5. The Congress shall have power to enforce, by appropriate legislation, the provisions of this article.

Amendment XV *(Ratified Feb. 3, 1870)*

Section 1. The right of citizens of the United States to vote shall not be denied or abridged by the United States or by any State on account of race, color, or previous condition of servitude.

Section 2. The Congress shall have power to enforce this article by appropriate legislation.

Amendment XVI *(Ratified Feb. 3, 1913)*

The Congress shall have power to lay and collect taxes on incomes, from whatever source derived, without apportionment among the several States, and without regard to any census or enumeration.

Amendment XVII *(Ratified Apr. 8, 1913)*

The Senate of the United States shall be composed of two Senators from each State, elected by the people thereof, for six years; and each Senator shall have one vote. The electors in each State shall have the qualifications requisite for electors of the most numerous branch of the State legislatures.

When vacancies happen in the representation of any State in the Senate, the executive authority of such State shall issue writs of election to fill such vacancies: *Provided,* That the legislature of any State may empower the executive thereof to make temporary appointments until the people fill the vacancies by election as the legislature may direct.

This amendment shall not be so construed as to affect the election or term of any Senator chosen before it becomes valid as part of the Constitution.

Amendment XVIII *(Ratified Jan. 16, 1919)*

Section 1. After one year from the ratification of this article the manufacture, sale, or transportation of intoxicating liquors within, the importation thereof into, or the exportation thereof from the United States and all territory subject to the jurisdiction thereof for beverage purposes is hereby prohibited.

Section 2. The Congress and the several States shall have concurrent power to enforce this article by appropriate legislation.

Section 3. This article shall be inoperative unless it shall have been ratified as an amendment to the Constitution by the legislatures of the several States, as provided in the Constitution, within seven years from the date of the submission hereof to the States by the Congress.

Amendment XIX *(Ratified Aug. 18, 1920)*

The right of citizens of the United States to vote shall not be denied or abridged by the United States or by any State on account of sex.

Congress shall have power to enforce this article by appropriate legislation.

Amendment XX *(Ratified Jan. 23, 1933)*

Section 1. The terms of the President and Vice President shall end at noon on the 20th day of January, and the terms of Senators and Representatives at noon on the 3d day of January, of the years in which such terms would have ended if this article had not been ratified; and the terms of their successors shall then begin.

Section 2. The Congress shall assemble at least once in every year, and such meeting shall begin at noon on the 3d day of January, unless they shall by law appoint a different day.

Section 3. If, at the time fixed for the beginning of the term of the President, the President elect shall have died, the Vice President elect shall become President. If a President shall not have been chosen before the time fixed for the beginning of his term, or if the President elect shall have failed to qualify, then the Vice President elect shall act as President until a President shall have qualified; and the Congress may by law provide for the case wherein neither a President elect nor a Vice President elect shall have qualified, declaring who shall then act as President, or the manner in which one who is to act shall be selected, and such person shall act accordingly until a President or Vice President shall have qualified.

Section 4. The Congress may by law provide for the case of the death of any of the persons from whom the House of Representatives may choose a President whenever the right of choice shall have devolved upon them, and for the case of the death of any of the persons from whom the Senate may choose a Vice President whenever the right of choice shall have devolved upon them.

Section 5. Sections 1 and 2 shall take effect on the 15th day of October following the ratification of this article.

Section 6. This article shall be inoperative unless it shall have been ratified as an amendment to the Constitution by the legislatures of three-fourths of the several States within seven years from the date of its submission.

Amendment XXI *(Ratified Dec. 5, 1933)*

Section 1. The eighteenth article of amendment to the Constitution of the United States is hereby repealed.

Section 2. The transportation or importation into any State, Territory or possession of the United States for delivery or use therein of intoxicating liquors, in violation of the laws thereof, is hereby prohibited.

Section 3. This article shall be inoperative unless it shall have been ratified as an amendment to the Constitution by conventions in the several States, as provided in the Constitution, within seven years from the date of the submission hereof to the States by the Congress.

Amendment XXII *(Ratified Feb. 27, 1951)*

Section 1. No person shall be elected to the office of the President more than twice, and no person who has held the office of President, or acted as President, for more than two years of a term to which some other person was elected President shall be elected to the office of the President more than once. But this Article shall not apply to any person holding the office of President when this Article was proposed by the Congress, and shall not prevent any person who may be holding the office of President, or acting as President, during the term within which this Article becomes operative from holding the office of President or acting as President during the remainder of such term.

Section 2. This Article shall be inoperative unless it shall have been ratified as an amendment to the Constitution by the legislatures of three-fourths of the several States within seven years from the date of its submission to the States by the Congress.

Amendment XXIII *(Ratified March 29, 1961)*

Section 1. The District constituting the seat of Government of the United States shall appoint in such manner as the Congress may direct:

A number of electors of President and Vice President equal to the whole number of Senators and Representatives in Congress to which the District would be entitled if it were a State, but in no event more than the least populous State; they shall be in addition to those appointed by the States, but they shall be considered, for the purposes of the election of President and Vice President, to be electors appointed by a State; and they shall meet in the District and perform such duties as provided by the twelfth article of amendment.

Section 2. The Congress shall have power to enforce this article by appropriate legislation.

Amendment XXIV *(Ratified Jan. 23, 1964)*

Section 1. The right of citizens of the United States to vote in any primary or other election for President or Vice President, for electors for President or Vice President, or for Senator or Representative in Congress, shall not be denied or abridged by the United States or any State by reason of failure to pay any poll tax or other tax.

Section 2. The Congress shall have power to enforce this article by appropriate legislation.

Amendment XXV *(Ratified Feb. 10, 1967)*

Section 1. In case of the removal of the President from

office or of his death or resignation, the Vice President shall become President.

Section 2. Whenever there is a vacancy in the office of the Vice President, the President shall nominate a Vice President who shall take office upon confirmation by a majority vote of both Houses of Congress.

Section 3. Whenever the President transmits to the President pro tempore of the Senate and the Speaker of the House of Representatives his written declaration that he is unable to discharge the powers and duties of his office, and until he transmits to them a written declaration to the contrary, such powers and duties shall be discharged by the Vice President as Acting President.

Section 4. Whenever the Vice President and a majority of either the principal officers of the executive departments or of such other body as Congress may by law provide, transmit to the President pro tempore of the Senate and the Speaker of the House of Representatives their written declaration that the President is unable to discharge the powers and duties of his office, the Vice President shall immediately assume the powers and duties of the office as Acting President.

Thereafter, when the President transmits to the President pro tempore of the Senate and the Speaker of the House of Representatives his written declaration that no inability exists, he shall resume the powers and duties of his office unless the Vice President and a majority of either the principal officers of the executive department or of such other body as Congress may by law provide, transmit within four days to the President pro tempore of the Senate and the Speaker of the House of Representatives their written declaration that the President is unable to discharge the powers and duties of his office. Thereupon Congress shall decide the issue, assembling within forty-eight hours for that purpose if not in session. If the Congress, within twenty-one days after receipt of the latter written declaration, or, if Congress is not in session, within twenty-one days after Congress is required to assemble, determines by two-thirds vote of both houses that the President is unable to discharge the powers and duties of his office, the Vice President shall continue to discharge the same as Acting President; otherwise, the President shall resume the powers and duties of his office.

Amendment XXVI *(Ratified July 1, 1971)*

Section 1. The right of citizens of the United States, who are eighteen years of age or older, to vote shall not be denied or abridged by the United States or by any State on account of age.

Section 2. The Congress shall have power to enforce this article by appropriate legislation.

Reference Notes

Introduction

1. Carl Van Doren, *The Great Rehearsal: The Story of the Making and Ratifying of the Constitution of the United States* (New York: The Viking Press, 1948), p. 35.

2. James Madison, Alexander Hamilton, and John Jay, *The Federalist Papers*, (New York: Mentor, 1961), p. 323.

3. *Ibid.*, p. 320.

4. *Ibid.*, p. 403.

5. Woodrow Wilson, *Congressional Government*, (Cleveland: Meridian, 1956), pp. 154-155.

6. Congressional Quarterly, *Watergate: Chronology of a Crisis*, pp. xv-xix.

Part I—Constitutional Beginnings

Chapter One—Colonial Background

1. Charles M. Andrews, *The Colonial Period of American History*, Vol. 1: *The Settlements* (New Haven: Yale University Press, 1934), p. 23.

2. *Ibid.*, p. 375.

3. *Ibid.*, p. 185.

4. *Ibid.*, p. 368.

5. Andrews, *The Colonial Period of American History*, Vol. 4: *England's Commercial and Colonial Policy*, p. 150.

6. Jack P. Greene, ed., *Great Britain and the American Colonies, 1606-1763* (New York: Harper Paperbacks, 1970), p. xxxix.

7. *Ibid.*, p. xli.

8. Edmund S. Morgan, *The Birth of the Republic 1763-89* (Chicago: University of Chicago Press, 1956), p. 31.

9. *Ibid.*, pp. 60-61.

10. L. H. Butterfield, ed., *Adams Family Correspondence,* Vol. 1: *December 1761-May 1776* (Cambridge, Mass.: The Belknap Press of Harvard University, 1963), p. 166.

11. Edmund Cody Burnett, *The Continental Congress* (New York: Norton, 1964), pp. 42-50.

12. *Ibid.,* p. 61.

Chapter Two—Revolution and Confederation

13. Burnett, *The Continental Congress,* pp. 85-87.

14. *Ibid.,* p. 127.

15. *Ibid.,* pp. 131-137.

16. *Ibid.,* p. 171.

17. Charles Ramsdell Lingley, *The Transition In Virginia From Colony to Commonwealth* (New York: Columbia University, 1910), p. 172.

18. Burnett, *The Continental Congress,* p. 171.

19. Andrew C. McLaughlin, *The Confederation and the Constitution 1783-1789,* with a Foreword by Henry Steele Commager (New York: Collier Books, 1962), p. 51.

Chapter Three—The Constitution

20. Charles Warren *The Making of the Constitution* (Boston: Little, Brown, 1928), p. 12.

21. *Ibid.,* pp. 6-7.

22. *Ibid.,* p. 8.

23. *Ibid.,* p. 23.

24. *Ibid.,* p. 25.

25. James Madison, *Notes of Debates in the Federal Convention of 1787,* with an Introduction by Adrienne Koch (Athens, Ohio: Ohio University Press, 1966), p. 30.

26. Warren, *The Making of the Constitution,* p. 150.

27. Madison, *Notes of Debates in the Federal Convention,* p. 36.

28. Warren, *The Making of the Constitution,* pp. 216-218. McLaughlin, *The Confederation and the Constitution 1783-1789,* p. 144.

29. Warren, *The Making of the Constitution,* p. 223.

30. *Ibid.,* p. 232.

31. *Ibid.,* p. 257.

Chapter Four—The Structure of Congress

32. *Ibid.,* p. 159.

33. *Ibid.,* pp. 160, 162.

34. *Ibid.,* p. 161.

35. *Ibid.,* p. 195.

36. Madison, *Notes on Debates in the Federal Convention,* p. 257.

37. Warren, *The Making of the Constitution,* p. 290.

38. *Ibid.,* p. 292.

39. *Ibid.,* pp. 294-298.

40. *Ibid.,* p. 345.

41. *Ibid.,* p. 242.

42. *Ibid.,* p. 243.

43. *Ibid.,* p. 401.

44. *Ibid.,* p. 409.

45. *Ibid.,* pp. 415-416.

46. *Ibid.,* p. 414.

47. *Ibid.,* p. 415.

48. *Ibid.,* p. 417.

49. *Ibid.,* pp. 418-419.

50. *Ibid.,* p. 426.

51 *Ibid.,* pp. 445-451.

52. Merrill Jensen, *The Articles of Confederation* (Madison: University of Wisconsin Press, 1940), p. 264.

53. *Ibid.*

54. Warren, *The Making of the Constitution,* p. 616.

55. *Ibid.,* pp. 615-616.

56. *Ibid.,* p. 431.

Chapter Five—Powers of Congress

57. *Ibid.,* p. 166.

58. *Ibid.,* p. 316.

59. Madison, *Notes of Debates in the Federal Convention,* p. 45.

60. Warren, *The Making of the Constitution,* pp. 314-315.

61. *Ibid.,* p. 469.

62. *Ibid.,* pp. 473-475.

63. *Ibid.,* p. 497.

64. *Ibid.,* p. 574.

65. *Ibid.,* p. 573.

66. *Ibid.,* p. 575.

67. *Ibid.*

68. *Ibid.,* p. 576.

69. *Ibid.,* p. 583.

70. Madison, *Notes of Debates in the Federal Convention,* pp. 475-477.

71. *Ibid.,* p. 482.

72. *Ibid.,* p. 580.

73. *Ibid.,* p. 516.

74. Warren, *The Making of the Constitution,* pp. 665-666.

75. Henry Steele Commager, ed., *Documents of American History*, Vol. 1: *To 1898* (Englewood Cliffs, N.J.: Prentice-Hall, 1973), p. 128.

76. Warren, *The Making of the Constitution*, p. 594.

77. *Ibid.*, pp. 594-595.

78. *Ibid.*, p. 661.

79. *Ibid.*, p. 662.

80. Madison, *Notes of Debates in the Federal Convention*, p. 471.

Chapter Six—Executive and Judiciary

81. Warren, *The Making of the Constitution*, p. 359.

82. *Ibid.*, pp. 174, 360.

83. *Ibid.*, pp. 174-175.

84. *Ibid.*, p. 525.

85. *Ibid.*, p. 360.

86. *Ibid.*, p. 358.

87. *Ibid.*, p. 623.

88. *Ibid.*, pp. 628-629.

89. Madison, *Notes of Debates in the Federal Convention*, p. 596.

90. Warren, *The Making of the Constitution*, pp. 635-638.

91. *Ibid.*, p. 638.

92. *Ibid.*, p. 530.

93. *Ibid.*, pp. 651-652.

94. *Ibid.*, p. 656.

95. *Ibid.*, p. 456.

96. *Ibid.*, pp. 326-327.

97. *Ibid.*, pp. 327-328.

98. Madison, *Notes of Debates in the Federal Convention*, pp. 536-537.

99. Warren, *The Making of the Constitution*, pp. 333-334.

100. *Ibid.*, p. 650.

101. *Ibid.*, p. 552.

Chapter Seven—Amendment and Ratification

102. *Ibid.*, p. 673.

103. *Ibid.*, p. 675.

104. *Ibid.*, p. 679.

105. *Ibid.*, pp. 679-680.

106. *Ibid.*, pp. 348-350.

107. *Ibid.*

108. *Ibid.*, p. 607.

109. *Ibid.*, p. 717.

110. *Ibid.*, p. 746.

111. *Ibid.*, p. 754.

112. *Ibid.*, p. 749.

Part II—History of the House

Chapter Eight—Formative Years

1. George B. Galloway, *History of the House of Representatives*, (New York: Crowell, 1969), p. 135.

2. *Ibid.*, p. 2.

3. *Ibid.*, p. 10.

4. *Ibid.*, p. 12.

5. *Ibid.*, p. 18.

6. Paul Leicester Ford, ed., *The Writings of Thomas Jefferson*, Vol. 6 (New York: G. P. Putnam's, 1895), p. 102.

7. Galloway, *History of the House of Representatives*, p. 18.

8. *Ibid.*, p. 129.

9. *Ibid.*, p. 71.

10. *Ibid.*, pp. 129-130.

Chapter Nine—Congressional Ascendancy

11. Bernard Mayo, *Henry Clay: Spokesman of the New West* (Boston: Houghton Mifflin, 1937), pp. 346-347.

12. *Annals of the Congress of the United States*, 18th Congress, 1st Session, Dec. 1, 1823, p. 795.

13. Galloway, *History of the House of Representatives*, p. 130.

14. *Ibid.*

Chapter Ten—A House Divided

15. *Ibid.*, p. 43.

16. Marie B. Hecht, *John Quincy Adams: A Personal History of an Independent Man* (New York: Macmillan, 1972), p. 545.

17. *Ibid.*, p. 547.

18. Asher C. Hinds, *Hinds' Precedents of the House of Representatives*, Vol. 4 (Washington: U.S. Government Printing Office, 1907), p. 278.

19. *Ibid.*, Vol. 5, pp. 354-355.

Chapter Eleven—New Complexities

20. Galloway, *History of the House of Representatives*, pp. 245-246.

21. Richard F. Fenno, Jr., *The Power of the Purse: Appropriations Politics in Congress* (Boston: Little, Brown, 1966), p. 8.

22. T. Harry Williams, *Hayes: The Diary of a President 1875-1881* (New York: David McKay Company, 1964), p. 206.

23. Woodrow Wilson, *Congressional Government* (Cleveland: Meridian, 1956), p. 76.

24. *Ibid.*, p. 82.

25. *Ibid.*, p. 80.

26. *Ibid.*, p. 85.

27. Neil MacNeil, *Forge of Democracy: The House of Representatives* (New York: David McKay Company, 1963), p. 185.

28. Galloway, *History of the House of Representatives*, p. 51.

29. MacNeil, *Forge of Democracy*, p. 76.

30. Galloway, *History of the House of Representatives*, p. 132.

31. *Ibid.*, p. 251.

32. *Ibid.*, p. 52.

33. *Ibid.*, p. 135.

34. *Congressional Record*, 51st Congress, 1st Session, Feb. 10, 1890, pp. 1172-1173.

35. Woodrow Wilson, *Congressional Government*, p. 63.

Chapter Twelve—Tyranny and Reaction

36. Galloway, *History of the House of Representatives*, pp. 54-55.

37. *Ibid.*, p. 55.

38. *Ibid.*, p. 139.

39. *Ibid.*, p. 140.

40. *Ibid.*, p. 108.

Chapter Thirteen—Republican Years

41. Paul DeWitt Hasbrouck, *Party Government in the House of Representatives* (New York: Macmillan, 1927), p. 15.

42. Floyd M. Riddick, *The United States Congress: Organization and Procedure* (Washington: National Capitol Publishers, 1949), p. 123.

43. Hasbrouck, *Party Government in the House of Representatives*, p. 20.

44. *Ibid.*, p. 99.

45. *Congressional Record*, 69th Congress, 1st Session, Dec. 7, 1925, p. 380.

46. Hasbrouck, *Party Government in the House of Representatives*, p. 164.

47. *Congressional Record*, 69th Congress, 1st Session, Dec. 16, 1925, p. 933.

48. Hasbrouck, *Party Government in the House of Representatives*, p. 23.

49. *Congressional Record*, 67th Congress, 3rd Session, Nov. 22, 1922, p. 26.

50. *Congressional Record*, 68th Congress, 2nd Session, Feb. 18, 1925, pp. 4009-4010.

51. *Congressional Record*, 69th Congress, 1st Session, March 25, 1926, p. 6313.

52. Galloway, *History of the House of Representatives,* p. 145.
53. *Ibid.*
54. *Congressional Record,* 67th Congress, 1st Session, Oct. 14, 1921, p. 6315.
55. *Congressional Record,* 69th Congress, 1st Session, April 8, 1926, p. 7148.

Chapter Fourteen—Democratic Years

56. *Congressional Record,* 73rd Congress, 2nd Session, Jan. 11, 1934, p. 481.
57. *Ibid.,* p. 485.
58. *The Public Papers and Addresses of Franklin D. Roosevelt,* Vol. 7 (New York: Macmillan, 1941), p. 489.
59. Richard Bolling, *Power in the House: A History of the Leadership of the House of Representatives* (New York: Dutton, 1968), p. 164.
60. *The Reorganization of Congress,* A Report of the Committee of Congress of the American Political Science Association (Washington: Public Affairs Press, 1945), pp. 80-81.
61. *Hearings Before the Joint Committee on the Organization of Congress,* 79th Congress, 1st Session, March 19, 1945, p. 109.
62. *Organization of the Congress,* Report of the Joint Committee on the Organization of Congress, 79th Congress, 2nd Session (Washington: U.S. Government Printing Office, 1946), p. 35.
63. *Ibid.,* p. 13.

Chapter Fifteen—Postwar Developments

64. MacNeil, *Forge of Democracy,* p. 129.
65. *Congressional Record,* 80th Congress, 2nd Session, Feb. 27, 1948, p. 1878.
66. *Ibid.,* Feb. 18, 1948, p. 1400.
67. *Congressional Record,* 81st Congress, 1st Session, Feb. 7, 1949, p. 880.
68. George B. Galloway, *The Legislative Process in Congress* (New York: Crowell, 1953), p. 659.
69. Fenno, *The Power of the Purse,* p. 629.
70. *Congressional Record,* 87th Congress, 2nd Session, July 9, 1962, p. 12899.
71. *Ibid.,* p. 12900.
72. *Ibid.,* Oct. 10, 1962, pp. 23014-23015.
73. *Ibid.,* Oct. 13, 1962, p. 23470.
74. *Congressional Record,* 82nd Congress, 1st Session, Jan. 3, 1951, p. 18.
75. *Ibid.,* p. 12.
76. *Ibid.,* p. 10.

77. James A. Robinson, *The House Rules Committee* (Indianapolis: Bobbs-Merrill, 1963), p. 72.

78. *Congress and the Nation, 1965-1968*, Vol. II (Washington: Congressional Quarterly Inc., 1969), p. 897.

79. *Ibid.*, p. 900.

80. Congressional Quarterly, *Congress and the Nation, 1969-1972*, Vol. III, p. 429.

Chapter Sixteen—Sweeping Reforms

81. Congressional Quarterly, *1973 Almanac*, pp. 905-917, 1007-1010; *1975 Almanac*, pp. 327-331, 801, 885-887.

82. *Congress and the Nation, 1969-1972*, Vol. III, pp. 382-396.

83. Congressional Quarterly, *1971 Almanac*, pp. 9-11; *1975 Almanac*, pp. 3-5.

84. Congressional Quarterly, *Inside Congress* (1976), pp. 1-16, 67-70, 74-91, 99-112, 127-133; *1971 Almanac*, pp. 723-724; *1974 Almanac*, p. 612.

85. *Inside Congress*, pp. 6-7; *1974 Almanac*, pp. 634-640.

86. Congressional Quarterly, *1972 Almanac*, pp. 419-442; *1973 Almanac*, pp. 243-256.

87. *1975 Almanac*, pp. 3-23.

88. *1974 Almanac*, pp. 867-902.

Part III—History of the Senate

Chapter Seventeen—Formative Years

1. George H. Haynes, *The Senate of the United States: Its History and Practice*, vol. 1 (Boston: Houghton Mifflin, 1938), p. vii.

2. Lindsay Rogers, *The American Senate* (New York, Knopf, 1926), pp. 9, 90.

3. James Madison, *Notes on Debates in the Federal Convention of 1787*, with an Introduction by Adrienne Koch (Athens, Ohio: Ohio University Press, 1966), p. 42.

4. Charles Warren, *The Making of the Constitution* (Boston: Little, Brown, 1929), p. 195.

5. *Ibid.*

6. Rogers, *The American Senate*, p. 18.

7. Haynes, *The Senate of the United States*, vol. 1, p. 11.

8. *The Federalist Papers*, with an Introduction by Clinton Rossiter (New York: Mentor, 1961), p. 377.

9. Rogers, *The American Senate*, p. 21.

10. Gaillard Hunt, ed., *The Writings of James Madison, 1787-1790*, vol. 5: (New York: G. P. Putnam's Sons, 1904), p. 276.

11. Roy Swanstrom, *The United States Senate, 1787-1801*, Senate Document No. 64, 87th Congress, 1st Session (Washington: U.S. Government Printing Office, 1962), p. 86.

12. Haynes, *The Senate of the United States,* vol. 1, p. 62.

13. *Ibid.,* pp. 63, 68.

14. *Ibid.,* pp. 192-194.

15. Swanstrom, *The United States Senate, 1787-1801,* pp. 192-194.

16. *Ibid.,* p. 247.

17. *Ibid.,* pp. 36-37.

18. *Ibid.,* p. 80.

19. *Ibid.,* p. 283.

20. *Congressional Directory,* U.S. Government Printing Office, Washington, D.C., 1976, p. 404.

21. Swanstrom, *The United States Senate, 1787-1801,* p. 271.

22. W. E. Binkley, *The Powers of the President* (New York: Russell & Russell, 1973), p. 52.

Chapter Eighteen—Emerging Senate

23. *Ibid.,* pp. 60-61.

24. Lauros G. McConachie, *Congressional Committees: A Study of the Origins and Development of our National and Local Legislative Methods* (New York: Burt Franklin Reprints, 1973), p. 312.

25. Haynes, *The Senate of the United States,* vol. 1, pp. 272-278.

26. *Ibid.*

27. *Ibid.,* vol. 2, p. 1003.

28. *Ibid.,* vol. 1, pp. 212-214.

Chapter Nineteen—The Golden Age

29. Alexis de Tocqueville, *Democracy in America,* vol. 1 (New York: Schocken Books, 1967) pp. 233-234.

30. Haynes, *The Senate of the United States,* vol. 2, p. 1002.

31. Binkley, *The Powers of the President,* p. 81.

32. *Ibid.,* p. 86.

33. Franklin L. Burdette, *Filibustering in the Senate* (New York: Russell & Russell, 1965), pp. 22-25.

34. Haynes, *The Senate of the United States,* vol. 1, p. 298.

Chapter Twenty—Party Government

35. Binkley, *The Powers of the President,* pp. 130-133.

36. *Ibid.,* p. 207.

37. David J. Rothman, *Politics and Power: The United States Senate 1869-1901* (Cambridge, Mass.: Harvard University Press), p. 188.

38. Woodrow Wilson, *Congressional Government* (Cleveland: Meridian, 1956), p. 147.

39. Rothman, *Politics and Power,* p. 44.

40. *Ibid.,* pp. 56-57.

41. *Ibid.,* p. 60.

42. *Ibid.,* pp. 24-25.

43. *Ibid.,* p. 97.

44. Haynes, *The Senate of the United States,* vol. 1, p. 85.

45. *Ibid.,* p. 95.

46. Rothman, *Politics and Power,* p. 146.

47. *Congressional Globe,* 37th Congress, 3rd Session, Mar. 3, 1863, p. 1491.

48. *Congressional Globe,* 38th Congress, 2nd Session, Feb. 25, 1865, p. 1108.

49. Haynes, *The Senate of the United States,* vol. 1, pp. 398-399.

50. *Ibid.,* p. 400.

51. Burdette, *Filibustering in the Senate,* p. 80.

52. George B. Galloway, *The Legislative Process in Congress* (New York: Crowell, 1953), p. 542.

53. Haynes, *The Senate of the United States,* vol. 1, p. 395.

54. *Ibid.,* pp. 395-396.

Chapter Twenty-one—Era of Reform

55. *Ibid.,* pp. 96-98.

56. *Ibid.,* pp. 100-104.

57. *Ibid.,* pp. 111-112.

58. *Ibid.,* pp. 112-115.

59. George B. Galloway, *Congress at the Crossroads* (New York: Crowell, 1946), p. 38.

60. Haynes, *The Senate of the United States,* vol. 1, p. 402.

61. *Ibid.,* pp. 402-403.

Chapter Twenty-two—Republican Stalemate

62. *Ibid.,* vol. 2, p. 973.

63. Binkley, *The Powers of the President,* p. 243.

64. Haynes, *The Senate of the United States,* vol. 1, p. 291.

65. Charles O. Jones, *The Minority Party in Congress* (Boston: Little, Brown, 1970), p. 144.

66. Haynes, *The Senate of the United States,* vol. 1, p. 411.

67. *Ibid.,* p. 416.

68. Haynes, *The Senate of the United States,* vol. 1, p. 286.

Chapter Twenty-three—Democratic Leadership

69. Randall B. Ripley, *Majority Party Leadership in Congress* (Boston: Little, Brown, 1969), p. 81.

70. *Ibid.,* p. 77.

71. *Congressional Record,* 78th Congress, 2nd Session, Feb. 23, 1944, p. 1966.

72. *Congressional Record,* 79th Congress, 1st Session, Jan. 18, 1945, p. 349.

73. Haynes, *The Senate of the United States,* vol. 1, p. 413.

Chapter Twenty-four—Postwar Developments

74. Jones, *The Minority Party in Congress,* p. 168.

75. *Congress and the Nation, 1945-1964,* vol. I, (Washington: Congressional Quarterly Inc., 1965), p. 1426.

76. *Ibid.,* p. 1427.

77. *Ibid.*

78. *Ibid.*

79. *Congress and the Nation, 1969-1972,* vol. III (Washington: Congressional Quarterly, Inc., 1973), p. 357.

80. *Congress and the Nation, 1945-1964,* vol. I, p. 1726.

81. *Ibid.,* p. 1774.

82. Galloway, *The Legislative Process in Congress,* p. 659.

83. *Ibid.*

84. *Congressional Record,* 87th Congress, 2nd Session, Oct. 13, 1962, p. 23470.

85. *Congress and the Nation, 1945-1964,* vol. I, p. 264.

86. *Ibid.,* p. 265.

87. *Ibid.,* p. 122.

88. *Ibid.,* pp. 132-133.

89. *Ibid.,* pp. 138-139.

Chapter Twenty-five—Liberal Advances

90. Arthur M. Schlesinger Jr., *The Imperial Presidency* (Boston: Houghton Mifflin Company, 1973), p. 201; *Congressional Record,* 90th Congress, 1st Session, July 31, 1967, pp. 20706, 20718; Congressional Quarterly, *1972 Almanac,* pp. 905-917; *1975 Almanac,* p. 5.

91. Congressional Quarterly, *1975 Weekly Report,* p. 2657; *1976 Weekly Report,* p. 507.

92. *Congress and the Nation 1969-1972,* pp. 382-396.

93. Congressional Quarterly, *Inside Congress* (1976), pp. 11-14; *1976 Weekly Report,* pp. 838-839.

94. *Inside Congress,* p. 15.

95. *Ibid.,* pp. 127-133; Congressional Quarterly, *1974 Almanac,* pp. 145-153.

96. Congressional Quarterly, *1971 Almanac,* pp. 875-896; *1974 Almanac,* pp. 611-633.

97. *The Washington Post,* 10 May 1976.

98. Congressional Quarterly, *1973 Almanac*, p. 1008; Congressional Quarterly, *Watergate: Chronology of a Crisis* (1975), pp. 192, 620.

99. *1973 Almanac*, pp. 905-917; *1975 Almanac*, pp. 291, 306-311, 344-349, 885-887.

Selected Bibliography
Part I—Constitutional Beginnings

Andrews, Charles M. *The Colonial Period of American History.* 4 vols. New Haven: Yale University Press, 1934.

Beard, Charles A. *An Economic Interpretation of the Constitution of the United States.* New York: Macmillan, 1935.

Beard, Charles A., ed. *The Enduring Federalist.* Garden City, N.Y.: Doubleday, 1948.

Brant, Irving, *James Madison: Father of the Constitution, 1787-1800.* Indianapolis: Bobbs-Merrill, 1950.

Burnett, Edmund C. *The Continental Congress.* New York: Macmillan, 1941.

Butterfield, L.H., ed. *Adams Family Correspondence.* Vol. 1: *December 1761-May 1776.* Cambridge, Mass.: The Belknap Press of Harvard University Press, 1963.

Commager, Henry Steele, ed. *Documents of American History.* Vol. 1: *To 1898.* Englewood Cliffs, N.J.: Prentice-Hall, 1973.

Elliot, Jonathan, ed. *The Debates in the Several State Conventions on the Adoption of the Federal Constitution.* 5 vols. Philadelphia: J.B. Lippincott, 1937.

Farrand, Max. *The Framing of the Constitution of the United States.* New Haven: Yale University Press, 1913.

_____, ed. *The Records of the Federal Convention of 1787.* 4 vols. New Haven: Yale University Press, 1973.

Greene, Jack P., ed. *Great Britain and the American Colonies, 1606-1763.* New York: Harper Paperbacks, 1970.

Jensen, Merrill. *The Articles of Confederation.* Madison, Wis.: University of Wisconsin Press, 1940.

Kelly, Alfred H. and Harbison, Winfred A. *The American Constitution: Its Origins and Development.* New York: Norton, 1955.

Lingley, Charles Ramsdell. *The Transition in Virginia From Colony to Commonwealth.* New York: Columbia University, 1910.

McLaughlin, Andrew C. *The Confederation and the Constitution, 1783-1789.* Foreword by Henry Steele Commager. New York: Collier Books, 1962.

Madison, James; Hamilton, Alexander; and Jay, John. *The Federalist Papers.* Introduction by Clinton Rossiter. New York: Mentor, 1961.

Madison, James. *Notes of Debates in the Federal Convention of 1787.* Introduction by Adrienne Koch. Athens, Ohio: Ohio University Press, 1966.

Morgan, Edmund S. *The Birth of the Republic.* Chicago, University of Chicago Press, 1956.

Nevins, Allan. *The American States During and After the Revolution, 1775-1789.* New York: Macmillan, 1924.

Rossiter, Clinton. *1787: The Grand Convention.* New York: Macmillan, 1966.

Smith, David G. *The Convention and the Constitution.* New York: St. Martin's Press, 1965.

Van Doren, Carl. *Benjamin Franklin.* Westport, Conn.: Greenwood Press, 1973.

_____, *The Great Rehearsal: The Story of the Making and Ratifying of the Constitution of the United States.* New York: Viking, 1948.

Warren, Charles. *The Making of the Constitution.* Boston: Little, Brown, 1928.

Wilson, Woodrow. *Congressional Government.* Introduction by Walter Lippmann. Cleveland: Meridian Books, 1956.

Wright, Benjamin F. *Consensus and Continuity, 1776-1787.* Boston: Boston University Press, 1958.

Part II—History of the House

Bolling, Richard H. *House Out of Order.* New York: Dutton, 1965.

————, *Power in the House.* New York: Dutton, 1968.

Brown, George Rothwell. *The Leadership of Congress.* New York: Arno Press, 1974.

Burns, James MacGregor. *Congress on Trial.* New York: Harper & Brothers, 1949.

Carroll, Holbert N. *The House of Representatives and Foreign Affairs.* Pittsburgh: University of Pittsburgh Press, 1958.

Chiu, Chang-Wei. *The Speaker of the House of Representatives Since 1896.* New York: Columbia University Press, 1928.

Clapp, Charles L. *The Congressman: His Work as He Sees It.* Washington: The Brookings Institution, 1963.

Congress and the Nation, 1945-1964. Vol. I. Washington: Congressional Quarterly Inc., 1965.

Congress and the Nation, 1965-1968. Vol. II. Washington: Congressional Quarterly Inc., 1969.

Congress and the Nation, 1969-1972. Vol. III. Washington: Congressional Quarterly Inc., 1973.

Congressional Record. Washington: U.S. Government Printing Office.

Fenno, Richard F., Jr. *The Power of the Purse:* Appropriations Politics in Congress: Boston: Little, Brown, 1966.

Follett, Mary P. *The Speaker of the House of Representatives.* New York: Burt Franklin Reprints, 1974.

Ford, Paul Leicester, ed. *The Writings of Thomas Jefferson.* Vol. 6. New York: G. P. Putnam's, 1895.

Froman, Lewis A., Jr. *Congressmen and their Constituencies.* Chicago: Rand McNally, 1963.

Galloway, George B. *History of the House of Representatives.* New York: Crowell, 1961.

————, *The Legislative Process in Congress.* New York: Crowell, 1953.

————, *Congress at the Crossroads.* New York: Crowell, 1946.

Griffith, Ernest S. *Congress: Its Contemporary Role.* New York: New York University Press, 1951.

Hasbrouck, Paul DeWitt. *Party Government in the House of Representatives.* New York: Macmillan, 1927.

Hecht, Marie B. *John Quincy Adams: A Personal History of an Independent Man.* New York: Macmillan, 1972.

Hinds, Asher C. *Precedents of the House of Representatives of the United States.* 8 vols. Washington. U.S. Government Printing Office, 1907.

Huitt, Ralph K., and Peabody, Robert L. *Congress: Two Decades of Analysis.* New York: Harper & Row, 1972.

MacNeil, Neil. *Forge of Democracy: The House of Reresentatives.* New York: David McKay Company, 1963.

McConachie, Lauros G. *Congressional Committees: A Study of the Origins and Development of Our National and Local Legislative Methods.* New York: Burt Franklin Reprints, 1973.

Mayo, Bernard. *Henry Clay: Spokesman of the New West.* Boston: Houghton Mifflin, 1937.

Riddick, Floyd M. *The United States Congress: Organization and Procedure.* Washington: National Capitol Publishers, 1949.

Ripley, Randall B. *Party Leaders in the House of Represenatives.* Washington: The Brookings Institution, 1967.

Robinson, James A. *The House Rules Committee.* Indianapolis: Bobbs-Merrill, 1963.

Williams, T. Harry. *Hayes: The Diary of a President 1875-1881.* New York: David McKay Company, 1964.

Wilson, Woodrow. *Congressional Government.* Cleveland: Meridian, 1956.

Young, Roland. *The American Congress.* New York: Harper & Brothers, 1958.

Part III—History of the Senate

Bates, Ernest Sutherland. *The Story of Congress, 1789-1935.* New York: Harper & Brothers, 1936.

Benton, Thomas Hart. *Thirty Years' View.* 2 vols. New York: Greenwood Press, 1968.

Binkley, Wilfred E. *The Powers of the President.* New York: Russell & Russell, 1973.

Burdette, Franklin L. *Filibustering in the Senate.* New York: Russell & Russell, 1965.

Clark, Joseph S. *Congress: The Sapless Branch.* New York: Harper and Row, 1964.

Clark, Joseph S. *The Senate Establishment.* New York: Hill and Wang, 1963.

Congress and the Nation, 1945-1964. Vol. I. Washington: Congressional Quarterly Inc., 1965.

Congress and the Nation, 1965-1968. Vol. II. Washington: Congressional Quarterly Inc., 1969.

Congress and the Nation, 1969-1972. Vol. III. Washington: Congressional Quarterly Inc., 1973.

Galloway, George B. *Congress at the Crossroads.* New York: Crowell, 1946.

_____. *The Legislative Process in Congress.* New York: Crowell, 1953.

Harris, Joseph P. *The Advice and Consent of the Senate.* New York: Greenwood Press, 1968.

Haynes, George H. *The Senate of the United States: Its History and Practice.* 2 vols. Boston: Houghton Mifflin, 1938.

Huitt, Ralph K., and Peabody, Robert L. *Congress: Two Decades of Analysis.* New York: Harper & Row, 1972.

Jones, Charles O. *The Minority Party in Congress.* Boston: Little, Brown, 1970.

Luce, Robert. *Legislative Procedure: Parliamentary Practices and the Course of Business in the Framing of Statutes.* New York: Da Capo Press, 1972.

Madison, James; Hamilton, Alexander; and Jay, John. *The Federalist Papers.* Introduction by Clinton Rossiter. New York: Mentor, 1961.

Madison, James. *Notes on Debates in the Federal Convention of 1787.* Introduction by Adrienne Koch. Athens, Ohio: Ohio University Press, 1966.

Matthews, Donald R. *U.S. Senators and Their World.* Chapel Hill, N.C.: University of North Carolina Press, 1960.

McConachie, Lauros G. *Congressional Committees: A Study of the Origins and Development of Our National*

and Local Legislative Methods. New York: Burt
Franklin Reprints, 1973.

Price, David E. *Who Makes the Laws? Creativity and
Power in Senate Committees.* Cambridge, Mass.:
Schenkman Publishing Co., 1972.

Ripley, Randall B. *Majority Party Leadership in Congress.*
Boston: Little, Brown, 1969.

Ripley, Randall B. *Power in the Senate.* New York: St. Martin's Press, 1969.

Rogers, Lindsay. *The American Senate.* New York: Knopf,
1926.

Rothman, David J. *Politics and Power: The United States
Senate, 1869-1901.* Cambridge, Mass.: Harvard University Press, 1966.

Swanstrom, Roy. *The United States Senate, 1787-1801.*
Senate Document 64, 87th Congress, 1st Session.
Washington: U.S. Government Printing Office, 1962.

Tocqueville, Alexis de. *Democracy in America.* 2 vols. New
York: Schocken Books, 1967.

Warren, Charles. *The Making of the Constitution.* Boston:
Little, Brown, 1929.

Wilson, Woodrow. *Congressional Government.* Introduction by Walter Lippmann. Cleveland: Meridian, 1956.

Index

A

B

Index

Index

Index